SCHMUCKISMUS

kuratiert von | curated by
Karen Pontoppidan

herausgegeben von | edited by
Angelika Nollert

Die Neue Sammlung
The Design Museum

Arnoldsche Art Publishers

Angelika Nollert

„Das Gegebene zu hinterfragen…“

Auf Einladung der Neuen Sammlung – The Design Museum kuratiert Karen Pontoppidan, Professorin für Goldschmiedekunst an der Akademie der Bildenden Künste München, eine Ausstellung, die sich dezidiert mit der Bedeutung von Autorenschmuck als Spiegel eines kritischen Diskurses auseinandersetzt.
Schmuck wird hier nicht verstanden als ein selbstreferentielles Instrument, sondern als Möglichkeit und Notwendigkeit zu einer Reflexion von gesellschaftsrelevanten Inhalten. Themen wie Ökologie, Konsumgesellschaft, Identitäten oder Feminismen werden direkt durch das Medium Schmuck ausgedrückt. Es geht hier nicht um die Findung einer einzigen richtungsweisenden Ausdrucksform in Bezug auf Motive oder Gestaltung, sondern um das Zulassen unterschiedlicher Äußerungen und Diversität im Bereich des Autorenschmucks.
„I don't favor a single truth environment“ ist ein bekennender Satz der in Dänemark geborenen und international renommierten Schmuckkünstlerin Karen Pontoppidan, die damit ihre Haltung als Künstlerin, Kuratorin und Lehrende definiert. Ihre eigene Arbeit hinterfragt die Bedeutung und die ethischen Werte von Schmuck, auch für ihre Besitzer*innen. Schmuck lässt nicht nur Fragen an ihre Träger*innen zu, sondern die Träger*innen von

“To Question the Given...”

Karen Pontoppidan, professor of jewelry art at Akademie der Bildenden Künste München, will be taking up an invitation by Die Neue Sammlung to curate an exhibition that rigorously engages with the significance of studio jewelry as a mirror to a critical discourse.
Jewelry is understood here not as a self-referential instrument, but as an opportunity to engage in the necessary reflection on socially relevant issues. Themes such as ecology, consumer society, identity and feminisms are directly expressed by the medium of jewelry. This is not about finding a single, trend-setting form of expression as relates to themes or design, but about allowing for a range of statements and diversity in the realm of studio jewelry.
Internationally renowned Danish jewelry artist Karen Pontoppidan's attitude as an artist, curator and professor is best encapsulated in her defining statement: “I don't favor a single truth environment.” Her own work questions the meaning and the ethical values of jewelry, which includes with regard to its owners. Jewelry not only allows for questions to be asked of those who wear it, but also gives its wearers the opportunity to raise questions related to their environment.

Schmuck stellen durch diesen auch Fragen an ihre Umgebung.
Der Titel „SCHMUCKISMUS“ spiegelt diese dialektische Haltung. Zunächst erscheint der Begriff „Schmuckismus“ als ein Paradoxon, denn gerade der Autorenschmuck will sich nicht einem Ismus unterordnen. Aber gerade in dieser bewusst pointierten scheinbaren Widersprüchlichkeit liegt das Potential des Begriffes, da er in diesem Kompositum eine Haltung beschreibt, die den Ismus als Vielfalt versteht bzw. diese Vielfalt durch einen so definierten Ismus geradezu einfordert.
Für die Ausstellung hat Karen Pontoppidan 30 Schmuckkünstler*innen einer jüngeren und mittleren Generation aus verschiedenen Ländern eingeladen, die auf ein eigenes, aber noch nicht abgeschlossenes Werk verweisen können. Ihre Arbeiten zeigen, wie unterschiedlich die jeweiligen Themen und Inhalte, die Materialien und die Herstellungsverfahren sind, und wie unterschiedlich auch die jeweils intendierte Rezeptionsmöglichkeit durch ein Publikum ist.
Das, was die Teilnehmer*innen miteinander verbindet, ist ihre grundsätzlich kritische Haltung, die Schmuck als ein Medium für gesellschaftspolitische und sozialrelevante Fragestellungen versteht, gerade auch, weil sie aus der jeweiligen individuellen Perspektive entwickelt werden.
Das Konzept der Ausstellung sieht vor, dass die Schmuckkünstler*innen jeweils zu ihren von Karen Pontoppidan ausgewählten Exponaten zusätzlich eine neue Arbeit entwickeln oder eine weitere Arbeit selbst aussuchen. So ergibt sich eine dialogische Zusammenschau von über 100 Objekten aus einem Zeitraum der letzten 15 Jahre.
Karen Pontoppidan hat ebenfalls die Ausstellung gestaltet. Ihre Vitrinen, die an der Brüstung und an den Pfeilern der Rotunde befestigt werden, sind aus einfacher Tischlerplatte hergestellt, die Objektbeschriftung wird unaufwändig angebracht. Damit erinnern die Ausstellungsdisplays gleichermaßen an einfache Informations-Schaukästen im öffentlichen Raum wie an selbst gefertigte improvisierte Träger, um alternative Stimmen zu kommunizieren. Wie der Titel so gibt auch die Ausstellungsarchitektur dezidiert Raum für eine nicht nur künstlerisch relevante Aussage des aktuellen Autorenschmucks.
Ein künstlerisches Werk in der Ausstellung stammt nicht von den eingeladenen Künstler*innen.
Bei der Arbeit *Körperschmuck Abwehrreaktion IV.* der österreichischen Künstlerin Brigitte Lang aus dem Jahr

The title “SCHMUCKISMUS” reflects this dialectic approach. To begin with, the term “Schmuckismus” appears paradoxical, for after all studio jewelry precisely does not want to be subsumed under an “ism” of any kind. However, it is precisely in this deliberately pointed, seeming discrepancy that the potential of the term lies, as the composite word describes an attitude that understands the “ism” to be a diversity, or actually calls for this diversity by deploying an “ism” defined this way.
For the exhibition Karen Pontoppidan has invited 30 jewelry artists from a range of countries who are members of a younger and middle generation, all of whom can look back on a distinctive oeuvre that is not yet complete. Their works show how different the themes and contents, the materials and production methods in question are, and also how great the differences are when it comes to how the jewelry artists intend the public reception of the works to be.
What the participants have in common is their fundamentally critical approach; they all regard jewelry as a medium for socio-political and socially relevant lines of enquiry, precisely because it is generated from the individual perspective in question.
The exhibition concept involves all of the jewelry artists participating creating a new work or themselves selecting a work, to be displayed alongside the pieces selected by Karen Pontoppidan. The result is a dialogic survey of around 100 objects created in the last 15 years.
Karen Pontoppidan has also designed the exhibition. Her showcases, attached to the balustrade and the pillars of the rotunda, are made of simple wood-core plywood, with the object labelling attached in a simple way. This makes the exhibition displays appear somewhat reminiscent of elementary information showcases in the public sphere, but also of a home-made improvised medium for communicating alternative voices. Like the title, the exhibition architecture thus clearly provides scope for the statements of current studio jewelry that go beyond being merely artistically relevant.
One piece in the exhibition was not made by the invited artists. The work *Körperschmuck Abwehrreaktion IV.* by Austrian artist Brigitte Lang, created in 1982, consists of a cross made up of metal braces. The ends of these feature round shapes and a triangle, all of which reference the neck, breasts and vulva. Worn on the naked skin, this body jewelry

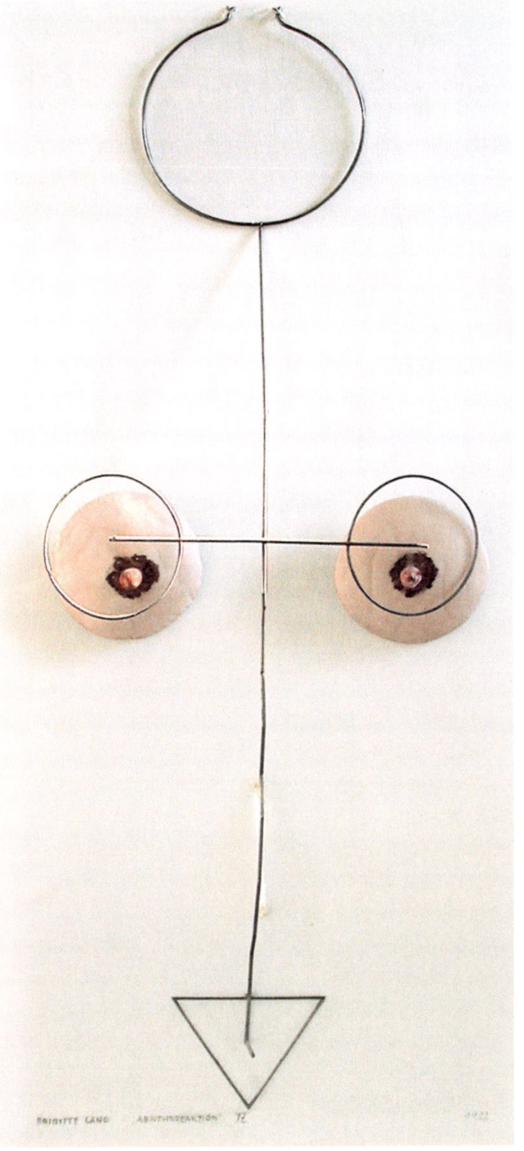

Brigitte Lang, Körperschmuck | body jewelry
Abwehrreaktion IV., 1982, Edelstahl, Messing, Baumwollstoff, Holz | stainless steel, brass, cotton, wood
68,9 × 35 × 13 cm, © Brigitte Lang / SAMMLUNG VERBUND, Wien

1982 handelt es sich um ein aus Metallstreben gebildetes Kreuz, an dessen Enden Kreismotive und ein Dreieck auf Hals, Brust und Vulva verweisen. Dieser Körperschmuck, auf der nackten Haut getragen, betont die Genitalien des weiblichen Körpers, aber er verwandelt sich durch seine Stacheln vor allem auch in eine Waffe, die sich gegen ein nahendes Gegenüber richtet.

Diese Arbeit, die für eine emanzipierte und genderbewusste Haltung steht, die gesellschaftliche Normen und Rollen hinterfragt, dient hier als Auftakt und Leitgedanke der Ausstellung.

Karen Pontoppidan führt eine weitere Bedeutungsebene in die Ausstellung ein, indem sie eine Sammlung von Ansteckplaketten ausstellt: Der niederländische Schmuckkünstler Paul Derrez und Willem Hoogstede haben seit den 1970er-Jahren eine umfangreiche Sammlung von Buttons zusammengetragen, weil sie an dem Phänomen und der Entwicklung dieses „Schmucktypus" als unmittelbares grafisches Medium der politischen Aussage interessiert sind.

Mit der Ausstellung „SCHMUCKISMUS" freut sich Die Neue Sammlung, einen weiteren und besonderen Beitrag zur Erforschung sowie zum Diskurs von Autorenschmuck leisten zu können. Nach umfangreichen Ausstellungen über die Arbeiten von Hermann Jünger, Gijs Bakker, Dorothea Prühl, Giampaolo Babetto, Peter Skubic, Otto Künzli, Anton Cepka, Thomas Gentille sowie Tone Vigeland wurden im letzten Jahr mit „Jablonec '68" die Pioniere des internationalen Autorenschmucks vorgestellt. Mit einem inhaltlichen Sprung von einem halben Jahrhundert zeigt die Ausstellung „SCHMUCKISMUS" einen aktuellen Schwerpunkt des heutigen internationalen Autorenschmucks und damit seine Entwicklung auf.

Neben den regelmäßig stattfindenden Ausstellungen präsentiert Die Neue Sammlung auch permanent in ihrer sogenannten Danner-Rotunde Schmuckobjekte aus dem reichen Fundus der Danner-Stiftung, die auch Werke von Karen Pontoppidan umfasst, sowie der eigenen Sammlung. Die Schmuckschauen auf der 1949 gegründeten und jährlich stattfindenden Internationalen Handwerksmesse sowie die sich durch Kontinuität auf hohem Niveau auszeichnende Klasse für Schmuck und Gerät der Akademie der Bildenden Künste – mit Prof. Karen Pontoppidan schließt sich auch hier dieser Kreis – und nicht zuletzt die Danner-Stiftung mit ihrer seit Mitte der 1980er-Jahre stetig wachsenden Sammlung von Autorenschmuck bilden – verbunden mit ihrer von Beginn an großzügigen Unterstützung für unser Haus – eine Trias, die mit der Neuen Sammlung symbiotisch zusammenwirkt.

emphasizes the genitalia, but with its spikes it can also be used as a weapon to ward off unwanted physical proximity.

The work stands for an emancipated and gender-sensitive stance that questions the social norms and roles and provides the starting point and central theme of the exhibition.

Karen Pontoppidan introduces a further level of meaning into the exhibition by showcasing a collection of badges: Since the 1970s, Dutch jewelry artist Paul Derrez and Willem Hoogstede have compiled a comprehensive collection of such items, following their interest in the phenomenon and the development of this "jewelry type" as a graphic medium for direct political expression.

Die Neue Sammlung is happy in the form of the exhibition "SCHMUCKISMUS" to be able to provide a further and a very special contribution to research and discussion in the field of studio jewelry. After comprehensive exhibitions on the works of Hermann Jünger, Gijs Bakker, Dorothea Prühl, Giampaolo Babetto, Peter Skubic, Otto Künzli, Anton Cepka, Thomas Gentille as well as Tone Vigeland, last year Die Neue Sammlung introduced the pioneers of international studio jewelry "Jablonec '68" to the broader general public. Leaping forward half a century in time and content, the "SCHMUCKISMUS" exhibition presents a topical focus of today's international studio jewelry and its development.

Alongside its temporary exhibition schedule, Die Neue Sammlung also presents on a permanent basis, namely jewelry items from the rich troves of the Danner Foundation collection as well as its own collection, (which also includes works by Karen Pontoppidan): in the Danner Rotunda. Then there are the jewelry exhibitions that take place at the annual international crafts fair Internationale Handwerksmesse (founded in 1949), not to mention the consistently high standard of creations by the Jewelry Class at Akademie der Bildenden Künste (things again come full circle, as Prof. Karen Pontoppidan heads the class) and not lastly the Danner Foundation itself with its collection of studio jewelry that is steadily growing since the mid-1980s and its generous support for the museum since the very beginning. Together with Die Neue Sammlung this trio forms a symbiotic jewelry focus in Munich.

We are most grateful to Waltraud Wiedenbauer, Die Neue Sammlung's registrar, and to the museum's

Ein großer Dank geht an Waltraud Wiedenbauer, Registrar der Neuen Sammlung, und an den Fotografen des Hauses, Alexander Laurenzo, sowie an alle Mitarbeiter*innen, die an der Realisierung beteiligt waren. Wir danken den Leihgebern für die hilfsbereite Zurverfügungstellung von Werken für die Ausstellung. Wir freuen uns, dass dieser Katalog erneut bei Arnoldsche Art Publishers erscheint, und danken persönlich Dirk Allgaier für die ausgezeichnete Zusammenarbeit. Ein Dank geht an Yvonne Quirmbach aus Berlin für die Gestaltung der Publikation, die kongenial den Geist der Ausstellung in das grafische Medium übersetzt hat. Ein weiterer großer Dank geht an Prof. Dr. Hanne Loreck und an Paul Derrez für ihre wichtigen Katalogbeiträge.

Der größte Dank geht an Karen Pontoppidan und die Künstler*innen der Ausstellung. Wir freuen uns, dass Karen Pontoppidan unserer Einladung mit Interesse und Begeisterung gefolgt ist, eine Ausstellung über zeitgenössischen internationalen Autorenschmuck zu kuratieren und ihren Blick darauf mit uns zu teilen. Wir danken den Künstler*innen für ihre wichtigen Beiträge, mit denen sie ihr Denken und Schaffen präsentieren und die Rezipient*innen zu einem Dialog über das politische Potential von Autorenschmuck einladen.

photographer, Alexander Laurenzo, as well as to all members of staff involved in realizing the exhibition concept. We would like to express our gratitude to the lenders for kindly making the works available for the exhibition. We are pleased that this catalog is once again being issued by Arnoldsche Art Publishers, with a personal thank you due to Dirk Allgaier for the excellent collaboration. Thank also goes to Yvonne Quirmbach from Berlin for designing the publication: She has congenially conveyed the spirit of the exhibition for the graphic medium. Our gratitude also goes to Prof. Hanne Loreck and Paul Derrez for their important catalogue contributions.

That said, our greatest thanks are due to Karen Pontoppidan and the artists in the exhibition. We are delighted that Karen Pontoppidan has responded to our invitation to curate an exhibition on contemporary international studio jewelry with both interest and enthusiasm and that she has shared her view of this marvelous field. We are grateful for the artists' substantive contributions, which present their thinking and their creative work and invite the viewers to enter into a dialogue on the political potential of studio jewelry.

Karen Pontoppidan

SCHMUCK-ISMUS

Schmuck wird öffentlich getragen. Er kann als eine Schwelle zwischen einer privaten und einer öffentlichen Identität des Einzelnen empfunden werden, oder er kann in seiner Gesamtheit als gesellschaftliches Phänomen betrachtet werden.

Die Ursprünge von Schmuck gehen Hand in Hand mit der Entstehung der frühesten Zivilisationen vor hunderttausend Jahren. Schmuck repräsentiert hierbei eine Markierung von spezifischer Gruppenzugehörigkeit gegenüber anderen Gemeinschaften und gleichzeitig ist er eine Kennzeichnung von individuellen Positionen innerhalb einer sozialen Gruppe.

Der amerikanische Anthropologe Randall White beschreibt, wie Körperverzierungen den Aufbau einer Vielfalt sozialer und persönlicher Identitäten ermöglichen. Weiter stellt Randall White fest, dass materialbasierte Kommunikationssysteme die ersten differenzierten Gesellschaften begleiteten und dass die symbolischen Verweise, die durch Schmuck entstanden, einen starken Einfluss auf die politischen und sozialen Beziehungen gehabt haben müssen.[1]

Die Vorstellung, wie Schmuck in den frühesten Zivilisationen entstand und allgemein wurde, gibt deutliche Hinweise auf die Bedeutung von Schmuck innerhalb

SCHMUCK-ISMUS

Jewelry is worn publicly. It may be perceived as a threshold between an individual's private and public identity or viewed as a social phenomenon in its entirety.

The origins of jewelry went hand in hand with the emergence of the earliest civilizations one hundred thousand years ago. In this context, jewelry represented a marker of specific group-belonging towards other communities and at the same time it is an indication of individual positions within a social group.

The American anthropologist Randall White describes how body adornment enables the establishment of a range of social and personal identities. He further determines that the earliest differentiated societies had material-based communication systems and that symbolic indications created through jewelry must have had a strong influence on political and social relationships.[1]

The notion of how jewelry first emerged in the early civilizations and how it became widespread provides clear evidence of its significance in social structures. The evolution of markers worn on the body that not only defined an individual's status and classification with respect to strangers, but also in relationship to other

sozialer Strukturen. Die Entwicklung von einer am Körper getragenen Markierung, als Status und Zuordnung des Einzelnen, nicht nur gegenüber Fremden, sondern auch gegenüber allen anderen Stammeszugehörigen, hat eine systematische, visuelle Ordnung geschaffen. Diese war auf vielen Ebenen hilfreich, vor allem innerhalb der Kulturen, in denen die Bevölkerung schnell gewachsen ist. Man braucht nur an das immer noch übliche Tragen von Eheringen zu denken, um zu verstehen, wie hilfreich eine solche Kommunikation sein kann (zum Beispiel bei der Partnersuche).

Natürlich wurden in den frühen Zivilisationen Körpermarkierungen auch auf andere Weise hergestellt. Bekannt sind Bemalungen und Tätowierungen, die jedoch im Vergleich zu Schmuck beide auf einer gesellschaftspolitischen Ebene weniger Flexibilität bieten. Körperbemalungen sind zeitintensiver, da sie immer wieder erneuert werden müssen, etwas, das sich vor allem in Zeiten der Unruhe als problematisch erweisen kann. Tätowierte Markierungen sind durch ihre Permanenz problematischer als Schmuck, wenn Gemeinschaften wachsen oder neue Bündnisse eingehen möchten. Zusätzlich bietet das Objekt Schmuck im Vergleich zu Bemalungen und Tätowierungen eine einfache Möglichkeit für Tausch und Handel.

Gesellschaftspolitisch gesehen war Schmuck also attraktiv, da er nicht nur die Manifestierung einer Vielfalt von sozialen Identitäten ermöglichte, sondern auch soziale Flexibilität anbot. Dies ist besonders wichtig bei Gemeinschaften im Wachstum oder im Wandel, bei denen Aufstieg oder Abstieg der Einzelnen sowie Bündnisse oder Feindschaften der Gruppe kommuniziert werden müssen. Sowohl innerhalb als auch außerhalb einer Gruppe schafft Schmuck ein erkennbares hierarchisches System, das zum Teil vergleichbar ist mit Militäruniformen, die Aufgabenbereich und Position des Einzelnen kommunizieren. Im Verhältnis zu Uniformen ist eine soziale Kommunikation durch Schmuck natürlich wesentlich komplexer und subtiler. Beide sind jedoch strukturierte Zurschaustellungen einer Gruppenzugehörigkeit, die gleichzeitig eine Selbstidentifikation ermöglichen.

Für das Individuum beinhaltet eine durch Schmuck kommunizierbare Gesellschaftsstruktur durchaus das Potenzial, eigenen Überzeugungen oder Widerwillen Ausdruck zu verleihen. Innerhalb der jeweiligen Normen gibt es Spielräume, die mit „Individualität" beschrieben werden können. Und doch ist der Akt des Schmückens seinem Wesen nach ein Ausdruck von grundlegenden sozialen Konstruktionen.

clan members, created a systematic visual order. This was helpful on many levels, most notably so in cultures with a rapidly growing population. One need only think of the still customary wearing of wedding rings to understand how helpful such communication can be (for example, in the search for partners).

Of course, in the early civilizations, body adornments were also created in other ways: Body painting and tattoos are well known. Yet in comparison to jewelry, both of these offer less flexibility on a sociopolitical level. Body painting is more time-intensive, with such adornments needing to be renewed time and again – something that may prove problematic, especially in turbulent times. The permanence of tattooed markers makes their use more problematic than jewelry in those instances where groups grow or want to form new alliances. In addition, compared to body painting and tattoos, jewelry objects offer the possibility of exchange and trade.

Jewelry was thus attractive from a sociopolitical viewpoint, as it not only enabled the manifestation of a range of social identities, but also offered social flexibility. This was especially important in growing or changing societies, in which the ascent or descent of individuals, as well as alliances or enmities of the group must be communicated. Jewelry creates a recognizable hierarchical system both within and outside a group that is partially comparable to military uniforms, which communicate an individual's area of responsibility and position. Of course, in comparison to military uniforms, social communication through jewelry is far more complex and subtle. Yet both are structured displays of group affiliation that simultaneously make self-identification possible.

For individuals, a social structure communicable through jewelry certainly has the potential to express their own convictions or reluctance. Within the applicable norms there is leeway that can be described as "individuality." Yet by its very nature the act of adorning oneself is an expression of fundamental social constructions.

In her article *Essential Adornment: Why Jewellery is Important in Society*, Talya Underwood writes that despite the extreme amount of time modern humans spend on their appearance, the crucial role jewelry plays in society is often underestimated. Personal ornaments have an effect beyond their purely aesthetic function; they associate individuals with communities as well as ethnic groups with one another. Talya Underwood

"There is now broad consensus that, among contemporary humans, material systems of personal ornamentation enable the construction of a diversity of social and personal identities. In large part, they do so by making reference to group histories, values and beliefs via profound metaphorical linkages between chosen materials and created forms on the one hand, and various agreed-upon social identities on the other. The initial invention of such material systems of personal ornamentation in the prehistoric past doubtless accompanied the first internally differentiated human societies. The metaphorical references alone must have been a powerful influence on political and social relations."
Randall White

Talya Underwood schreibt in ihrem Artikel *Essential Adornment: Why Jewellery is Important in Society*, dass, obwohl moderne Menschen extrem viel Zeit auf ihr Äußeres verwenden, die entscheidende Rolle, die Schmuck in der Gesellschaft spielt, unterschätzt wird. Persönliche Ornamente wirken über eine rein ästhetische Funktion hinaus, sie verbinden sowohl Individuen mit Gemeinschaften als auch ethnische Gruppen miteinander. Für Talya Underwood ist Schmuck grundsätzlich ein wichtiger Teil unseres Kommunikationsrepertoires.[2]

In der heutigen Zeit wird Schmuck oft als ein individueller Ausdruck von Persönlichkeit angesehen. Hierbei wird Schmuck der Privatsphäre zugeordnet, anstatt als ein wichtiges kulturelles Merkmal gelesen zu werden. Dadurch könnte vermutet werden, dass der Schmuck im Laufe der Entwicklungsgeschichte der westlichen Kulturen an gesellschaftlicher Bedeutung verloren hat. Allerdings hat die deutsche Uhren- und Schmuckindustrie einen Jahresumsatz von über einer Milliarde Euro,[3] demnach gibt es einen großen individuellen Bedarf nach dem Medium Schmuck, der durchaus eine ökonomische Bedeutung für die Gemeinschaft hat. Der heutige kommerzielle Erfolg von Schmuck kann jedoch leicht dazu führen, dass andere kulturelle Kommunikationsebenen

essentially sees jewelry as an important part of our communication repertoire.[2]

In present times jewelry is often regarded as an individual expression of personality. Jewelry is thus attributed

to the private sphere rather than being read as an important cultural characteristic. This could lead us to the assumption that the historical development of Western cultures, jewelry had lost its significance in social contexts. Yet the German watch and jewelry industry has sales in excess of one billion euros.[3] As such, one can assume that there is a large individual demand for the medium jewelry, which is certainly of economic importance for society. However, the commercial success jewelry currently enjoys may easily lead to other levels of cultural communication being upstaged. What remains perceptible is a personal preference or an economic value, yet jewelry is primarily an expression of group affiliation.

The significance of jewelry has undergone great social changes over the course of history. One example of this is the changing image of masculinity, which as a consequence of the French Revolution evolved rapidly in the late 18th century. Male fashion abruptly eschewed

"For all the time we spend on our appearance, the importance of jewellery is often underestimated, and the crucial role jewellery plays in society is usually overlooked. In actuality, personal ornaments act beyond a simply aesthetical function, instead they tie together individuals, societies, and ethnic groups. Fundamentally, it is also an important part of our communication repertoire, acting as a visual mechanism to convey information important to social relationships or to store information in a similar way to writing."
Talya Underwood

in den Hintergrund gedrängt werden. Sichtbar bleibt eine persönliche Vorliebe oder ein ökonomischer Wert, dabei ist Schmuck vorrangig ein Ausdruck von Gruppenzugehörigkeit.

Die Bedeutung von Schmuck erfuhr im Lauf der Geschichte große gesellschaftliche Wandlungen. Ein Beispiel hierfür ist das veränderte Männerbild, das sich als Folge der Französischen Revolution Ende des 18. Jahrhunderts rasch entwickelte: Die Herrenmode verzichtete abrupt auf Extravaganzen, wahrscheinlich als eine Bemühung des Adels, sozial engagierter zu erscheinen. Der Schmuck verschwand dadurch nicht, weder vom männlichen noch vom weiblichen Körper. Schmuck für Männer wurde mit Technik und Funktion getarnt und der extravagante Schmuck wurde fortan nur den Frauen zugeschrieben.

Ted Polhemus schreibt in *Body Styles*, dass die westliche Gesellschaft Schmuck in den letzten Jahrhunderten hauptsächlich als unbedeutende Freizeitbeschäftigung abgetan hat mit der Folge, dass schmückende Aktivitäten oft als „weiblich" kategorisiert werden.[4]

Die Kategorisierung von Schmuck als „weiblich", die in patriarchalen Strukturen häufig als eine Gleichsetzung mit etwas Niedlichem oder sogar Unseriösem gilt, scheint

extravagances, presumably as an effort on the part of the nobility to appear more socially engaged. Yet this did not mean that jewelry disappeared altogether, from the male or female body. Jewelry for men was camouflaged with technology and function, while from that time onwards more extravagant jewelry was assigned to women.

In *Body Styles*, Ted Polhemus describes how in recent centuries Western society has for the most part written off jewelry as a meaningless leisure activity, and how this has in turn resulted in adorning activities often being categorized as "feminine."[4]

The categorization of jewelry as "feminine," which in patriarchal structures is often equated to cuteness or even non-seriousness, appears to be having a lasting impact on the significance of jewelry. Nevertheless, the complexity of the relationship between jewelry and society can hardly be described without including different social developments, such as religious or political ones.

It is relevant to ask whether, for instance, the consequences of colonialization are a factor that has contributed to the devaluation of the conscious approach to jewelry as a social marker. The exploitation of

nachhaltig einen Einfluss auf die Bedeutung von Schmuck zu haben. Die Komplexität des Verhältnisses zwischen Schmuck und Gesellschaft kann allerdings kaum beschrieben werden, ohne andere gesellschaftliche Entwicklungen einzuschließen, wie religiöse oder politische.
Es ist relevant zu fragen, ob zum Beispiel die Folgen der Kolonialisierung ein Faktor sind, der zur Abwertung des bewussten Umgangs mit Schmuck als einem gesellschaftlichen Zeichen beigetragen hat.
Die Ausbeutung fremder Kulturen ermöglichte eine Aneignung von ursprünglich aus Asien, Afrika oder Südamerika stammenden Materialien, Formen und Bildsprachen. Die angeeigneten Materialien erhielten zwar eine neue Bedeutungsebene in der westlichen Welt, etwa um Macht, Weltoffenheit oder Abenteuerlust auszudrücken, aber die symbolische Kraft, welche die Materialien in ihrem ursprünglichen kulturellen Kontext besaßen, wurde weitgehend ignoriert. Diese Aushöhlung könnte für die Lesbarkeit von Schmuck als einem gesellschaftlichen Zeichen einschneidend gewesen sein, denn die Kommunikation von Schmuck beruht auf der Verständlichkeit seiner Bestandteile. Schmuck erhält seine Narrative durch die Verknüpfung kultureller Bedeutungsebenen von Material und Form. Randall White formuliert es treffend, wenn er feststellt, dass Schmuck sich auf die Werte und Überzeugungen der jeweiligen Gemeinschaft bezieht und dass Schmuck durch die tiefgreifenden metaphorischen Verknüpfungen zwischen geschaffenen Formen und ausgewählten Materialien entsteht.[5] Da jedoch die Bedeutung eines Materials selten universell ist, unterliegt die Sprache von Schmuck eben den jeweiligen gesellschaftlichen Normen.
Es gibt also deutliche Anzeichen für eine Verwässerung der kulturellen Bedeutungsebene des Schmucks, aber auf keinen Fall wird die Zeichenkraft ausgelöscht, die Schmuck in der westlichen Welt hat. Es ist vielleicht eher so, dass wir in der westlichen Kultur die nach wie vor existierende Signifikanz gerne ignorieren möchten, da sie womöglich in ihrer Komplexität unseren Drang, uns „schön" zu schmücken, stören und dadurch auch die Massentauglichkeit und Kommerzialisierung von Schmuck beeinflussen könnte.
Sich „schön" zu schmücken erscheint individuell, jedoch wird spätestens durch die Entwicklung von Queer- und Gendertheorien klar, dass das Aussehen des Einzelnen nie ausschließlich als ein individueller Ausdruck von Persönlichkeit gelesen werden darf. Diese Theorien weisen darauf hin, dass normative Denkstrukturen tagtäglich das Spektrum, in dem Menschen sich schmücken und

foreign cultures made it possible to assimilate materials, shapes and imagery that were originally from Asia, Africa and South America. While the appropriated materials to some extend gained a new meaning in the Western world, e.g. in expressing power, a cosmopolitan attitude or an adventurous spirit, the symbolic power these materials had in their primary cultural context was for the most part ignored. This erosion could have been decisive for the legibility of jewelry as a social marker, as the communication of jewelry relies on the comprehensibility of its components. Jewelry gains its narrative through the correlation of cultural semantic levels of material and form. Randall White puts it very aptly when he states that jewelry relates to the values and beliefs of the society in question and that jewelry is created from the profound metaphorical links between the forms created and the materials chosen.[5] As the meaning attached, for instance, to a material is rarely universal, the language of jewelry is in turn subject to the social norms in question.
It can thus be said that there are clear signs of a watering-down of sorts of the cultural semantic level of jewelry, whereas the symbolic power of jewelry in the Western world is in no way obliterated. It is perhaps, rather, the case that we in Western cultures would like to ignore the persisting significance of jewelry, as in its complexity it may influence or hinder us when it comes to our urge for "beautyfication", which could in turn also have an impact on the suitability for the masses and commercialization of jewelry.
To adorn oneself "beautifully" appears to be individual, yet at the very latest through the development of queer and gender theories it has been made clear that the appearance of an individual can never solely be seen as an individual expression of personality. These theories point to the fact that normative thought patterns regulate the spectrum on which humans adorn and groom themselves on a daily basis. Jewelry is a part of a comprehensive system that conveys social values, and the right to a "queer" appearance is therefore not simply an individual matter, but something political that has been at least in some cases hard won. This makes it clear that jewelry has a great significance in contemporary Western culture, too, and that its potential is needed now more than ever.
In his article *The Social Skin*, Terence S. Turner states that the characteristic element of jewelry lies in its direct addressing of the construction of the individual as a social actor. As this construction is a fundamental

zurechtmachen, regulieren. Schmuck ist Teil eines umfassenden Systems, das gesellschaftliche Werte vermittelt, und das Recht auf ein „schräges" Erscheinungsbild ist deswegen nicht einfach etwas Individuelles, sondern etwas Politisches und zum Teil auch etwas hart Erkämpftes. Dadurch wird verdeutlicht, dass Schmuck auch in der zeitgenössischen westlichen Kultur eine große Aussagekraft besitzt und dass dieses Potenzial mehr denn je benötigt wird.

Terence S. Turner schreibt in seinem Artikel *The Social Skin*, dass das Charakteristische des Schmucks darin besteht, dass er sich unmittelbar mit der Konstruktion des Individuums als sozialem Akteur befasst. Da diese Konstruktion ein grundlegendes Anliegen aller Gemeinschaften ist, wird das Tragen von Schmuck ausnahmslos für alle Gesellschaften zu einer ernsthaften Angelegenheit, egal ob ihre Mitglieder als Einzelne dieses bewusst ernst nehmen oder nicht.[6]

Gerade die Diskrepanz, dass Schmuck in der heutigen Zeit oft als belanglos betrachtet wird, anstatt ernsthaft als gesellschaftliches Sinnbild wahrgenommen zu werden, macht ihn zu einer großartigen Ausdrucksform, um kritische Gedanken zu formulieren. Durch die Verharmlosung von Schmuck entstehen vielfältige Optionen, seine omnipotente Präsenz zu nutzen. Sich öffentlich durch Schmucktragen zu äußern, bedeutet nicht ausschließlich, einen privaten Standpunkt kundzutun, sondern sich auch für oder wider Normen zu positionieren. Durch den Akt des Schmückens erhält jeder die Möglichkeit einer öffentlichen Wahrnehmung, indem er von seinem sozialen Umfeld Aufmerksamkeit einfordert, die ihm sonst verwehrt bleibt. Schmuck dient essentiell der Beschreibung von Gesellschaftsstrukturen, und hierauf bezugnehmend können Arbeiten entstehen, die das Potenzial von Schmuck für kritische Diskurse betonen.

Innerhalb der Entwicklung des Autorenschmucks der letzten fünfzig Jahre gibt es etliche Arbeiten, die kritische Ansätze formulieren, zum Beispiel gegenüber Wertesystemen. Die meisten dieser Arbeiten haben ihren Ursprung in einem Diskurs, der Teil einer kritischen Beobachtung von Schmucktraditionen ist, also die Reflexion des eigenen Mediums in einem künstlerischen Prozess voraussetzt.

In den letzten Jahren kann ein weiterer Ansatz im Schmuck beobachtet werden. In den Arbeiten einer aktuellen Generation von Künstler*innen hat der Schmuck sich weitgehend aus der Selbstreflexion gelöst und stattdessen wird Schmuck direkt als Instrument zur gesellschaftlichen Reflexion verwendet. Themen wie Ökologie,

concern of all societies, the wearing of jewelry is without exception for all social groups a serious matter, regardless of whether its members individually regard it as such or not.[6]

It is precisely the discrepancy between jewelry nowadays often being regarded as trivial and genuinely perceived as a social allegory that makes it a magnificent form of expression for formulating critical thought. The trivialization of jewelry gives rise to a range of options for harnessing its omnipotent presence. Expressing oneself publicly by wearing jewelry does not exclusively mean communicating a private viewpoint, but also positioning oneself for or against norms. By the act of adornment everyone gets the possibility of being perceived in public, demanding attention from the social environment, which otherwise could be denied. Jewelry essentially serves to describe social structures, and in reference to this works can be created that emphasize the potential of jewelry for critical discourse.

In the development of studio jewelry over the past fifty years there have been numerous works that formulate critical approaches, for example with regard to value systems. Most of these originate from a discourse that is part of a critical observation of jewelry traditions that presupposes reflection on one's own medium in an artistic process.

In recent years there has been evidence of a further approach to jewelry. In the works of a current generation of artists, jewelry has for the most part disentangled itself from self-reflection and is instead directly used as an instrument for social reflection. Topics such as ecology, consumer society and feminisms are expressed directly through the medium of jewelry, as are more individual concerns, which are however expressive of no less relevant topics, such as questions on the formation of identity or the condition of being human in the 21st century.

It is reasonable to presume that it was the works of earlier generations that paved the way for the current generation of jewelry artists to view jewelry as a natural medium for critical discourse. At any rate, a new approach can be observed now that is increasingly employing other methods for making statements through jewelry. The cultural meaning of the materials used often serves as a fundamental citation in the works, and this approach may be applied comprehensively, in order to reference globalization or cultural norms. Questioning the craft as a social phenomenon or deliberately subverting expectations generally held

"For the last few hundred years Western society has, in the main, dismissed body decoration, adornment, fashion and style as unimportant leisure activities which only the frivolous relish and which only the foolish take seriously. (Put another way, this has usually meant that we in the West categorise such activities as 'feminine'.)"
Ted Polhemus

Konsumgesellschaft oder Feminismen werden direkt durch das Medium Schmuck ausgedrückt und ebenso individuellere Belange, die jedoch nicht weniger relevante Themen ausdrücken wie etwa Fragen zur Identitätsbildung im Sinne der Postmoderne oder zum Ist-Zustand des Menschseins im 21. Jahrhundert.

Es ist anzunehmen, dass die Werke der früheren Generationen von Schmuckkünstler*innen es erst ermöglicht haben, dass die heutige Generation Schmuck als ein selbstverständliches Medium für einen kritischen Diskurs betrachtet. Jedenfalls kann ein neues Vorgehen beobachtet werden, das verstärkt andere Methoden einsetzt, um Aussagen im Schmuck zu treffen. Häufig dient die kulturelle Bedeutung der verwendeten Materialien als tragendes Zitat innerhalb der Arbeiten, ein Ansatz, der sehr umfassend eingesetzt werden kann, zum Beispiel, um auf die Globalisierung oder auf kulturelle Normen zu verweisen. Ein anderer erkennbarer Ausgangspunkt ist, das Handwerk als ein gesellschaftliches Phänomen zu hinterfragen oder Erwartungen an handwerkliche Methodik bewusst zu untergraben. Es gibt auch Beispiele von Künstler*innen, die polarisierenden Themen durch ihren Schmuck Ausdruck verleihen, sie weisen auf die Weltpolitik oder auf die Komplexität von Rassismus hin,

of craft methods is another discernible starting point. There are also examples of artists who express their views on polarizing topics through their art, for example through references to world politics or the complexity of racism, in order to thus address the construction of the individual as a social actor.

The exhibition "SCHMUCKISMUS" showcases works by international jewelry artists who question social phenomena in various ways.

The exhibition concept emerged from the conviction that we are living in an era in which rigid political and religious isms need to be rigorously questioned. At the same time, we live at a time in which opinions thoughtlessly posted in social media are confused with truths. This is why we need pieces of jewelry that address the profound questions we face in our world today and that enable their wearers to express substantiated thoughts.

"Bodily adornment, considered as a symbolic medium, is not unique in these respects: every society has a number of such media or languages, the most important among which is of course language itself. The distinctive place of the adornment of the body among these is that it is the medium most directly and concretely concerned with the construction of the individual as social actor or cultural 'subject'. This is a fundamental concern of all societies and social groups, and this is why the imposition of a standardised symbolic form upon the body, as a symbol or 'objective correlative' of the social self, invariably becomes a serious business for all societies, regardless of whether their members as individuals consciously take the matter seriously or not."
Terence S. Turner

um sich dadurch mit der Konstruktion des Individuums als sozialem Akteur zu befassen.
Die Ausstellung und Publikation „SCHMUCKISMUS" zeigt Arbeiten von internationalen Schmuckkünstler*innen, die auf verschiedene Weise gesellschaftliche Phänomene hinterfragen.
Das Konzept entstand aus der Überzeugung, dass wir in einer Zeit leben, in der starre politische und religiöse Ismen gründlich hinterfragt werden müssen. Gleichzeitig leben wir aber in einer Zeit, in der unüberlegte Meinungen in sozialen Medien leicht mit Wahrheiten verwechselt werden. Deswegen sind Schmuckobjekte notwendig, die sich tiefgreifend mit der Welt auseinandersetzen und die es der Trägerin oder dem Träger ermöglichen, fundierte Gedanken auszudrücken.

1: Randall White, *Systems of Personal Ornamentation in the Early Upper Palaeolithic: Methodological Challangers and New observations*, in: Paul Mellars, Katie Boyle, Ofer Bas-Yosef und Chris Stringer (Hg.), Rethinking the Human Revolution. New Behavioural and Biological Perspectives on the Origin and Dispersal of Modern Humans, Cambridge, UK: Mc Donald Institute for Archaelogical Resyearch 2007, S. 287–302
2: Vgl. Talya Underwood: *Essential Adornment: Why Jewellery is Important in Society*, in: The Triple Helix 1 (13/2011), S. 18–20.
3: Umsatz der Uhren- und Schmuckindustrie in Deutschland in den Jahren 2008 bis 2017; https://de.statista.com (zuletzt 21.11.2018).
4: Vgl. Ted Polhemus, *Body Styles*, Colchester: TBS 1989, S. 30.
5: Vgl. Randall White, op. cit.
6: Vgl. Terence S. Turner: *The Social Skin*, in: HAU: Journal of Ethnographic Theory 2 (2/2012), S. 486–504, Zitat 502.

1: Randall White, *Systems of Personal Ornamentation in the Early Upper Palaeolithic: Methodological Challenges and New Observations*, in: McDonald Institute Monographs (Ed.): Rethinking the Human Revolution: New Behavioural and Biological Perspectives on the Origin and Dispersal of Modern Humans, Cambridge, 2007, p. 287.
2: Talya Underwood: *Essential Adornment: Why Jewellery is Important in Society*, edition: The Triple HelixEaster 2011, The Triple Helix Inc., Cambridge, p. 18.
3: Sales in the watch and jewelry industry in Germany in 2008 to 2017, figures as at November 21, 2018, https://de.statista.com.
4: Ted Polhemus, *Body Styles*, TBS The Book Service Ltd., Colchester, 2018, p. 91 (first edition: Lennard Publishing, London, 1988).
5: Randall White, op. cit.
6: Terence S. Turner: *The Social Skin*, in: HAU: Journal of Ethnographic Theory 2 (2/2012), Cornell University, p. 486–504, quotation p. 502.

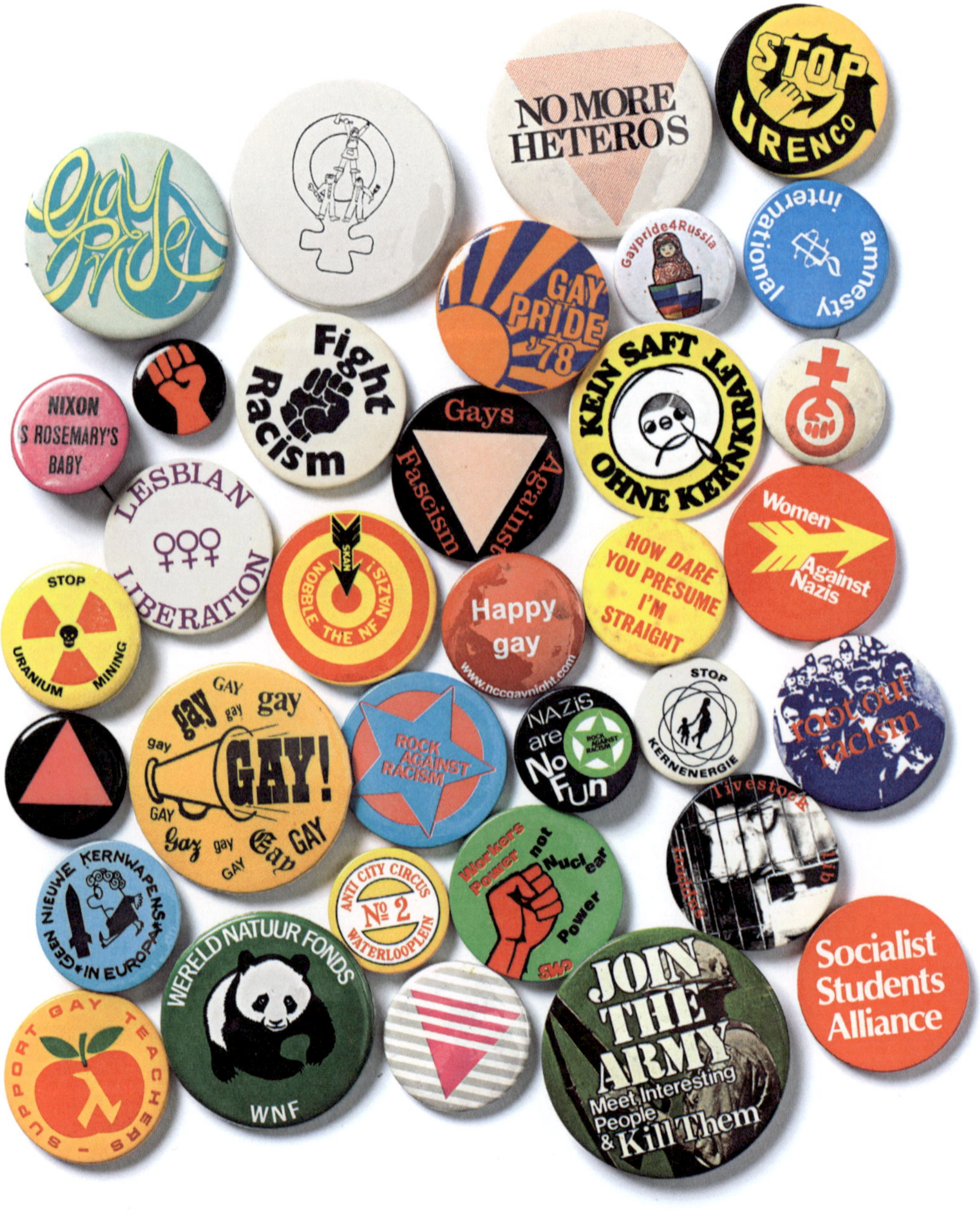
NO MORE HETEROS
STOP URENCO
Gaypride4Russia
amnesty international
GAY PRIDE '78
Fight Racism
NIXON S ROSEMARY'S BABY
Gays Against Fascism
KEIN SAFT OHNE KERNKRAFT
LESBIAN LIBERATION
Women Against Nazis
HOW DARE YOU PRESUME I'M STRAIGHT
STOP URANIUM MINING
NOBBLE THE NF NAZIS
Happy gay
www.nccgaynight.com
GAY! gay GAY
ROCK AGAINST RACISM
NAZIS are No Fun
STOP KERNENERGIE
root out racism
Livestock
GEEN NIEUWE KERNWAPENS IN EUROPA
ANTI CITY CIRCUS № 2 WATERLOOPLEIN
Workers Power not Nuclear Power
SWP
WERELD NATUUR FONDS
WNF
JOIN THE ARMY Meet Interesting People & Kill Them
Socialist Students Alliance
SUPPORT GAY TEACHERS

Paul Derrez

Ansteckbuttons Schmuck mit Botschaft

Paul Derrez und Willem Hoogstede haben in den 1970er-Jahren begonnen, Ansteckbuttons mit politischen Botschaften zu sammeln. Sie wurden 1979 in einer Ausstellung mit dem Titel *BADGES, idealistic jewellery* in der Galerie Ra, Amsterdam, gezeigt. Im Anschluss wurde die Sammlung mit über 300 Buttons im Museum of Modern Art im niederländischen Arnhem und an weiteren Orten ausgestellt. In diesem Beitrag soll auf das Phänomen eingegangen werden, das von den Buttons ausgeht.

Diese spezielle Form einer Anstecknadel hat ihren Ursprung in den USA und tauchte in einer eher einfachen Version erstmals Ende des 18. Jahrhunderts auf. Die ersten Buttons bestanden aus Stoff und wurden entweder aufgenäht oder als Anhänger getragen. Der Ansteckbutton, wie wir ihn kennen, mit seiner durchsichtigen Zelluloidfolie, die das darunter liegende Bild schützt, wurde 1893 patentiert. Damals stellte man die Anstecker in größeren Mengen her, um auf diese Weise insbesondere Werbung für Kandidaten bei Präsidentschaftswahlen zu machen. Innerhalb kürzester Zeit setzte man sie auch für andere Zwecke ein, so etwa für die Vermarktung von Tabakwaren, Süßigkeiten und Kaugummi. Die Buttons wurden wie andere Werbegeschenke – z.B. Bildkarten mit Athleten, Politikern und anderen populären Motiven – schnell zu

Buttons Jewelry with a Message

During the 1970s, Paul Derrez and Willem Hoogstede collected pin-back buttons with political messages. These were shown at Ra Gallery, Amsterdam in 1979, in an exhibition titled *BADGES, idealistic jewellery*. After the exhibition, the collection of over 300 buttons went on tour to the Museum of Modern Art in Arnhem and other venues. Forty years on, Paul Derrez looks back on the phenomenon.

The button originates from the USA and made its first primitive appearance towards the end of the 18th century. The name derived from the English word button, and the first were self-made and sewn on or worn as a pendant. The button as we know it, with a transparent celluloid film to protect the image, was patented in 1893. In those days, buttons started to be produced on a larger scale to endorse candidates in presidential elections. Other applications followed soon after, for instance as merchandise for products like tobacco, sweets and chewing gum. Buttons were a natural addition to other collectable promotion prizes, like picture cards featuring athletes, politicians and other popular subjects. The graphic design of these early prize buttons was often very beautiful. They were highly coveted and definitely helped to sell products.

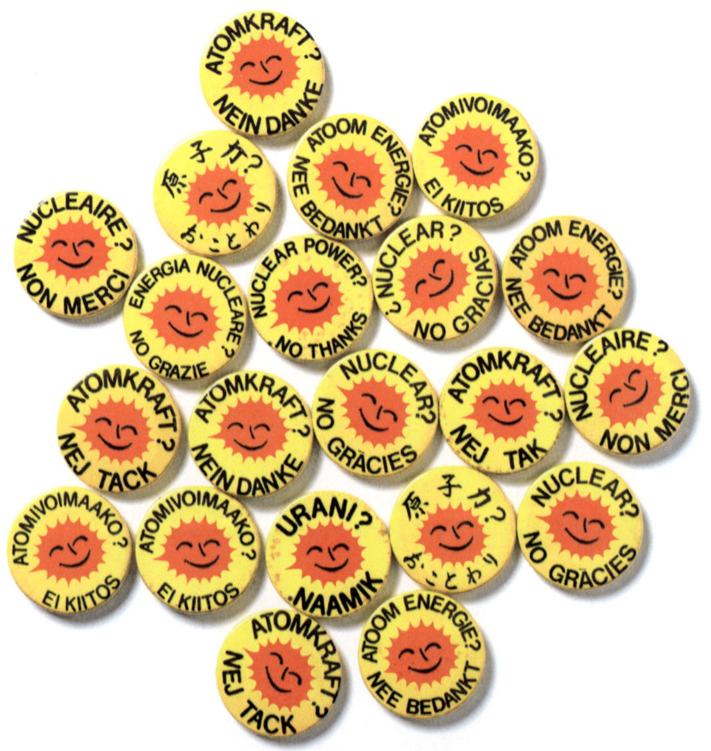

gesuchten Sammlerobjekten. Diese frühen Werbebuttons besaßen oftmals eine ausgesprochen hohe grafische Qualität und Ästhetik, was sie nicht nur sehr begehrt machte, sondern sicherlich auch zu einem gesteigerten Verkauf dieser Produkte führte.

Durch Veränderungen im Herstellungsprozess, die Buttons wurden nun zunehmend aus zuvor bedrucktem Weißblech gestanzt, konnte sowohl ihre Auflagenhöhe wesentlich gesteigert, als auch eine Mannigfaltigkeit bei der Motivauswahl generiert werden. Die mit den neuen Fertigungsprozessen verbundene Einschränkung in der Farbwahl und die weniger aufwändige Herstellung führten jedoch zu einem Verlust der vormals grafischen Qualität. Ab 1910 erlaubten neue fotografische Techniken das Drucken und Reproduzieren von Fotografien auf Metall, was völlig neue Möglichkeiten bezüglich der Produktion von Unikaten und personalisierten Memorabilien eröffnete, wie das Abbilden beliebter Persönlichkeiten oder von Tieren.

Für die Herstellung von Ansteckbuttons entwickelte sich sehr bald ein standardisiertes Verfahren: Nach dem Ausstanzen des Metallplättchens wird der Rand nach Innen umgeschlagen, so dass eine Rückseite entsteht. Innerhalb dieser meist etwas konkav gewölbten Rückseite wird eine Nadel im Sinne einer Broschierung angebracht, so dass das Metallplättchen – der Button –

By stamping buttons from pre-printed tinplate, producers were able to substantially increase their variety and production numbers, though the graphic quality suffered owing to the less sophisticated production process and use of colours. From 1910 onwards, new photographic techniques enabled photographs to be printed on metal, which opened up a world of possibilities for the production of unique and personal memorabilia, like buttons featuring popular people and animals.

The pin-back button's construction was standardized: After stamping the metal plate from the sheet, a folded rim is attached to it. A wire pin inserted into the concave opening at the back or behind the closed back enables the badge to be worn. The diameter can vary from two to ten centimetres.

Originally, various types of buttons were used in the USA during presidential elections, but in later years they were also worn during times of war and conflict. With a button, the wearer could show his engagement with and support of a cause, party or person: *Truman for President.* Conversely, the message on the badge could also address an enemy: *Hitler, wanted for murder.*

In the 1950s and 1960s, buttons saw a revival as a political tool used by activists, especially in America.

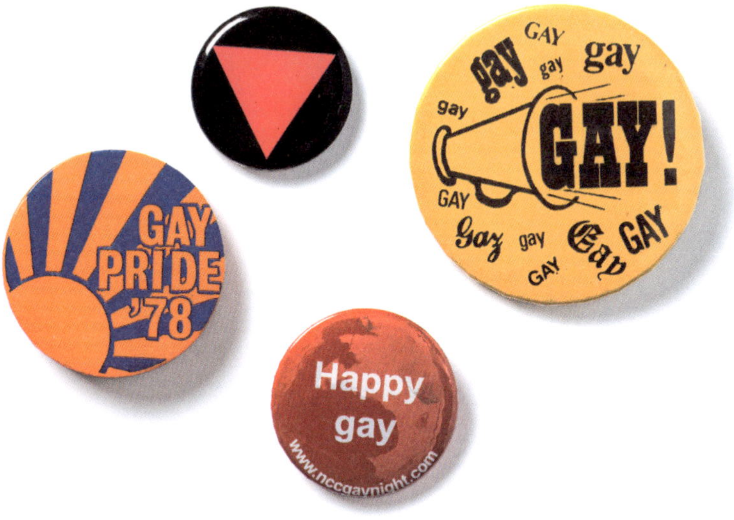

jetzt angesteckt werden kann. Der Durchmesser des Ansteckbuttons kann bei dieser Herstellungsart zwischen zwei bis zehn Zentimetern variieren.

Ursprünglich wurden in den USA vor allem während der Präsidentschaftswahlen Buttons getragen, später vor allem jedoch auch in Zeiten, die durch politische Konflikte und Kriegsgeschehen geprägt waren. Mit einem Button konnte der Träger seine Unterstützung für ein bestimmtes Anliegen, eine Partei oder Persönlichkeit zeigen, wie bei *Truman for President*. Umgekehrt konnte mit der Botschaft auf der Anstecknadel aber auch ein Gegner bzw. Feind benannt werden, wie etwa *Hitler, wanted for murder*.

In den 1950er- und 1960er-Jahren wurden die Buttons vor allem in Amerika von Aktivisten als politisches Instrument wiederentdeckt. Anstatt die nationale Politik zu unterstützen, wurde nun gegen die Politik der Regierung protestiert: *Jobs, Not Guns*. Der höchstumstrittene Vietnamkrieg löste eine enorme Protestwelle aus – Anstecknadeln, die diesen Krieg gutgeheißen haben, gab es kaum.

Gegen Ende der 1960er-Jahre wurden die Buttons als Träger politischer Botschaften auch auf dem europäischen Kontinent populär. Politische Meinungen und Überzeugungen waren nicht länger Privatsache – so war das Zeichen der weltweit agierenden Friedensbewegung allgegenwärtig. In den 1970er-Jahren war es die Punk- und

Instead of supporting national politics, buttons were now protesting the government's policies: *Jobs, Not Guns*. The controversial Vietnam War prompted massive protests. Buttons defending this war are rare.

Towards the end of the 1960s, buttons gained popularity as carriers of political messages in Europe, too. Political leanings and convictions were no longer kept private. The peace symbol was ubiquitous. In the 1970s, the button's popularity rode on the waves of the punk and squat movement: *Geen Woning Geen Kroning (no housing, no coronation)*.

The introduction of relatively cheap button-making machines opened up the possibility for people to make their own individual button to promote their personal, political or anarchistic views. Yet buttons were also mass-produced. In 1976, some 20–30 million *Nuclear Power? No Thanks* buttons were distributed worldwide. *Stop the Neutron Bomb* was also popular. In addition to politics and the environment, the support for liberation movements and gay and women's rights was a source of button slogans: *Gay, Proud and Angry*.

Naturally, buttons also continued to serve more mundane functions. They were hugely popular as pop star merchandise and were used at events and conferences for practical purposes.

Hausbesetzer-Szene, in der der Ansteckbutton erneut eine wichtige Kommunikationsrolle übernahm: *Geen Woning Geen Kroning* (*keine Wohnungen, keine Krönung*).
Durch technologische Weiterentwicklungen und das Aufkommen relativ günstiger Fertigungsmaschinen für die Button-Herstellung konnten individuelle Anstecker mit persönlichen, politischen oder anarchistischen Botschaften in einem Maße produziert werden wie nie zuvor. Der Button wurde zum Massenprodukt. 1976 wurden weltweit 20 bis 30 Millionen Buttons mit der Aufschrift *Nuclear Power? No Thanks* (*Atomkraft? Nein Danke!*) vertrieben. Sehr populär war auch *Stop the Neutron Bomb*. Neben Politik und Umweltschutz spielten auch Slogans für die Unterstützung von Befreiungsbewegungen sowie für die Rechte von Homosexuellen und Frauen zunehmend eine Rolle: *Gay, Proud and Angry*. Ansteckbuttons wurden aber natürlich auch für banalere Zwecke eingesetzt, beispielsweise für Merchandisingzwecke von Popstars oder für Events und Konferenzen.
Heutzutage lassen sich Ansteckbuttons für jeden Anlass einfach und billig produzieren. Dabei spiegeln sie genauso Entwicklungen im Grafikdesign, von politischen Bewegungen oder in Mode und Musik wider. Wie alle kulturellen Ausdrucksformen unterliegen Kleidung, Schmuck, Frisuren und Tattoos bestimmten Codes. Symbole, die am Körper getragen werden, funktionieren in der Regel nur, wenn sie von Träger*innen/Kommunikator*innen und von Beobachter*innen/Rezipient*innen erkannt und verstanden werden. Der Button ist dabei ein sehr einfaches Mittel, um den eigenen Standpunkt und die Zugehörigkeit zu einer bestimmten (Sub-)Kultur zu kommunizieren. Das Tragen von Anstecknadeln mit widersprüchlichen Botschaften oder absurden Texten – *Down with Gravity* oder *Elvis was Gay* – nutzt das künstlerische Mittel der Verwirrung beim Betrachten aus, um eine erneute Aufmerksamkeit auf ein vermeintlich bekanntes Thema zu erzeugen.
Schmuck hat immer eine Botschaft, die meisten Ansteckbuttons vermitteln diese auf sehr explizite Weise. Dass Ansteckbuttons mit sehr freimütigen Slogans als provokant empfunden werden und sogar ein Trage-Verbot herbeiführen können, ist nichts Neues in der Geschichte dieser Schmuckform. Angesichts der stark polarisierten, politischen Diskussion der letzten Jahre überlegt es sich heutzutage der Einzelne sehr genau, ob er politische, religiöse oder soziale Symbole mit Hilfe eines Buttons zur Schau tragen will. Eine zunehmende Intoleranz führt dabei mehr und mehr zu einer Selbstzensur.
Wer würde schließlich heute noch einen Buttons mit der Aufschrift *Wir schaffen das!* tragen wollen?

Buttons are easy and cheap to produce, for any cause. They reflect developments in the graphic industry and political movements, as well as trends in fashion and music. Just like any expression of culture, clothes, jewelry, hairstyles and tattoos are subject to certain codes. Symbols that are worn on the body usually work only when they are recognized and understood both by the wearer/transmitter and the observer/receiver. A button is a fairly straightforward means to show what you stand for and which (sub)culture you belong to. That said, wearing buttons with contradictory messages or absurd texts like *Down with Gravity* or *Elvis was Gay* may cause some confusion.
Jewelry communicates something, and most pin-back buttons do so quite explicitly. There is nothing new in considering outspoken buttons provocative and even prohibiting people from wearing them. Still, in recent years, it seems that the polarized public debate makes people think twice about wearing political, religious and social symbols and texts. Increased intolerance leads to self-censuring. Who is going to wear a button now that says: *Wir schaffen das!*?[1]

1: Angela Merkel, federal press conference, 31.08.2015

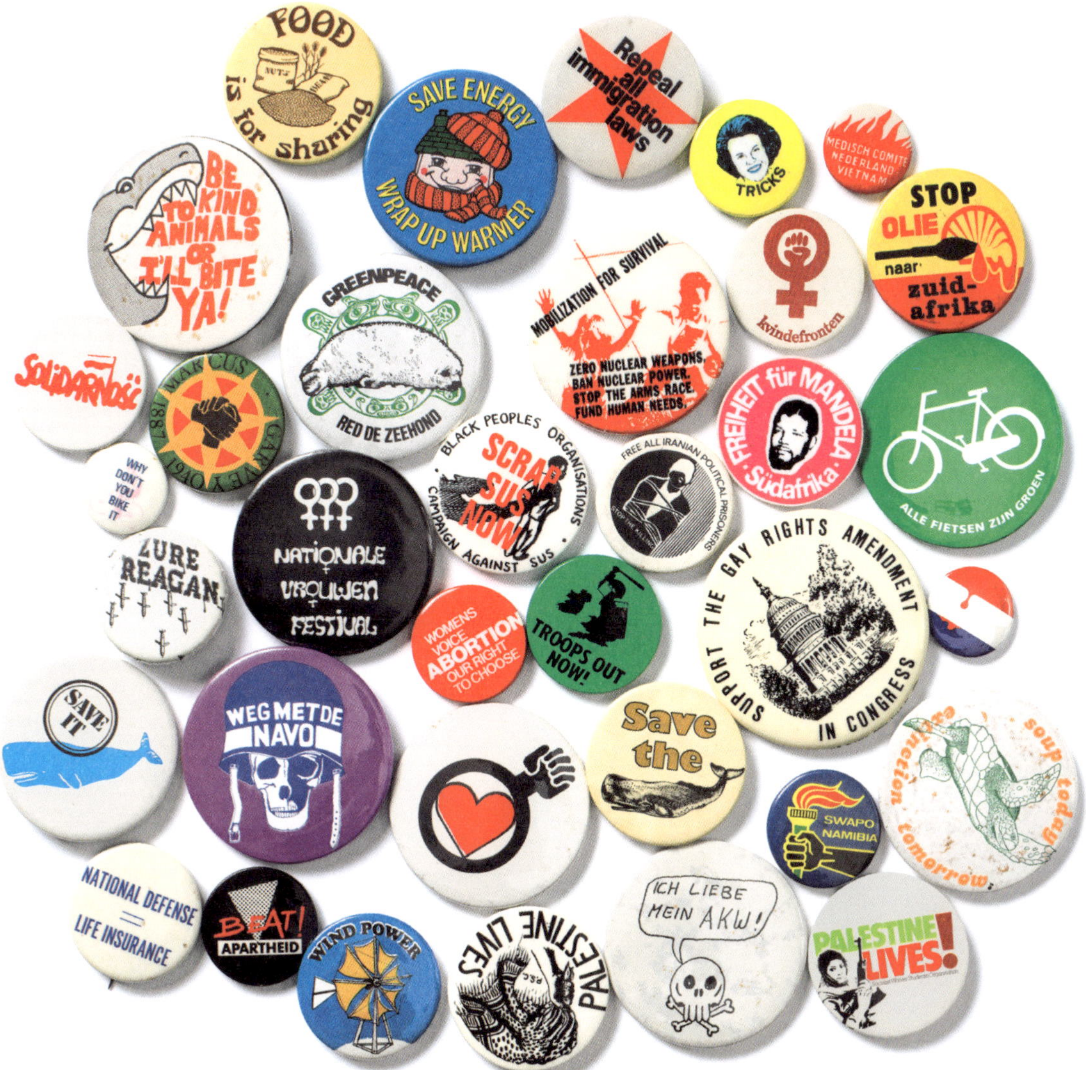
FOOD is for sharing
SAVE ENERGY WRAP UP WARMER
Repeal all immigration laws
TRICKS
MEDISCH COMITE NEDERLAND VIETNAM
STOP OLIE naar zuid-afrika
BE KIND TO ANIMALS OR I'LL BITE YA!
GREENPEACE RED DE ZEEHOND
MOBILIZATION FOR SURVIVAL
ZERO NUCLEAR WEAPONS. BAN NUCLEAR POWER. STOP THE ARMS RACE. FUND HUMAN NEEDS.
kvindefronten
SOLIDARNOŚĆ
MARCUS GARVEY 1887 1940
FREIHEIT für MANDELA Südafrika
ALLE FIETSEN ZIJN GROEN
WHY DON'T YOU BIKE IT
NATIONALE VROUWEN FESTIVAL
BLACK PEOPLES ORGANISATIONS CAMPAIGN AGAINST SUS
SCRAP SUS NOW
FREE ALL IRANIAN POLITICAL PRISONERS
ZURE REAGAN
SUPPORT THE GAY RIGHTS AMENDMENT IN CONGRESS
WOMENS VOICE ABORTION OUR RIGHT TO CHOOSE
TROOPS OUT NOW!
SAVE IT
WEG MET DE NAVO
Save the
extinction tomorrow soup today
SWAPO NAMIBIA
NATIONAL DEFENSE = LIFE INSURANCE
BEAT APARTHEID
WIND POWER
PALESTINE LIVES
ICH LIEBE MEIN AKW!
PALESTINE LIVES!

Hanne Loreck

Das Persönliche ist immer wieder politisch

Das SCHMUCKISMUS-Projekt schon im Kopf, sah ich jüngst eine Ausstellung der Künstlerin Kerstin Drechsel. *Ohne Titel* aus der Arbeit *E-Werk*, 2018, eine mehrteilige Risografie auf rosa Papier, zeigte sich mir in dieser Perspektive als Allegorie neuer Schmuckweisen. Grundlage des großformatigen Drucks ist ein kleinformatiges, realistisch ausgeführtes Aquarell eines weiblichen Torsos. Wie ein Schmuckstück hängt ein etwa handygroßes technisches Gerät mit kleinem Display an seinem Band zwischen den nackten Brüsten; etliche Schläuche führen zu Elektroden, die am Oberkörper kleben. Die Figur ist verkabelt, Körper und Maschine sind aneinander angeschlossen, um Biodaten zu liefern. Visuell bilden das Organische und das Anorganische einen Kreislauf, aber das Bild stellt nicht klar, ob es dabei um eine medizinische Diagnose oder um eine Behandlung geht, es sich um eine externalisierte Organfunktion bzw. eine Prothese oder vielleicht sogar um ein Toy zur sexuellen Stimulierung handelt.

Das Gehänge teilt mit einem Schmuckobjekt verschiedene Eigenschaften, pragmatische wie symbolische: Es wird getragen und fügt also dem Subjekt etwas hinzu, es unterstreicht, es zeigt an, es transformiert, es stellt in Frage. Und doch lässt sich anhand dieses Beispiels auch

Time and Again, the Personal is Political

Already preoccupied with the SCHMUCKISMUS project, I recently saw an exhibition of the work of artist Kerstin Drechsel. With the above in mind, *Ohne Titel* (Untitled) from her *E-Werk*, 2018, a multipart risograph on pink paper, appeared to me as an allegory of new approaches to decoration. Her large-format print was based on a small-format, realistic watercolor of a female torso. A technical appliance about the size of a cellphone with a small display on its cord is hanging between her naked breasts like a piece of jewelry; a number of tubes lead to two electrodes stuck onto her upper body. The figure is wired up; her body and the machine are connected to each other to provide biodata. In visual terms the organic and the inorganic form a closed loop, but the image does not make it clear whether the figure is involved in medical diagnostics or is being treated, whether what we are looking at is an externalized organ function, an artificial organ replacement or perhaps even a sex toy to stimulate sexual arousal.

The pendant has various characteristics in common with a piece of sculptural jewelry, both on pragmatic and on symbolic levels. It is being worn, thus adding something to the subject, it underscores, it indicates,

ein gravierender Unterschied zwischen der Wahrnehmung dieses Kunstwerks und derjenigen künstlerischen Schmucks festmachen: *E-Werk* bleibt in der Rezeption mehr oder weniger ausgeprägt mit der Künstlerin, ihrer Ideenwelt und ihren bekannten Realisierungspraxen verbunden, ein Kunstschmuckstück hingegen löst sich aus der ästhetisch-ideellen Bindung an die Produzent*in. Nach seinem Erwerb stehen die Träger*innen im Mittelpunkt; sie sind es, die in Verbindung mit dem un-gewöhnlichen Objekt gebracht werden, ganz besonders dann, wenn es eine Art von Herausforderung in Bezug auf Größe, Gewicht, Material, Machart, vor allem aber in Hinsicht auf Symbolik und Narration darstellt. Die erste Frage des Gegenübers ist nicht diejenige danach, was sich der/die Künstler*in wohl gedacht, sondern vielmehr, was eine Träger*in zu ihrer Wahl bewogen habe und welche Aussage sie in der Koexistenz mit dem ‚piece' machen wolle; weniger gibt die Künstler*in ein Statement ab oder provoziert, sondern vielmehr die Träger*in. Dabei sei unter Träger*in keine individuelle ‚User*in', sondern eine von einer konkreten Person losgelöste Trageoption verstanden.

Anstecken (Ring, Brosche), Umhängen (Kette), Anklipsen oder Stecken (Ohrringe), vielleicht sogar Implantieren – das Verhältnis des Objekts zum Körper ist je verschieden. Ob auf der Haut, auf der Bekleidung, unter der Haut oder durch die Haut hindurch, Schmuckstücke gehen unterschiedlich enge Beziehungen mit dem Körper ein. „Welches Potenzial bergen uns umhüllende Kleidungsstücke, Geräte und Prothesen, die Grenzen unseres Körpers neu zu formen und zu denken?", fragt das Konzept der Ausstellung *Touch* (nGbK, Berlin 2018), und die Fortsetzung im Text lässt sich auf Schmuckstücke übertragen, denn die „zitathaft aufgegriffenen Objekte und Materialitäten" beziehen sich allesamt auf den „Körper in einem Verhältnis von Anhaftung oder Abstoßung, von Formung und Geformtwerden"[1]. Exemplarisch sichtbar werden aktives Gestalten und gleichermaßen aktives Form-Annehmen in ihrer Relation zur (nackten) Haut: Jeder Schmuck widersteht ihr, transzendiert sie und kollaboriert mit ihr. Das heißt, er berührt. In unserem Kontext hat die Kontaktform Berühren vornehmlich Anteil an zwei disziplinären Kontexten: dem anthropologischen bzw. kulturhistorischen und dem medialen (der sinnesphysiologische spielt hier keine Rolle).

Doch beginnen wir physisch-materiell. Dann zeigt sich Berühren als Form von Verbindung oder Kombination zweier oder mehrerer Elemente oder Positionen über eine gemeinsame Schnittstelle. Anthropologisch gesehen, geht

it transforms and questions. And yet this example highlights an important difference between the perception of this work of art and that of artistic jewelry: Our reception of *E-Werk* remains, to a greater or lesser extent, associated with the artist, her world of ideas and her familiar way of implementing them. By contrast, a piece of artistic jewelry disengages itself from its aesthetic and ideational ties to its maker. After it has been purchased it is its wearer who is in the limelight; it is s/he who will be associated with this unusual item, particularly when it represents a kind of challenge in terms of size, weight, material, design and most especially with regard to its symbolic value and the story it has to tell. The first question asked about it is usually not what the artist will have been thinking, but instead what will have caused its wearer to choose it and what kind of statement the latter wishes to make by their coexistence with the 'piece'; it is not so much the artist who is making a statement or being provocative, but rather the piece's wearer. In the above context the wearer does not mean any particular 'user,' but a wearing option completely unattached to any particular person.

Pinning on (brooch), putting on or clipping on (ring, chain, earrings), perhaps even implanting – the relationship between the object and the body varies a great deal depending on situation. The closeness of the relationship that our bodies enter into with different pieces of jewelry always depends on whether the latter are placed against our skin, on our clothes, under our skin or through our skin. "What is the potential of the devices, prostheses and garments which envelop us to reshape and rethink the boundaries of our bodies?" asks the concept behind the exhibition *Touch* (nGbK, Berlin, 2018), and what the text goes on to say can be transferred to the relevant piece of jewelry, because "the objects and materialities cited by and incorporated into the works have a relationship of attachment or repulsion to the body, of molding and being shaped."[1] Both actively designing and actively taking shape become apparent in the example of jewelry's relationship with (bare) skin: All jewelry resists the latter, transcends it and collaborates with it. This means that it touches it. In our context the form of contact known as touching plays an important role in the context of two disciplines – anthropology or cultural history and the media (sensory physiology does not need to be taken into consideration here).

solches Berühren über das Individuum hinaus in Richtung der Stiftung einer Gruppenidentität oder zumindest einer überindividuellen Verbindlichkeit. Pauschal gesagt, schließen sich hier außereuropäische Ethnografie und westliche Modegeschichte kurz, wenn Schmuck und sein Gegenteil, Schmucklosigkeit, das Verhältnis zwischen dem Einzelnen und der Gemeinschaft markieren. John Carl Flügel, britischer Psychoanalytiker und Kulturtheoretiker, stellte 1930 die modetheoretisch zwar ausgefallene, aber gut nachvollziehbare These von der Verkehrung der Kleiderordnung infolge der Französischen Revolution auf: Männliche Aristokraten hätten wesentliche sichtbare und erotisch anziehende, aber auch „Rang und Wohlstand"[2] zur Schau stellende *Privilegien* wie Schmuck, Perücken, Spitze oder Samt ablegen müssen, um, nunmehr gleich den (männlichen) Bürgern, ihre (militärischen) *Leistungen* in Form von Abzeichen den jeweiligen Dienstanzügen anzuheften. Die bis dato lustvoll individuelle Stilisierung, ja Exzentrik innerhalb des qua Geburt garantierten adeligen Standesbewusstseins war bei den Männern der Uniform, dem Gleichmachenden gewichen. Erst das bürgerliche Zeitalter kürte die (reich behängte) Frau zum Schmuckstück und (ökonomischen, kulturellen) Potenzausweis ihres Gatten, der im Gegenzug nunmehr mit einer diskreten (nach wie vor freilich distinguierenden) ‚Funktionskleidung' angetan auftrat. „Gleichheit, Freiheit, Brüderlichkeit" hatte die männliche Homosozialität und ihre gesellschaftlich machtvolle Verbindlichkeit gefestigt, und die neuen, nüchtern-schlichten Standards für die Männerbekleidung hatten das Soziale auch optisch figuriert. Über Jahrhunderte zwar ein wenig dezenter und schamhafter als der Mann gekleidet, war die Frau aber in Sachen erotischer und sexualisierender Ausstrahlung spätestens ab der Einführung des Dekolletés zu Ende des Mittelalters in nahezu gleichem Maß wie er ausstaffiert. Wir sehen, auch hier spielt die Haut eine Rolle, ob ausgestellt oder imaginiert – denn Haut sei unter einem Frauenkleid derart präsent, dass Flügel erklären kann, die Intention sei einzig, ausgezogen zu werden.

Zählen heute Frauen wie Männer zu den Träger*innen von künstlerischem oder Autorenschmuck, so mag in dieser gewissen Gleichverteilung der Dekoration auf die Geschlechter auch ein Verweis auf jene ‚Mode vor der Mode' aufscheinen und die spielerische Reappropriation von erotischen Formeln und Selbstdekoration durch beide Geschlechter als ästhetisch-emanzipatorisches Zeichen ihrer Gleichberechtigung gelten. Schon 1930 hatte Flügel in seiner psychohistorischen Modeanalyse einen

Yet let us start with the physical or material aspect. In this context, touching represents a kind of distribution or combination of two or more elements or positions via a common interface. From an anthropological viewpoint this kind of touching goes beyond the individual, approaching the creation of a kind of group identity or at least a supra-individual commitment.

Broadly speaking, non-European ethnography meets Western fashion history at the point where jewelry and its opposite, lack of adornment, characterize the relationship between the individual and the community. In 1930, John Carl Flügel, the British psychoanalyst and cultural theoretician, put forward the admittedly unusual but easy-to-understand theory of the reversal of the dress code subsequent to the French Revolution, a theory that stated that male aristocrats had had to adapt and to divest themselves of all their basic, visible and erotically attractive *privileges*, including those that showed off their "rank and wealth,"[2] such as jewelry, wigs, lace or velvet and, like ordinary (male) citizens, pin their (military) *decorations* to their various uniforms in the form of medals. The hitherto greatly relished individual stylization, or even eccentricity as part of the awareness of the nobility conferred by birth, was replaced, in men, by the leveler that was uniform. It was only the age of the bourgeoisie that started considering a (richly embellished) woman to be an adornment and a symbol of the (economic, cultural) power of her husband who would, in turn, be attired in discreet (but nonetheless distinguished) 'functional clothing.' "Equality, liberty, *fraternity*" had consolidated male homosociality with its socially powerful and binding character, and the new, simple and sober standards in male clothing had also become a visible indication of social standing. Although, over a period of centuries, women dressed a little more unobtrusively and modestly than men, in terms of erotic and sexualizing charisma, as of the introduction of the décolletage at the end of the Middle Ages at the very latest, women rivaled their male counterparts. As we can see, here too skin has its role to play, independent of whether it is showed off or imagined – after all, even when hidden, skin is so present that Flügel can declare that the sole intention of a woman's dress is to be removed.

Nowadays, with both women and men opting to wear artistic or studio jewelry, this somehow equal distribution in the incidence of decoration among both sexes

geschlechtersolidarischen Akt angeregt, beugte ein Mann sich nicht der homosozialen Uniformierung: „[…] und hier kann der Mann bewusst versuchen, sich mit einer Frau zu identifizieren“[3]. In diesem Sinn können spezifische das Dekorative betreffende Oberflächenoperationen heute als queerfeministische und – unter postkolonialen Vorzeichen – ebenso als interkulturelle Statements politisch gewertet werden.

Wenn wir nun die Frage des Berührens vertiefen, so gilt die Vertiefung dem Medienaspekt der Berührung. Er hat für ein aktuelles Schmuckdenken die größte Relevanz, haben sich doch die Funktion und die Präsenz der Medien seit den 1960er-Jahren, das heißt zeithistorisch seit den Anfängen des Autorenschmucks, maßgeblich gewandelt und seine Ideen und Materialisierungen beeinflusst. Längst haben sich die Medien vom klassischen binären Sender-Empfänger-Modell der Telekommunikation ins Digitale hinein multipliziert, übertragen aufs Psychosoziale und auf kulturelle Zusammenhänge zugleich aber auch diversifiziert. Als Sinneswahrnehmungen, im physischen Sinn oftmals mit den Händen, im übertragenen Sinn mit dem Blick, stellen Berühren und Tasten weit mehr als jenes simple Interface zwischen Subjekt und Objekt, organischer und anorganischer Materie her, das einen Datenfluss ermöglicht. Philosophisch gesehen öffnet vielmehr die Sinneserfahrung das Subjekt in Richtung des Anderen. Wie die Quantenfeldphysikerin und feministische Philosophin Karen Barad schreibt: „Bei einer Berührung geschieht so vieles: Eine Unendlichkeit von Anderem – anderen Wesen, anderen Räumen, anderen Zeiten – wird erweckt.“[4] Während wir meinen, uns anzunähern oder uns etwas über den tastenden Blick zu erschließen, steht etwas grundsätzlich Fremdes, Unbestimmtes im Raum.[5] Mehr noch ist die Anerkennung dieses Nicht-Menschlichen, so Barad in ihrer philosophischen Wendung, die Voraussetzung für Mitgefühl und die „Möglichkeit der Berührung und des Berührt-Werdens“[6]. Auf die Touchscreen-Epoche bezogen und auf sie hin stark vereinfacht: Dass die Stärke des Streichens oder Wischens physikalisch bemessen ist, sagt natürlich nichts über die Affizierung der Betrachter*innen durch die aufgerufenen Inhalte. Diese sind, im übertragenen Sinn, berührend oder, stärker, sogar erschütternd, vielleicht auch animierend, denken wir an einen Porno, an jüngste Wahlergebnisse oder an Bilder von sinnlos im Mittelmeer Ertrunkenen. SHACHAR COHENs Broschen in den abstrahierten Umrissen von Gewaltdarstellungen in den Medien greifen das Informationszeitalter auf und konzipieren das Gegenüber als jemanden, der sich mit seinem Blick auf das

might just represent a reference to that ‘fashion before fashion’ and the playful reappropriation of erotic formulas and self-decoration by both sexes as an aesthetic and emancipatory symbol of their gender equality. Back in 1930, in his psycho-historical analysis of fashion Flugel suggested an act of solidarity between the sexes if a man did not bow to homosocial uniformization: “[…] and here the man may consciously seek to identify himself with a woman.”[3] In this context, specific surface operations for decorative purposes can be evaluated on a political level and seen as queer feminist and – from a postcolonial viewpoint – as intercultural statements, as well.

If we now look more closely at the question of touching, this in-depth appraisal is concerned with the media aspect of touching. This aspect is of great relevance to the current attitude to jewelry, particularly because since the 1960s, i.e., in historical terms since the early days of studio jewelry, the function and the presence of the media have undergone a dramatic transformation, influencing the former’s ideas and its appearance. The media have long since expanded from the classic binary broadcaster/listener model of telecommunication into the digital sphere, projecting themselves simultaneously onto the psychosocial sphere and cultural contexts as well as diversifying. As sensory perceptions, in concrete terms often through touching with our hands and in the figurative sense through looking, touching and feeling represent far more than that simple interface between a person and a thing, between organic and inorganic material, of the kind which makes an information flow possible. Instead, in philosophical terms, sensory perception opens a person up to the existence of the “other.” As quantum physicist and feminist philosopher Karen Barad writes: “So much happens in a touch: an infinity of others – other beings, other spaces, other times – are aroused.”[4] Although we think that we are getting closer to or acquiring a feel for something by touching it, there is something fundamentally foreign, uncertain about it.[5] What’s more, as Barad sees it from her philosophical viewpoint, recognizing this inhuman quality is a prerequisite for empathy and the “possibility of touching and being touched.”[6] In terms of the touchscreen era and greatly simplified with the latter in mind, the fact that the intensity of the scrolling or swiping movement is measured physically does not, of course, say anything about the extent to which the content accessed affects the people reading it. This

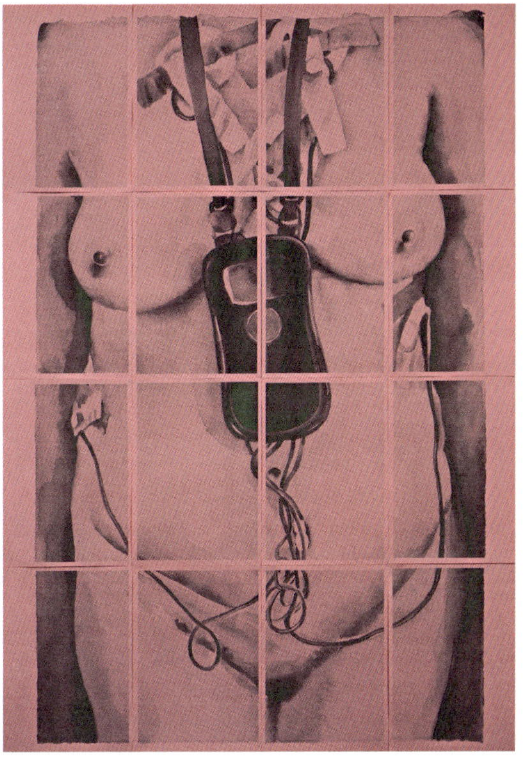

Kerstin Drechsel, o.T. aus der Serie
untitled from the series "E.Werk",
2018, Risografie | risograph
168 × 118,8 cm

hochglanzpolierte Objekt nicht so einfach narzisstisch widerspiegeln wird, sondern sich, ob wissentlich oder unbewusst, inmitten einer brutalen Szene wiederfindet, oder sein Abbild in einer Blutlache erkennen muss. Halsschmuck, für den DANA HAKIM Hardware-Material, genauer feines Siebblech aus Metall, aus Überwachungskameras zu einer Art Perlen biegt und mit Fäden wie ein Gewebe bestickt, greift auf die politische Realität der Kontrollgesellschaft zurück, setzt ihr aber in der Weiterbearbeitung auch das Potenzial des Ästhetischen entgegen (*My Four Guardian Angels – Blue Series 1*, 2011–2014).
Ohne sich mit einigen Konditionen des digitalen Zeitalters befasst zu haben, ist keine Theorie zeitgenössischen Schmucks denkbar. Denn die Medien stehen nicht nur in einem unmittelbaren Zusammenhang mit dem Wandel des Körper- und Geschlechterverständnisses und haben das Verhältnis zwischen Öffentlichkeit und dem privaten Raum fundamental verändert, sie haben auch Werte im materiellen wie im ideellen Sinn transformiert.
In seinem Essay *Gold und Geist. Prolegomena zu einer Theorie des Schmucks* (2015) diagnostiziert der Philosoph und Kulturtheoretiker Pravu Mazumdar unsere Zeit als eine „entfesselte[r] Oberflächen"[7] und bezieht sich dabei

content can, in a figurative sense, be moving or, to put it more strongly, even harrowing and sometimes stimulating – just thinking about porn, the latest election results or pictures of the people who have drowned meaninglessly in the Mediterranean Sea. SHACHAR COHEN's brooches with their abstract contours referencing the portrayals of violence in the media take up the subject of the information age, seeing the interlocutor as somebody who, in his perspective on this mirror-finish object, is not simply reflected in a narcissistic way but finds himself, knowingly or unconsciously, in the middle of a brutal scene or is forced to recognize his own image in a pool of blood. The necklaces for which DANA HAKIM shapes hardware material, in this case fine metal meshing from surveillance cameras, to make a kind of beading which she then embroiders with threads like a fabric, reference the political reality of the society of control, which she then contrasts with the potential offered by the aesthetic (*My Four Guardian Angels – Blue Series 1*, 2011–2014).
Formulating a theory of contemporary jewelry is inconceivable without having looked into a number of the conditions of the digital age. After all, the media

auf die aktuelle inflationäre Präsenz von Haut. Photogeshopt überzieht die eine Haut den menschlichen Körper, der seinerseits autoplastisch geformt ist: Fitnesstraining, Kosmetik und Schönheitschirurgie modellieren ihn nahezu nach Wunsch – vorausgesetzt das sogenannte Fleisch spielt mit und unterwirft sich den Disziplinarmaßnahmen. Entschiedener Widerstand gegen solche soziokulturellen Zwangsverpflichtungen zur Selbstgestaltung, aber auch Alter, Krankheit oder Unfall deformieren den Körper entgegen jedem Ideal und entziehen ihn der öffentlichen Visualisierung. Die andere Haut ist die Oberfläche smarter Geräte, gleichermaßen transparent wie undurchdringlich.
Solches Haut-Werden einer Epoche hat freilich nicht nur eine technische, sondern auch eine Geistesgeschichte. Mit Nietzsche veränderte sich das Verhältnis zwischen dem Wesen, in der Vormoderne immer in der Tiefe verortet, und der Oberfläche. Seine berühmte Denkformel, wie die Griechen Tiefe *zu haben*, erübrige die fortwährende Reklamation von Tiefe und eines grundsätzlich im Verborgenen gehüteten Wesenskerns, mache mithin die idealistische Abwehr des disqualifizierenden Urteils von Oberflächlichkeit überflüssig. Vormals galt die Körperoberfläche nicht als autonom, sondern immer als Transzendenz-Resultat. Seit der Moderne ist sie dann keine Erscheinung mehr, taucht nicht länger aus der Wesenstiefe auf, die umgekehrt jederzeit durch das Fenster namens Haut einen Einblick in Seele und Charakter eröffnete: Nunmehr ist sie Bild, Spiegelbild, Reflex. Dieser Wandel bestimmt sich keineswegs ausschließlich metaphysisch. Vielmehr hatte die Leitwissenschaft des 19. Jahrhunderts, die Biologie, mit dem Gewebe eine Struktur entdeckt, die den gesamten Organismus, unterschiedslos ob ‚Tiefe' oder Oberfläche, sein Innen wie sein Außen, durchzieht und lediglich graduell unterschiedlich, nämlich in Dichte und Funktion differierend, vorliegt: Die Tiefe ist zu einer „Falte in der Oberfläche"[8] geworden. Auf das 20. Jahrhundert bezogen findet sich eine vergleichbar weitreichende lebenswissenschaftliche Entdeckung einer übergeordneten, den Organismus durchwirkenden Struktur, die der DNA. Hier entwickeln sich die spezifische Zellfunktion und entsprechend unterschiedliche Charakteristika nach dem Muster der Chromosomen- und Proteinfaltung.
Mit dieser säkularen Oberflächenbestimmung soll hier in Bezug zu Schmuck weitergedacht werden, bildet Schmuck doch eine Trias mit der Kleidung und dem Körper und insbesondere der Haut. Auf der Relation von Haut und Schmuck liegt unser Hauptaugenmerk,

are not only directly connected with the change in our understanding of the body – and the sexes. They have not only fundamentally changed the relationship between the public and the private sphere; they have also transformed values in both the material and the nonmaterial sense.
In his essay *Gold und Geist. Prolegomena zu einer Theorie des Schmucks* (Gold and Mind: Prolegomena towards a Philosophy of Jewelry, 2015) philosopher and cultural theorist Pravu Mazumdar describes the era in which we live as one of "unleashed surfaces,"[7] referencing the currently excessive focus on the skin. Photoshopped skin covers the human body which is, in turn, shaped by a kind of autoplasty – by fitness training, cosmetics and aesthetic surgery capable of modifying it more or less to order, provided that the so-called flesh plays along and submits to the relevant disciplinary measures. However, not only determined resistance to these kinds of forced socio-cultural obligations to design ourselves, but also age, illness or accidents can deform the body in a manner that goes against every ideal and refuses to subject it to public standards. The other kind of skin is the user interface in smart appliances, as transparent as it is impenetrable.
Yet this way of an era becoming skin does not only have a technical history; it also has a cultural history. With Nietzsche the relationship changed between the essence – in the premodern era always believed to be situated in the depths – and the surface. The philosopher's famous formula for thinking of *having* depth like the Greeks denied the need for perpetually claiming depth and for a carefully hidden essence, thus rendering superfluous the idealist defense of the disqualifying judgment of superficiality. Previously, the surface of the body had been considered not autonomous, but always a result of transcendence. But since the dawn of the modern age it has no longer been a phenomenon, has no longer emerged from the depths of a being and been able, vice versa, to open up insights into a person's soul and character at any time via the window that goes by the name of skin. It is now an image, a mirror image, a reflection. And the reasons for this change are by no means exclusively metaphysical. Instead, in tissue, the 19th century's leading science, biology, discovered a structure which infuses the entire organism indiscriminately, be this in its 'depths' or on its surface, in the body's insides or on its exterior, one whose presence merely gradually

und zwar nicht nur deshalb, weil ein großes Schmucksegment direkt auf der Haut getragen und häufig so auch fotografisch repräsentiert wird, sondern auch weil Schmuckkünstler*innen sie als organisches Material verwenden und, vielmehr noch, mit dem ‚Hautigen' im Sinn von Oben und Unten, Showseite und Rückseite, Transparenz und Dichte, Zeigen und Verbergen operieren.

Immer wird Haut als Grenze und Kontaktzone verstanden, das heißt nach innen in Richtung des Organismus wie nach außen hin zum Anderen gedacht. Genau als solche ist ihr Verständnis gleich nicht länger derart abstrakt, wie gerade hergeleitet, lassen sich doch ihre Ein- und Ausstülpungen, die Körperöffnungen beispielsweise, unterschiedlich begehren. Sexuelle Identität wiederum wird im politischen Raum soziokulturell unterschiedlich gewertet: Heteronormativität und Homophobie gegenüber selbstbewusster Queerness. In diesem Sinn zeigen sich YASAR AYDINs Broschen mit ihren ledernen Faltungen und ‚Löchern', ihren farbigen Akzenten von aufreizendem Pink und analem Braun als solidarische Sticker mit Aspekten (homo)sexueller Lust. Einem Kleidungsstück angeheftet, kehren sie eine erotische Zone aus der Intimität nach außen, drehen die Funktion der Kleidung als Hülle und Verhüllung um in die Grundlage für ein Display, für eine Demonstration von etwas sehr Persönlichem-als-Politisches.

Ähnlich funktioniert die Logik hinter NANNA MELLANDs überdimensionierter Halskette aus Verhütungsspiralen in Rottönen, rot wie altes Blut. In die Gebärmutter eingesetzt, sollen sie die Einnistung des befruchteten Eis verhindern. In der aufgereihten Masse der kleinen funktionalen, vor allem aber gebrauchten und im Allgemeinen nicht ästhetisch wahrgenommenen Objekte entsteht ein ambivalentes Bild von der Verantwortung der Frauen für Sex ohne ungewünschte Schwangerschaft. Die Künstlerin veröffentlicht das medizinische Instrument, zeigt das Genießen, aber auch die Verantwortung von Frauen. Derart wird die Diskretion der Intimität durchbrochen, denn die Ketten entziehen sich dem gesellschaftlichen Imperativ der säuberlichen Trennung von Innen und Außen, von privat und politisch. Und lenken damit zumindest meinen Blick auf eine im Kunstkontext rezipierte historische, explizit feministische Position: Hannah Wilkes ausgekaute Kaugummis von *S.O.S. – Starification Object Series*, 1975, aus denen sie kleine Vaginas formte und sich auf das schöne Gesicht und den Oberkörper klebte, um sich mit den Popeln zu fotografieren – ein Beispiel, das verdeutlichen mag, wie viel aktuelle Schmuck-

differs, i.e. in its density and function. Depth had become a fold in the surface.[8] Making a comparison with the 20th century, the discovery of a structure which pervades the organism and boasts overarching importance and similarly wide-reaching implications for the world we live in was the discovery of DNA. In this case, the specific function of the cells and correspondingly their different characteristics develop according to the pattern of the relative chromosome and protein folding.

Bearing in mind the secular definition of surface, our intention here is to think a little more about jewelry, particularly since jewelry, clothing and the body – in particular the skin – form a trinity. Our main focus is on the relationship between skin and jewelry, not only because a large percentage of jewelry sits directly on the skin and is frequently photographed in such situations, but also because jewelry artists use it as an organic material and, what's more, operate with aspects of the skin, in the sense of top and bottom, the right side and the reverse, transparency and opacity, showing and hiding.

Skin is repeatedly seen as a boundary and a contact zone, i.e. what separates the inside of the organism itself from its outside, the side shown to other people. And it is as such that it is immediately no longer seen as so very abstract as we have just deduced it to be, since its indentations and protrusions, the various orifices of the body for instance, generate different desires. Sexual identity is, in turn, assessed differently in the political context: heteronormativity and homophobia compared with self-assured queerness. With this in mind, YASAR AYDIN's brooches with their leather folds and 'holes,' their splashes of provocative pink and anal brown, are like stickers showing solidarity with aspects of (homo)sexual lust. Pinned to an item of clothing, they invert an erotic zone, transferring it from the intimate sphere to the outside, turning the function of clothing as a sheath and a covering inside out and making it the basis of a kind of display, a demonstration of something very personal as something political.

The logic behind NANNA MELLAND's outsized necklace made of contraceptive coils in shades of red, red like old blood, works in a similar way. Inserted into the womb, the coils are intended to prevent the implementation of a fertilized egg in the wall of the uterus. This string of small, functional and above all used items which are generally not perceived as

praxen mit künstlerischen Konzepten und Artefakten zu tun haben.
Gleichermaßen traditionelle wie aktuelle populäre Körperschmucktechniken wie Tätowierungen oder Piercings erweitern die Körpergrenze optisch und physisch durch ikonische, fetischistische, kodierte Applikationen. Einmal wird Farbe in die zweite Hautschicht gestochen oder gespritzt, wobei die Bildzeichen minimal unter der Hautoberfläche angeordnet werden, das andere Mal wird die Haut durchlöchert. 1908 unterschied Georg Simmel in seiner intersubjektiv angelegten *Psychologie des Schmucks* die Grade der Verbindung des Schmucks mit dem Körper und kategorisierte die Tätowierung als „unbedingt enge[n] Schmuck", unlösbar mit der geschmückten Person verbunden, im Gegensatz zum „Metall- und Steinschmuck, der absolut unindividuell ist"[9]. Tattoos wie Piercings greifen die westlich ideologisch-theologisch verordnete Ganzheit des Menschen an und entwerten das kulturelle Gebot gezielt. Die biologisch-organische Porosität der Haut und die anatomischen, gesellschaftlich legitimen Körperöffnungen werden in den genannten Schmuckprozessen entgegen einer Idee von Natürlichkeit sozioästhetisch vermehrt. Und sie werden umgedeutet. Derart lassen sich Zugehörigkeit bzw. Abgrenzung oder Protest aus der subkulturellen Perspektive (vor allem Punk) signalisieren, das Subjekt stilisiert sich selbstgewählt oder stimuliert sich und/oder andere sexuell. Solche kulturellen Schmuck-Gesten, -Handlungen und -Visualitäten befragen einen traditionellen symbolischen Kanon von Unverletzlichkeit, von Sichtbarkeit und Unsichtbarkeit, Tiefe und Oberfläche, stellen Wert und Nutzen von Materialien in Frage. Zugleich schlagen sie eine Umdeutung wertproduzierender Techniken vor. Statt Gold fachgerecht kunstvoll zu schmieden, werden Alltagsgegenstände gefunden und gesammelt, um sie als Ready-mades zu kombinieren oder handwerklich zu modifizieren. Pravu Mazumdar zeigt auf überzeugende Weise, dass Gold deshalb derart ‚strahlen' und Macht materialisieren konnte, weil es als Spiegel der Gottheit Sonne galt; der symbolische Wert übertraf bei weitem den substanziellen. Spätestens mit der Aufhebung der Geldbindung an die Goldwährung 1976 ist das Material Gold autark geworden. Was die ausbeuterischen, überwiegend noch immer kolonialen Umstände seiner Gewinnung betrifft, stehen ihm Mineralien wie Lithium[10], die Metalle Nickel und Kobalt oder der fossile Energieträger Rohöl, bezeichnenderweise auch Schwarzes Gold genannt, allerdings in nichts nach (KATRIN SPRANGER, *Best Before*, 2012). Heute sind deren Preise Indikatoren

aesthetically pleasing presents an ambivalent picture of the responsibility of women for sex without the risk of unwanted pregnancy. The artist displays this medical instrument, focusing on the pleasure involved as well as on womankind's responsibility. The artist thus cuts through the discretion of intimacy because the chains do not conform with the social imperative of a clear distinction between the inside and the outside, the private and the political. And they thus direct at least my attention to a historically accepted, explicitly feminist position in the context of art – the chewed gum in Hannah Wilke's *S.O.S. – Starification Object Series*, 1975, from which she molded little vaginas and stuck them onto her beautiful face and her upper body, before taking photographs of herself with them – one example that might make it clear how many current jewelry practices are linked to art concepts and artifacts.
Techniques in body decoration such as tattoos and piercings, the kind of techniques that are not only traditional but also popular today, extend the boundaries of the body both visually and physically by means of iconic, fetishist, coded inscriptions. For tattoos, dye is engraved or injected into the second layer of the skin, with the pictographs being placed slightly under the surface of the skin, while piercing involves perforation of the skin. In his 1908 text *Psychologie des Schmucks* (The Psychology of Jewelry), which he approached from an intersubjective angle, Georg Simmel distinguished between different degrees of connection between jewelry and the body, categorizing tattooing as "extremely close jewelry," permanently linked to the decorated person, in contrast to "metal and stone jewelry which is absolutely not individualized."[9] Both tattoos and piercings assault the integrity of man in ideological or theological terms and purposely devalue the dictates of culture. The skin's biological or organic porosity and the anatomical, socially legitimate orifices of the body are aggrandized socio-aesthetically through the above-mentioned decorative processes which stand in contrast to the idea of naturalness. And they are reinterpreted. In this way, the fact of belonging, distancing oneself or even protesting, from the subcultural perspective, can be announced (one of the best examples of the latter being the punk movement); the person in question stylizes herself in her own way or stimulates herself and/or others sexually. These kinds of cultural decoration gestures, actions and illustrations query a traditional symbolic canon of

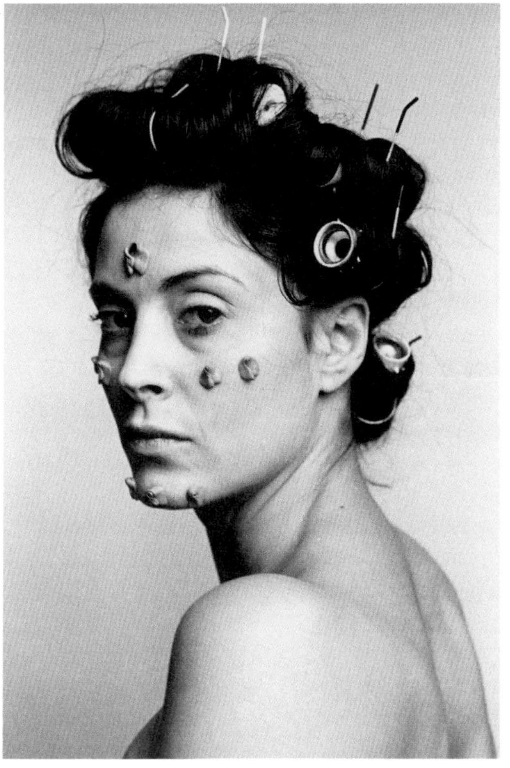

Hannah Wilke, S.O.S. – Starification Object Series (Lockenwickler I Curlers),1975
Silbergelatineabzüge mit Kaugummi-Skulpturen
Gelatin silver prints with chewing gum sculptures
101,6 × 148,6 × 5,7 cm
Museum of Modern Art, New York

für die Wirtschaftsentwicklung. Solche Materialien für die Schmuckproduktion einzusetzen, entlockt den Stoffen nicht nur überraschende ästhetische Eigenschaften. In anderem Maß als die in die Zeitlosigkeit der Konvention getriebenen Edelmetalle Gold und Silber transportieren die jüngst in der Autorenschmuck-Produktion eingesetzten ‚Kunststoffe' ihre historischen, ökonomischen und sozialen Kontexte. Der Abbau solchen Goldersatzes fällt mit dem Anthropozän zusammen, mit der gewaltsamen geologischen Umgestaltung der Erde in den letzten zwei Jahrhunderten.

Gehen wir einen Schritt zurück zur Ornamentierung von Haut, die bereits beim Tattoo Thema war, und fügen ihr eine fantastische Variante hinzu. Unermüdlich arbeitet die US-amerikanische Biologin, Philosophin und utopische Feministin Donna Haraway an Fiktionen, an *SF* wie *speculative fiction* oder *science fiction*, die der un-/menschlichen Destruktion im Anthropozän Achtsamkeitsmodelle im sogenannten Chthuluzän, einem Kompost- oder Humuszeitalter, entgegensetzen wollen. In ihrer Textsammlung *Unruhig bleiben. Die Verwandtschaft der Arten im Chthuluzän*[11] handelt eine futuristische Kurzgeschichte vom menschlichen Wesen Camille, dem vor der Geburt einige Gene des Monarchfalters eingesetzt

inviolability, one of visibility and invisibility, depth and surface, question the value and use of materials. At the same time, they suggest a reinterpretation of value-enhancing techniques. Here it is not a question of hammering gold artistically and in an expert fashion, but instead everyday items are found and collected, then combined into ready-mades or modified by skilled craftspeople. Pravu Mazumdar convincingly demonstrates that gold was able to 'gleam' so brightly and embody power because it was considered a mirror of the deity that was the sun; its symbolic value far exceeded its material one. When money ceased to be linked to the gold standard in 1976 at the very latest, the material gold became self-sufficient. And the exploitative, predominantly still colonial circumstances in which it is mined are matched by those in evidence for minerals such as lithium,[10] the metals nickel and cobalt and the fossil fuels crude oil, significantly known as black gold (KATRIN SPRANGER, *Best Before*, 2012). Nowadays, their prices are indicative of economic development. And it is not only the case that using these kinds of materials for jewelry production teases surprising aesthetic qualities from them. The 'synthetic materials' used in the recent past for

wurden und das daher das Muster der Schmetterlingsflügel auf der Haut trägt. Der Folgegeneration sind bereits feine Fühler gewachsen. Verbunden mit dieser Manipulation ist ein zunehmendes Gespür für die Befindlichkeit anderer Arten und ein von Generation zu Generation wachsendes Einfühlungsvermögen in eben jene Schmetterlingsart, die vom Aussterben bedroht ist. Haraways *SF* zeigt sich als ein vehementes Plädoyer für „companion species" (Gefährtenarten), mithin für Beziehungen quer zu biologisch fundierter Verwandtschaft und dafür, Menschen, Tiere, Pflanzen, Bakterien, Pilze, aber auch Maschinen in einer humusartigen Kollaboration zu sehen: „‚My' Chthulucene [...] entangles myriad temporalities and spatialities and myriad intra-active entities-in-assemblages – including the more-than-human, other than human, inhuman, and human-as-humus."[12] Bezogen auf ein alternatives Schmuckdenken steht hier geradezu die Forderung im Raum, die traditionell genealogisch-familial praktizierte Vererbung von Schmuck – von der Großmutter auf die Mutter auf die Tochter – zu durchbrechen. Es ist, als sollte das sozio-genetische Band im Erbe von Diamantringen oder Perlenketten durch andere Materialien, Konzepte und Assemblagen für queere Wahlverwandtschaften sensibilisiert, ja manipuliert werden.

EUNMI CHUNs Nachbildungen von Tieren, *Panda*, 2015, und *Gorilla*, 2011, kommen in den Sinn. Aus pergamenten präpariertem Kuhdünndarm konstruiert, haben diese Wesen feinste Tentakel aus Menschenhaar, um sich als Schmuckstück zwischen Kleid, Haut und Welt zu orientieren. Aber auch NICOLA SCHOLZs Kordel aus Spinnweben oder ihre Goldkette mit Tarantelbeinen, *o.T.*, 2010, lässt sich als ein gleichermaßen kunstvoller wie irritierender Hinweis auf Haraways utopisches Kompost-Zeitalter interpretieren. Zu einer formal klassisch anmutenden Kordel gedreht und um den Hals gehängt, mutieren Spinnwebfäden vom ekeligen Störfaktor zum delikaten Material. Extrem elastisch und reißfest, liegen in der Spinnenseide neben der zum Schmuck umgearbeiteten Solidarität mit anderen Lebewesen aber auch alternative biologische und technische Qualitäten in Kombination vor. Bionik und Medizin experimentieren erfolgreich mit diesem Stoff als Nervenersatz.[13] Metaphorisch gesprochen ist die Spinnenseide also ‚Gold wert' – denn ist die umfängliche Funktion der Nerven für den Organismus nicht wertvoller als alle Diamanten zusammen?

Inhaltlich nicht völlig anders, aber in anderer Materialität ausgeführt, spielen HANNA HEDMANs urzeitliche kleine

the production of studio jewelry reveal their historical, economic and social contexts to a different degree compared to the precious metals gold and silver, which have been driven into the timelessness of convention. However, mining this kind of replacement gold coincides with the Anthropocene, with the violent geological reconfiguration of the Earth over the past two centuries.

Let us take one step backwards to the ornamentation of the skin, which was already an issue in the case of tattooing, and let us add a fantastic element to this. American biologist, philosopher and utopian feminist Donna Haraway is tirelessly at work on various types of fiction, on *SF* as in both *speculative fiction* and science fiction, aimed at contrasting the non-human/human destruction in the Anthropocene with the consciousness model in the era known as the Chthulucene, an age of compost or humus. In her collection of texts *Staying with the Trouble: Making Kin in the Chthulucene*,[11] a futuristic short story tells of the human being Camille, into whom some of the genes of the monarch butterfly were implanted before birth and whose skin therefore bears the pattern of a butterfly wing. The following generation has already evolved delicate feelers. This manipulation was connected with an increasing feel for the sensitivities of other species and a capacity, which grew from generation to generation, for empathy particularly with those species of butterfly threatened with extinction. Haraway's *SF* turned out to be a vehement plea for "companion species" and therefore for relationships contrary to those with their roots in biology and for seeing people, animals, plants, bacteria, fungi and even machines in a humus-like collaboration: "'My' Chthulucene [...] entangles myriad temporalities and spatialities and myriad intra-active entities-in-assemblages–including the more-than-human, other than human, inhuman, and human-as-humus."[12] Applying this to an alternative approach to jewelry positively calls upon us to break through the family tradition of passing on jewelry from the grandmother to the mother to the daughter. It is as if the socio-genetic bond in evidence when bequeathing diamond rings or strings of pearls in this way should be sensitized, indeed manipulated by means of other materials, concepts and assemblages for queer elective affinities.

EUNMI CHUN's replicas of animals, *Panda*, 2015, and *Gorilla*, 2011, spring to mind. Constructed from the prepared small intestines of bovines and papery

Schuppenpanzer *While they await extinction*, 2011, auf ausgestorbene Tierarten an. Um den Hals gehängt, entsteht ein unmittelbares Statement zur Naturgeschichte und zur Bedrohung von Biodiversität, ein implizites Plädoyer für den Verantwortungsverbund in einem „Planthumanimal"[14] und der „companion species". JASMIN MATZAKOW verzwirnt Brennnesseln für die Serie *Ecotechnomagic*, 2018, arbeitet mit einem populären Nahrungs- und Heilmittel, spielt aber auch auf eine Stofffaser für das sogenannte Arme-Leute-Leinen an; alte Nutzeigenschaften, aber auch die Sozialgeschichte einer Pflanze und ihrer Verwendung zu signalisieren, mündet nunmehr in eine alternativ definierte Kostbarkeit.

Autorenschmuck, möchte ich gezeigt haben, ist emanzipatorisch. Er kann (selbst)ermächtigend wahrgenommen werden, gerade weil er eine traditionelle Kategorie von (sogenannter angewandter) Kunst und ästhetischer Produktion samt ihren spezifischen handwerklichen Techniken als Grundlage nimmt. In Akzeptanz der Kategorie Form wie zugleich in Auseinandersetzung mit den selbstbezüglichen Aspekten von Schmuck bezieht er sich auf die Welt – im Sinn eines scharfsinnig-kritischen Bewusstseins vom Heute in all seiner gesellschaftlichen, kulturellen, ökologischen und politischen Fragilität, aber auch in seiner Potenzialität. Dabei haben kulturelle Vorstellungen vom Körper große Bedeutung. Wird Schmuck getragen, hat er schließlich immer eine Beziehung zu seiner Oberfläche; Schmuck trianguliert die Elemente Bekleidung hier und Körper da; als Drittes hat er mit beiden zu tun und transformiert die Rolle von Sichtbarkeit und Positionierung des Subjekts. Wobei der Diskurs der Oberfläche in den vergangenen etwa 150 Jahren selbst schon die klassische Opposition von Außen und Innen ins topologische Denken von Nachbarschaften und Intensitäten überführte. Das Potenzial des derart verschobenen Denkens ist auch eine veränderte Aufmerksamkeit für das mächtige Gefälle zwischen Rändern und Mitte. Gesellschaftlich konkretisiert waren und sind es keineswegs ausschließlich, aber in besonderem Maß, Frauen und nichtheterosexuelle Menschen, die ihr Aussehen und ihr Ansehen in Frage gestellt gesehen haben und noch immer sehen. Verallgemeinern wir das Verhältnis zwischen Marginalem und Hegemonialem in Richtung alles Gefährdeten und Unterdrückten bzw. Verdrängten, das eine Anwaltschaft benötigt. Schmuck kann eine Artikulation dieser Verhältnisse sein. Ob seine Ideen und seine Anfertigungen geschätzt, ja wertgeschätzt werden oder nicht, Autorenschmuck ist Gesprächsgegenstand. Er kommuniziert mit einem nachgerade

in texture, these beings have the most delicate tentacles of human hair and, as jewelry pieces, can be placed somewhere between a dress, skin and the world. NICOLA SCHOLZ's cord made of cobwebs and her gold chain with tarantula, *Untitled*, 2010, can also be interpreted as an equally artistic and disconcerting reference to Haraway's utopian compost age. Twisted to form a cord that is classic in appearance and hung around the neck, the cobweb threads mutate from something disgusting and disturbing into a delicate material. Spider silk is not only extremely elastic and tear-proof but also, along with its solidarity with other living creatures, which has been translated into jewelry, contains combinations of alternative biological and technical qualities. Bionics and the medical field are both conducting successful experiments with this material as a nerve replacement.[13] Metaphorically speaking, spider silk is 'worth its weight in gold' – after all, is it not the case that the manifold functions of the nerves are more valuable to an organism than all the diamonds in the world?

Not entirely different in content, but executed in other materials, HANNA HEDMAN's primeval small pieces of scale armor *While they await extinction*, 2011, allude to extinct animal species. When wearers hang them around their necks they are making a statement about natural history and the threat to biodiversity, a veiled plea for a network of responsibility in a "planthumanimal"[14] and the "companion species." JASMIN MATZAKOW twists stinging nettles for her series *Ecotechnomagic*, 2018, working with a popular foodstuff and remedy but also referencing a vegetable fiber for something once known in Germany as "poor man's linen." Now, pointing out old uses for the fiber as well as referencing the social history of the plant have resulted in an alternative definition of the word precious.

As I hope to have demonstrated, studio jewelry has something emancipatory to it. It can be perceived as (self-)empowering, particularly because it is a traditional category of (so-called applied) art on the basis of aesthetic production including all the specific craft techniques of the trade. In accepting the category of form, whilst simultaneously investigating the self-referential aspects of decoration, the craft references the world – through its shrewd, critical awareness of the age we live in with all its social, cultural, ecological and political fragility, but also its potential. The cultural notions of body play an important role in this. When

unbegrenzten Spektrum an ästhetisch betörenden, aber auch provozierenden Mitteln. Sie artikulieren ihre Mitteilung als Abweichung vom Konventionellen und Gewohnten, das gleichwohl als Referenz bestehen bleibt. Da die Schmuckstücke dabei die Trägerin und den Träger physisch berühren und auch die Betrachter*innen aus der Nähe und nicht aus der Distanz schauen, wird die Kommunikation, ob real oder imaginär, sehr persönlich sein und unweigerlich die feministische Aufbruchsformel der 1970er-Jahre „Das Persönliche ist politisch" aktualisieren.

1: Bakri Bakhit, Nadja Quante u.a., *Touch*, Broschüre zur gleichnamigen Ausstellung in der nGbK Berlin 2018; https://www.ngbk.de/images/stories/PDF/booklet_touch_2018.pdf (zuletzt 11.11.2018).
2: John Carl Flügel, *Die Psychologie der Kleidung* (1930). In: Gertrud Lehnert, Alicia Kühl und Katja Weise (Hgg.), Modetheorie. Klassische Texte aus vier Jahrhunderten, aus dem Engl. von Matthias Müller, Bielefeld: transcript 2014, S. 117–129, wieder in Barbara Vinken (Hg.), Die Blumen der Mode. Klassische & neue Texte zur Philosophie der Mode, Stuttgart: Klett-Cotta 2016, S. 256–264, Zitat S. 258.
3: Ebd., S. 264.
4: Karen Barad, Berühren – das Nicht-Menschliche, das ich also bin. In: Kerstin Stakemeier und Susanne Witzgall (Hgg.), *Macht des Materials – Politik der Materialität*, Zürich, Berlin: diaphanes 2014, S. 163–176, Zitat S. 163.
5: Physikalisch betrachtet sind dies erst einmal Elektronen.
6: Karen Barad 2014, S. 176.
7: Pravu Mazumdar, *Gold und Geist. Prolegomena zu einer Theorie des Schmucks*, Berlin: Matthes & Seitz 2015, S. 15 ff., Zitat S. 15.
8: Vgl. Michel Foucault, *Die Geburt der Klinik. Eine Archäologie des ärztlichen Blicks* (1963), aus dem Franz. von Walter Seitter, Frankfurt am Main: Suhrkamp 1988, S. 140.
9: Georg Simmel, Psychologie des Schmuckes. In: *Der Morgen. Wochenschrift für deutsche Kultur*, begründet und hrsg. von Werner Sombart zusammen mit Richard Strauß, Georg Brandes u.a., Berlin, 2. Jg., Nr. 15 vom 10. April 1908, S. 454–459; http://socio.ch/sim/verschiedenes/1908/schmuck.htm (zuletzt 09.11.2018).
10: In Thomas Melles Buch *Die Welt im Rücken*, Berlin 2016, lernte ich Lithium auch als starkes und effektives Psychopharmakon kennen, eingesetzt bei bipolaren Störungen. Dieser Zusammenhang verleiht STEFAN HEUSERs aus Medikamenten gefertigten Selbstporträts *A Master of Selfcontrol Narrated*, 2010, eine spezifische Rezeption.
11: Donna J. Haraway, Camilles Geschichten. Die Kinder der Kompostisten. In: dies., *Unruhig bleiben. Die Verwandtschaft der Arten im Chthuluzän*, aus dem Amerik. von Karin Harrasser, Frankfurt am Main: Campus Verlag 2018, S. 134–168, 215–228.
12: Donna Haraway, Anthropocene, Capitalocene, Plantationocene, Chthulucene: Making Kin. In: *Environmental Humanities*, vol. 6, 2015, S. 159–165; www.environmentalhumanities.org (zuletzt 29.10.2018). Verwandtschaft findet sich exemplarisch in der Semiose des Begriffs der Brut: menschliche Nachkommenschaft, tierischer Laich und Myzelfäden eines Pilzes in eins.
13: Yvonne Maier, Nerven aus Spinnenseide, https://www.br.de/themen/wissen/spinne-spinnenseide-bionik-108.html, 24.02.2014 (zuletzt 11.11.2018).
14: Hanne Loreck, Einführung. In: dies.. Andrea Klier und Sara Lindeborg (Hgg.) *(Mit) Pflanzen kartografieren / Mapping (with) Plants*, Hamburg: Material-Verlag 2017, S. 77–80, Zitat S. 79.

jewelry is worn, at the end of the day it always has a relationship with the surface beneath it; jewelry triangulates the elements of clothing on the one hand and body on the other. Ultimately, it has something to do with both these aspects, transforming the role of its wearer's visibility and positioning. It should not be forgotten that over the past approximately 150 years the discourse on surface has taken even the classic contrast between outside and inside out into a topological sphere, in order to consider neighborhoods and intensities. One of the possibilities afforded by thinking in this skewed manner is a changed attention to the great gap between the edge and the center. In concrete social terms it has been and still is, by no means exclusively but to a large extent, women and the non-heterosexual who have considered and still consider their appearance and their reputations called into question. Let us generalize the relationship between the marginal and the hegemonic in terms of anything that is endangered or suppressed and is in need of advocacy. Jewelry can be one way of articulating such circumstances. Independent of whether its ideas and its concrete dimensions are valued or even appreciated or not, studio jewelry is a topic of discussion. It communicates by means of a well-nigh unlimited range of elements that are aesthetically beguiling, but also provocative. They articulate their message as a deviation from the conventional and familiar, one which nevertheless remains in existence as a point of reference. And since these jewelry pieces touch their wearers physically and since even those who look at them see them from close up rather than from a distance, what they communicate, whether in real or imagined terms, will be very personal and is bound to update the feminist rallying cry of the 1970s "The personal is political."

1: Bakri Bakhit, Nadja Quante et al., *Touch*, brochure accompanying the exhibition of the same name at nGbK Berlin, 2018; https://www.ngbk.de/images/stories/PDF/booklet_touch_2018.pdf (last accessed November 11, 2018).
2: John Carl Flügel, *The Psychology of Clothes*, (London: Hogarth Press, 1930), p. 111.
4: Karen Barad, "On Touching – The Inhuman That Therefore I Am," in: Kerstin Stakemeier and Susanne Witzgall (eds.), *Power of Material – Politics of Materiality*, (Zurich, Berlin: diaphanes, 2018), pp. 153–164, quotation p. 153.
5: Physically speaking, to begin with we are talking about electrons.
6: Karen Barad 2014, p. 164.
7: Pravu Mazumdar, *Gold und Geist. Prolegomena zu einer Theorie des Schmucks*, (Berlin: Matthes & Seitz, 2015), pp. 15ff, quotation p. 15, (trans.).
8: Cf. Michel Foucault, *The Birth of the Clinic: An Archaeology of Medical Perception* (1963), translated from the French by A. M. Sheridan Smith, (New York: Pantheon Books, 1973), p. 127.
9: Georg Simmel, "Psychologie des Schmuckes," in: *Der Morgen. Wochenschrift für deutsche Kultur*, established and ed. by Werner Sombart with Richard Strauß, Georg Brandes et al., Berlin, vol.2, no. 15 dated April 10, 1908, pp. 454–459; http://socio.ch/sim/verschiedenes/1908/schmuck.htm (last accessed November 9, 2018).

10: In Thomas Melle's book *Die Welt im Rücken* (Berlin, 2016), I discovered that in one of its guises lithium is a strong and effective psychotropic which is used for bipolar disorders. This context has furnished STEFAN HEUSER's self-portrait constructed from pharmaceuticals *A Master of Selfcontrol Narrated*, 2010, with a specific reception.
11: Donna J. Haraway, "The Camille Stories. Children of Compost," in: *Haraway, Staying with the Trouble. Making Kin in the Chthulucene*, (Durham: Duke University Press, 2016) pp. 134–68 and 215–228.
12: Donna Haraway, "Anthropocene, Capitalocene, Plantationocene, Chthulucene: Making Kin," in: *Environmental Humanities*, vol. 6, 2015, pp. 159–165; www.environmentalhumanities.org (last accessed October 29, 2018). One good example is to be found in the semiosis of the term brood: the descendants of human beings are children, those of animals are young and those of fungi are spawn.
13: Yvonne Maier, "Nerven aus Spinnenseide," https://www.br.de/themen/wissen/spinne-spinnenseide-bionik-108.html, February 24, 2014 (last accessed November 11, 2018).
14: Hanne Loreck, "Einführung," in: Loreck, Andrea Klier and Sara Lindeborg (eds.), *(Mit) Pflanzen kartografieren / Mapping (with) Plants*, (Hamburg: Material-Verlag, 2017), pp. 77–80, quotation p. 79.

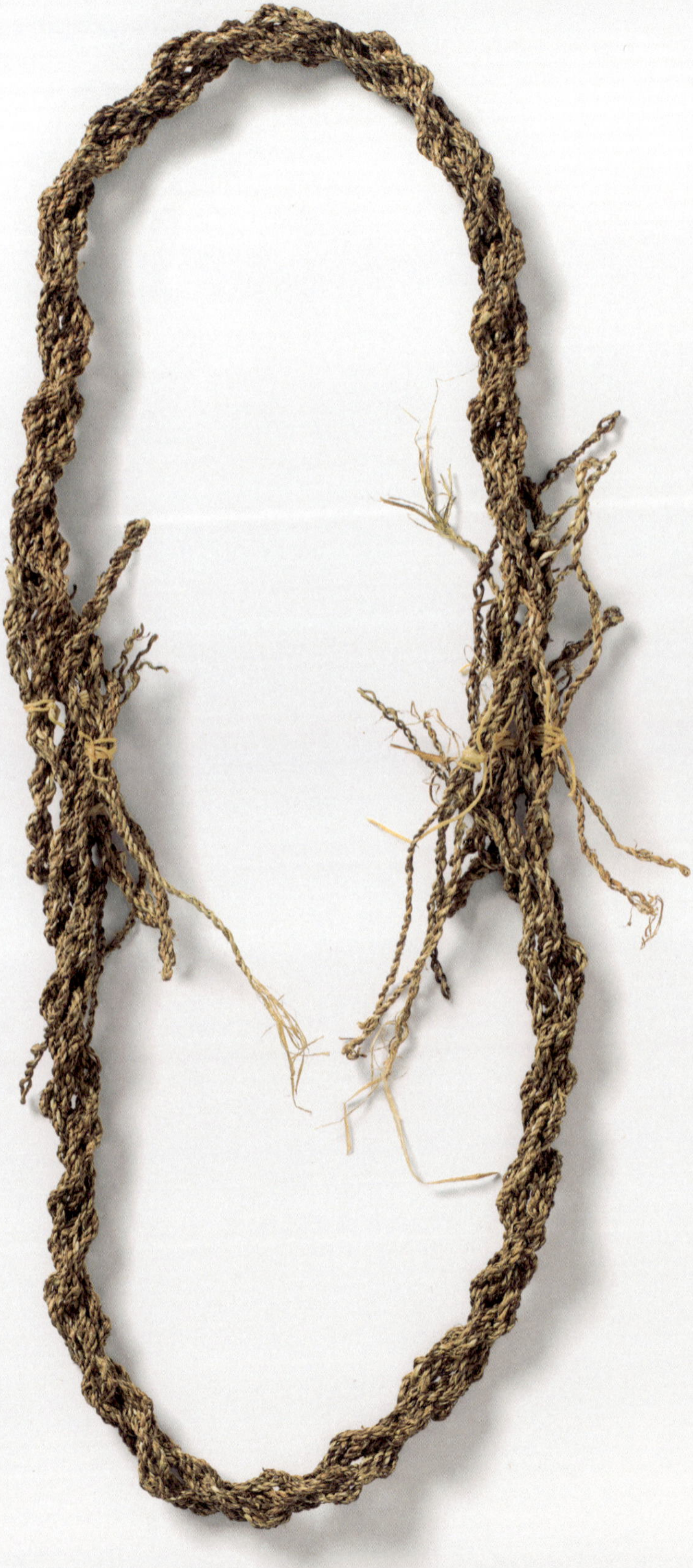

JASMIN MATZAKOW

40
Halsschmuck „Alliance“ aus der Serie | necklace "Alliance" from the series "Ecotechnomagic-Ritual", 2019
125 Brennnesseln, gezwirnt; Schweinedarm
125 stinging nettles, twisted; pig intestines
73 × 20 × 8 cm

42
Halsschmuck „Untamable“ aus der Serie
necklace "Untamable" from the series
"Ecotechnomagic", 2018, 75 Brennnesseln, gezwirnt
75 stinging nettles, twisted, 40 × 15 × 3 cm

43
Halsschmuck „Time“ aus der Serie
necklace "Time" from the series
"Ecotechnomagic", 2018, 50 Brennnesseln, gezwirnt
50 stinging nettles, twisted, 55 × 10 × 1 cm

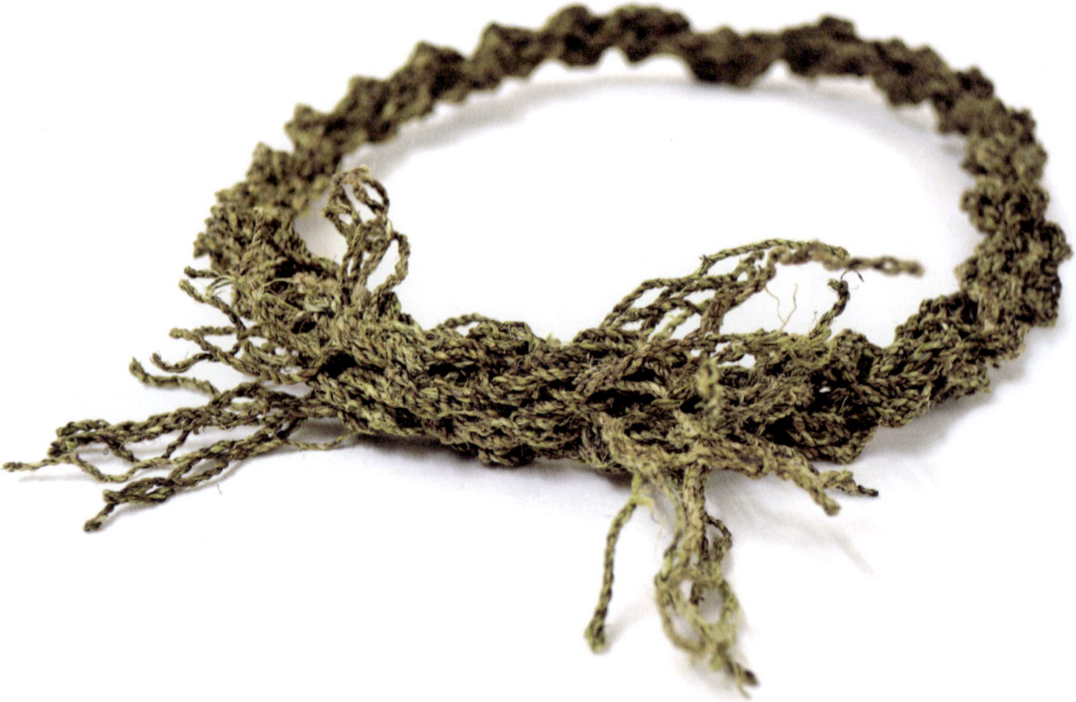

Die Werke von Jasmin Matzakow sind aus dem Material Brennnessel hergestellt. Ein Fokus innerhalb der Arbeiten ist die Nutzung von Materialien, die nur am Rande oder gänzlich außerhalb der Finanzsysteme der westlichen Kultur existieren und trotzdem für Menschen von großer Nützlichkeit sein können. Die Rolle der Künstlerin ist es hierbei, eine Art performative Stellvertreterin der Gesellschaft zu sein. Ähnlich funktionieren die Schmuckstücke als Zeugen eines Prozesses, der Diskurs über Machtsysteme und Kommerzialisierung anregen soll. Dabei wird der Schmucktragende aufgefordert, sich unmittelbar mit der Rolle des Einzelnen als sozialem Akteur auseinanderzusetzen. KP

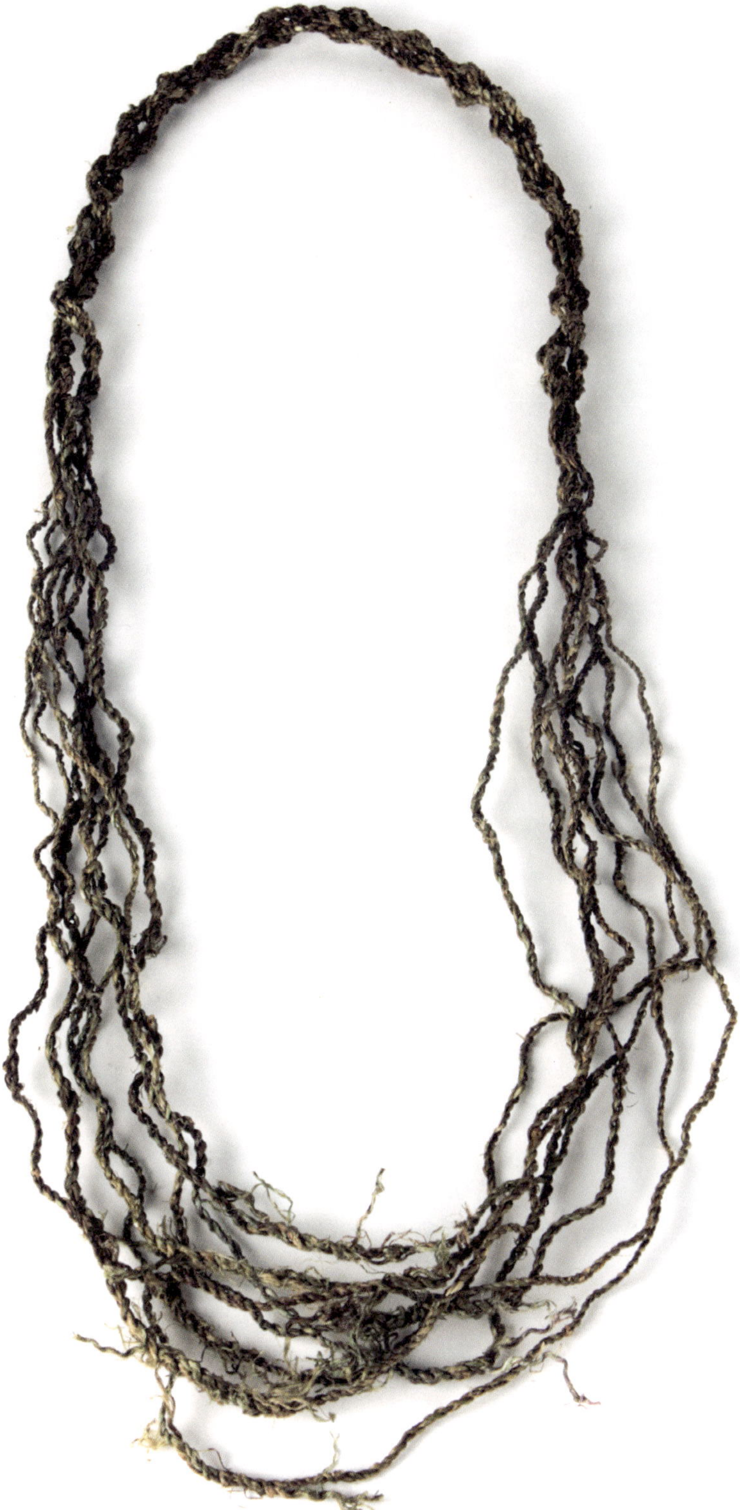

Jasmin Matzakow uses stinging nettles as a material. One point of focus in her work is the use of materials that exist on the margins of or entirely outside the financial systems of Western culture, but which can nevertheless be of great utility to human beings. The role that the artist assumes is that of a performative representative of society. Similarly, the jewelry provides evidence of a process intended to stimulate discourse on power systems and commercialization. In doing so, the wearer is challenged to face her or his actual role as social actor. KP

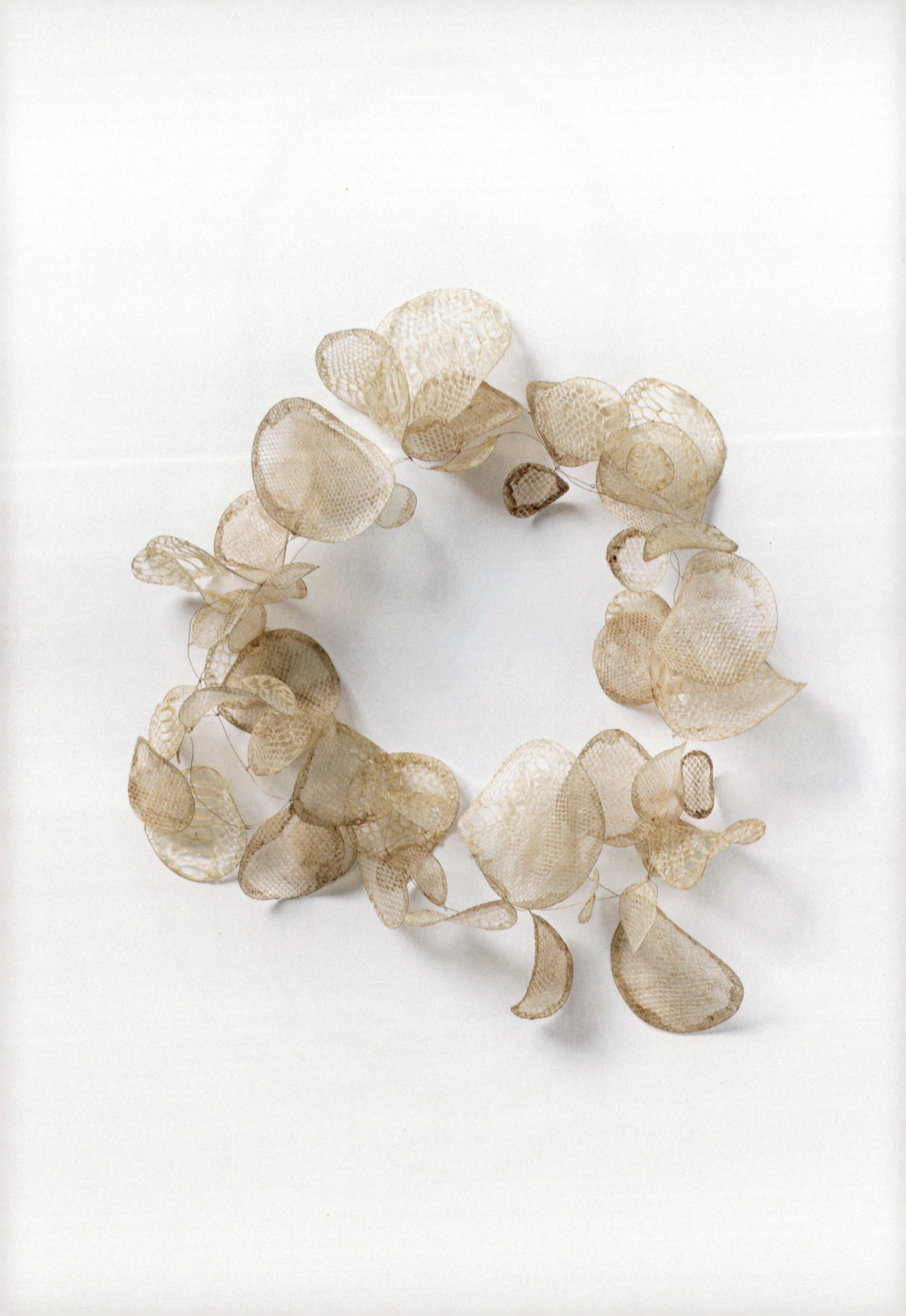

44
Halsschmuck o.T. | necklace untitled, 2019
Schlangenhaut, Gold | snakeskin, gold
Ø ca. 38 cm

47
Anhänger o.T. | pendant untitled, 2010
Vogelspinne (lat. Theraphosidae), Gold
tarantula (Theraphosidae), gold, 12 × 12 × 9 cm

Nicola Scholz formt aus abgestoßenen Beinen einer Tarantel einen Anhänger, der an einer Goldkette hängt. Nicht nur bei an Arachnophobie leidenden Menschen löst die Vorstellung, eine große Spinne am Hals zu tragen, Abneigung aus. Dabei sind die Spinnenbeine nur eine leere Haut, ein hohles Gebilde, ein Signal der Gefahr ohne Inhalt. Die Angst und der Ekel vor befremdlichen Materialien und Begegnungen, oder wie hier durch eine fremde „Haut" ausgelöst, ohne dass konkrete Gefahr besteht, können versteckte Vorurteile offenbaren. Vielleicht kann hierdurch ein Bewusstsein geschaffen werden, das mehr denn je benötigt wird, um gesellschaftliche Entwicklungen kritisch zu betrachten. KP

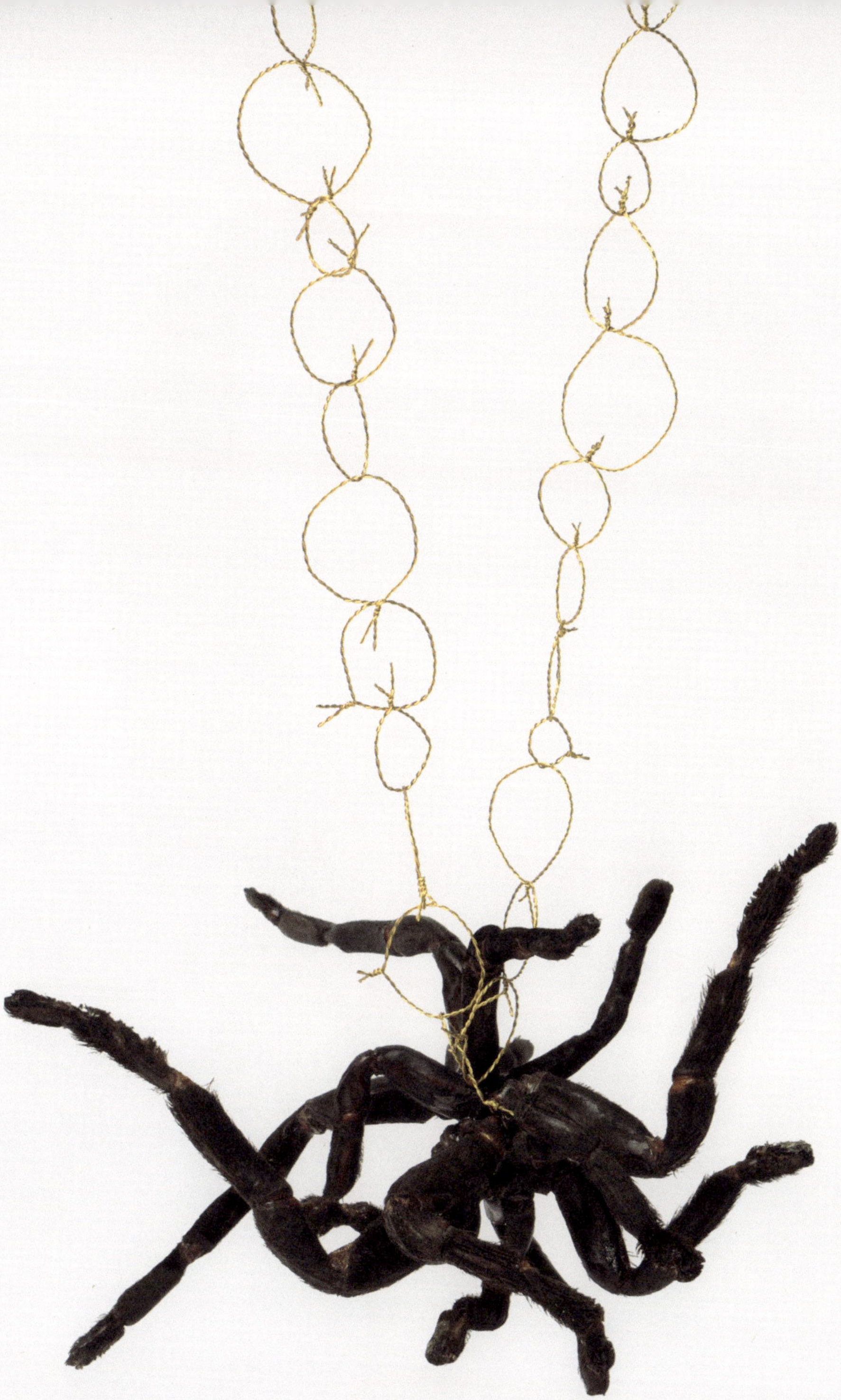

Nicola Scholz has created a necklace consisting of a golden chain and a pendant made from the husks of tarantula legs. It is not only in people suffering from arachnophobia that the idea of wearing a large spider around one's neck causes discomfort. Yet the spider legs are nothing but empty skin, a hollow structure, a signal of danger without real content. The fear of and disgust felt towards strange materials and encounters, or in this case triggered by a foreign "skin" without the presence of concrete danger, can reveal hidden prejudices. Perhaps reflecting on this fact can help raise awareness, something that is needed more than ever to critically examine social developments. KP

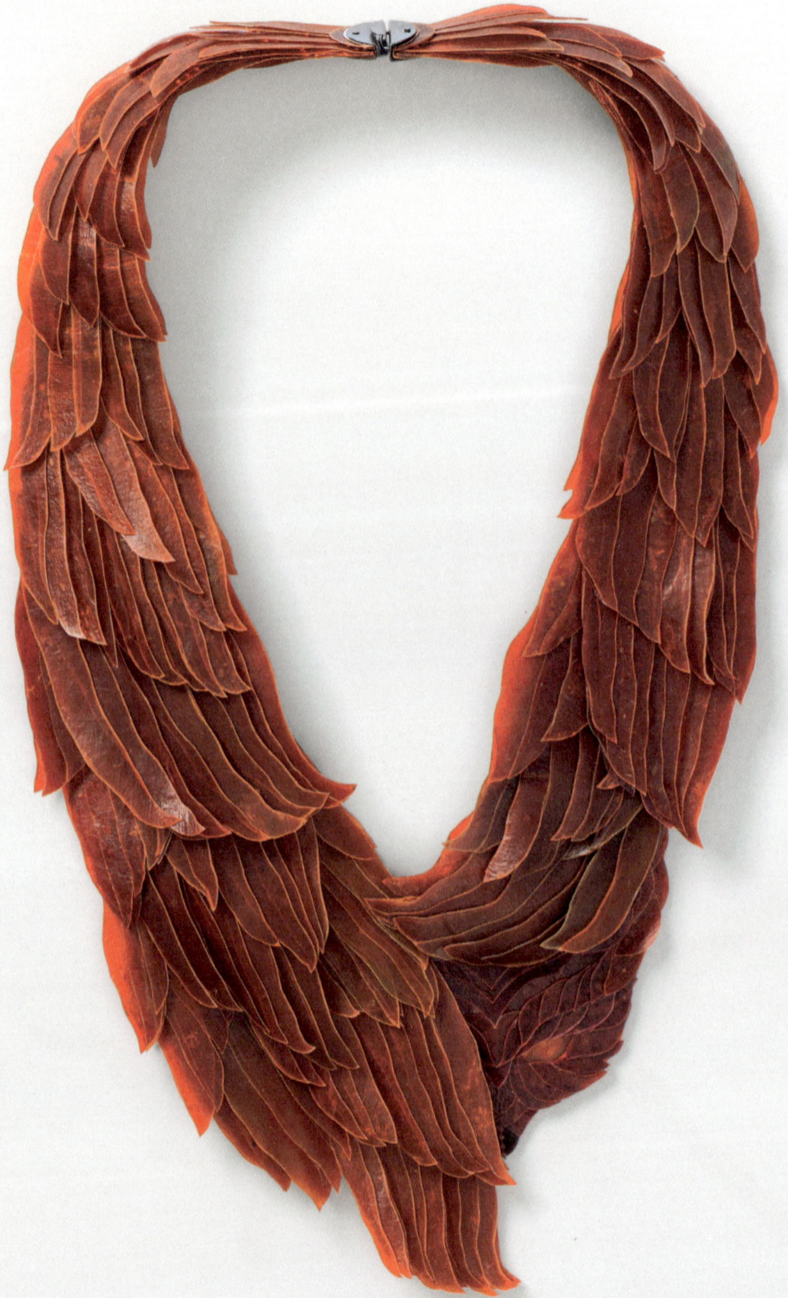

EUNMI CHUN

48
Halsschmuck | necklace "Tails of legendary fox", 2018
Darm, Faden, Tinte, Silber | intestine, thread, ink, silver
38 × 23 × 4 cm

50
Brosche | brooch "Panda", 2015
Menschliches Haar, Dünndarm einer Kuh, Samen, Silber
human hair, small intestine of cow, seeds, silver
9 × 14 × 10 cm

51
Brosche | brooch "Gorilla", 2011
Menschliches Haar, Dünndarm einer Kuh, Samen, Silber
human hair, small intestine of cow, seeds, silver
15 × 15 × 10 cm
Die Neue Sammlung – The Design Museum

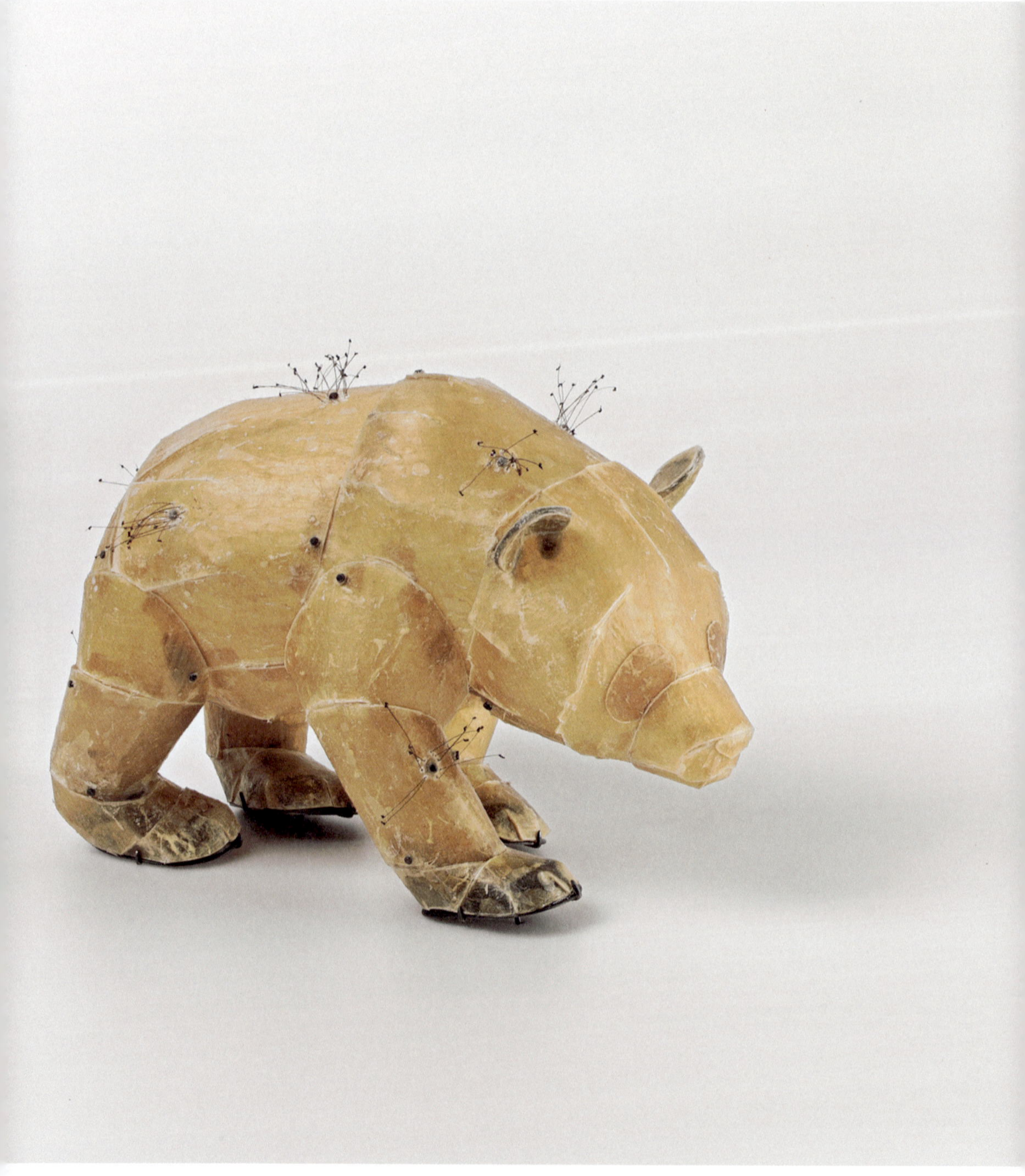

Aus dem Dünndarm einer Kuh hergestelltes Pergament, Samen und menschliche Haare sind die tragenden Materialien für das Narrative in Eunmi Chuns Broschen. Gezeigt werden ein Gorilla und ein Panda, beide Tierarten sind durch das Handeln der Menschen vom Aussterben bedroht. Auch die von der Künstlerin gesammelten, ausgefallenen Haare sprechen von einem bedrohlichen Zyklus, der nur durch die eingeschlossenen Samen erträglicher wird. Sich in die Haut des anderen versetzen zu können, ist die Basis von Empathie. Das Werk von Eunmi Chun zeigt diesen Gedanken nicht nur auf einer persönlichen Ebene, sondern die Aussagekraft hat auch auf einer gesellschaftlichen Ebene Bestand. KP

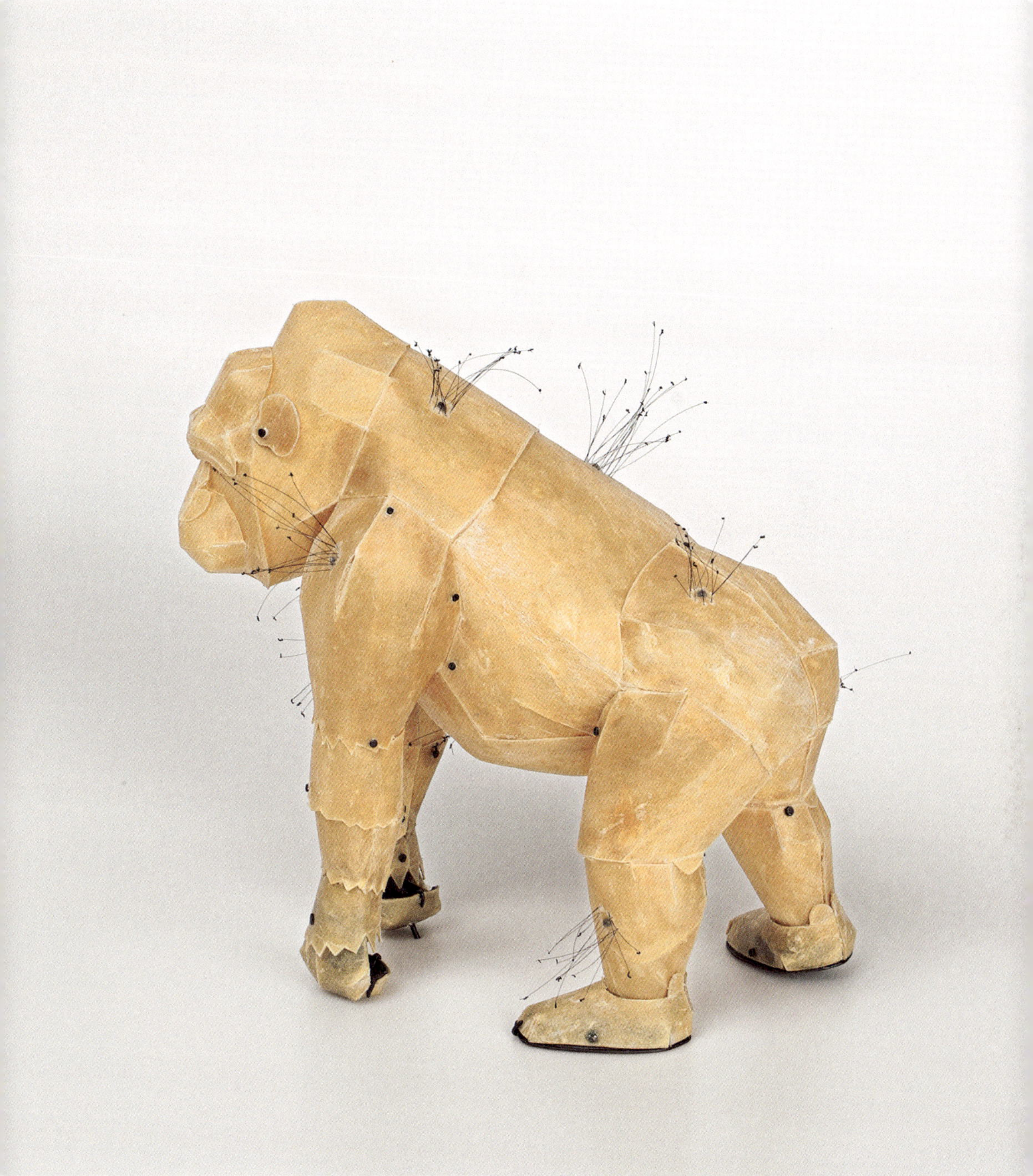

Vellum made from a cow's small intestine, seeds, and human hair are the materials that carry the narrative in Eunmi Chun's brooches. Pictured are a gorilla and a panda, both species that are threatened with extinction by the actions of human beings. The dead hair collected by the artist also speaks of a menacing cycle that is made more bearable only by the enclosed seed. Being able to imagine oneself in the skin (situation) of others is the bedrock of empathy. Eunmi Chun's work not only expresses this thought on a personal level; its significance exists on a societal level, too. KP

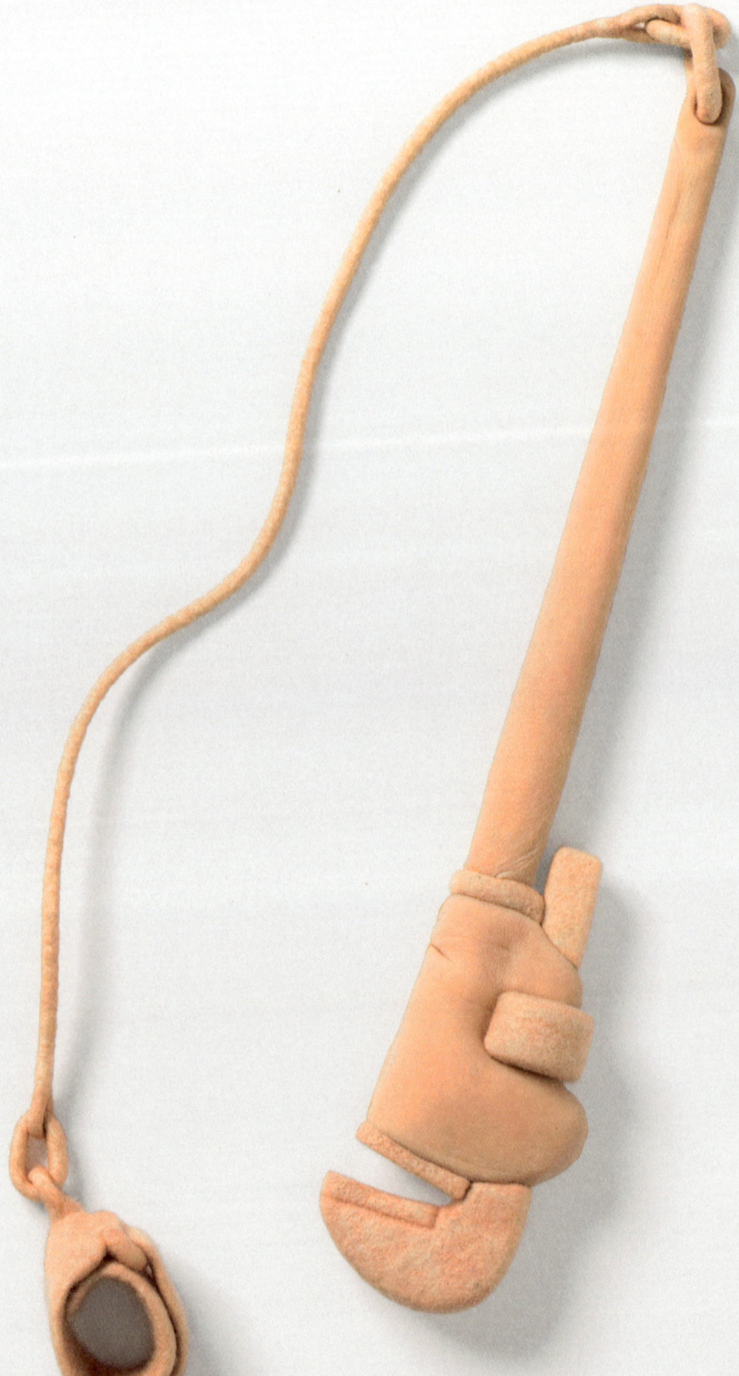

TOBIAS ALM

52
Armschmuck | bracelet, 2018
Werkzeug (Rohrschlüssel), Wollfilz, Silikon
tool (pipe wrench), wool felt, silicone
62 × 34,5 cm

54
"Châtelaine no 13 – Hammer or Flashlight Holder", 2017
Leder; Silber, vergoldet; Rubin; Stahl; Samt; Nylon
leather; silver, gilded; ruby; steel; velvet; nylon
20 × 30 × 10 cm

55
Brosche | brooch "Châtelaine no 14 –
Hammer or Flashlight Holder", 2017
Leder; Silber, vergoldet; Rubin; Stahl
leather; silver, gilded; ruby; steel
9 × 9 × 5 cm

Brosche | brooch "Châtelaine no 15 –
Quick release Tool Snap", 2017
Silber, vergoldet; Stahl | silver, gilded; steel
11 × 7 × 3 cm

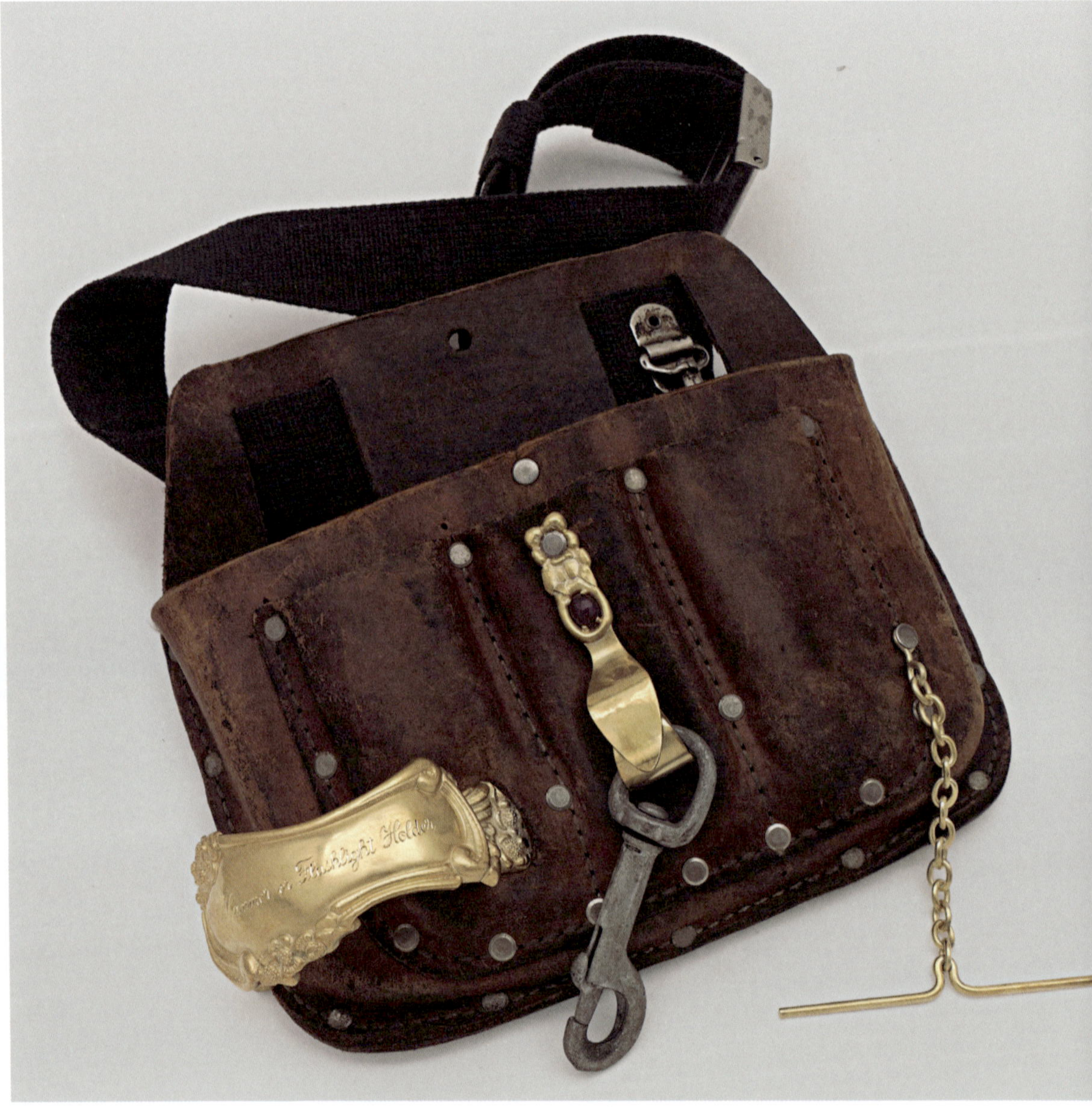

Innerhalb eines kulturellen Kontextes, dessen vorherrschende Vorstellung Männlichkeit als Gegensatz zu einem „Sich-Schmücken“ definiert, findet Tobias Alm den Ausgangspunkt für seine Arbeiten. Er hinterfragt, ob Werkzeuggürtel inmitten misogyner und patriarchalischer Strukturen als eine Art lebendige Schmuckkultur beschrieben werden könnten. In seinen Arbeiten wird stereotypische Männlichkeit als eine normative Geschlechteridentität offenbart, wodurch allgemeine Geschlechterrollen und gesellschaftliche Machtstrukturen beleuchtet werden. KP

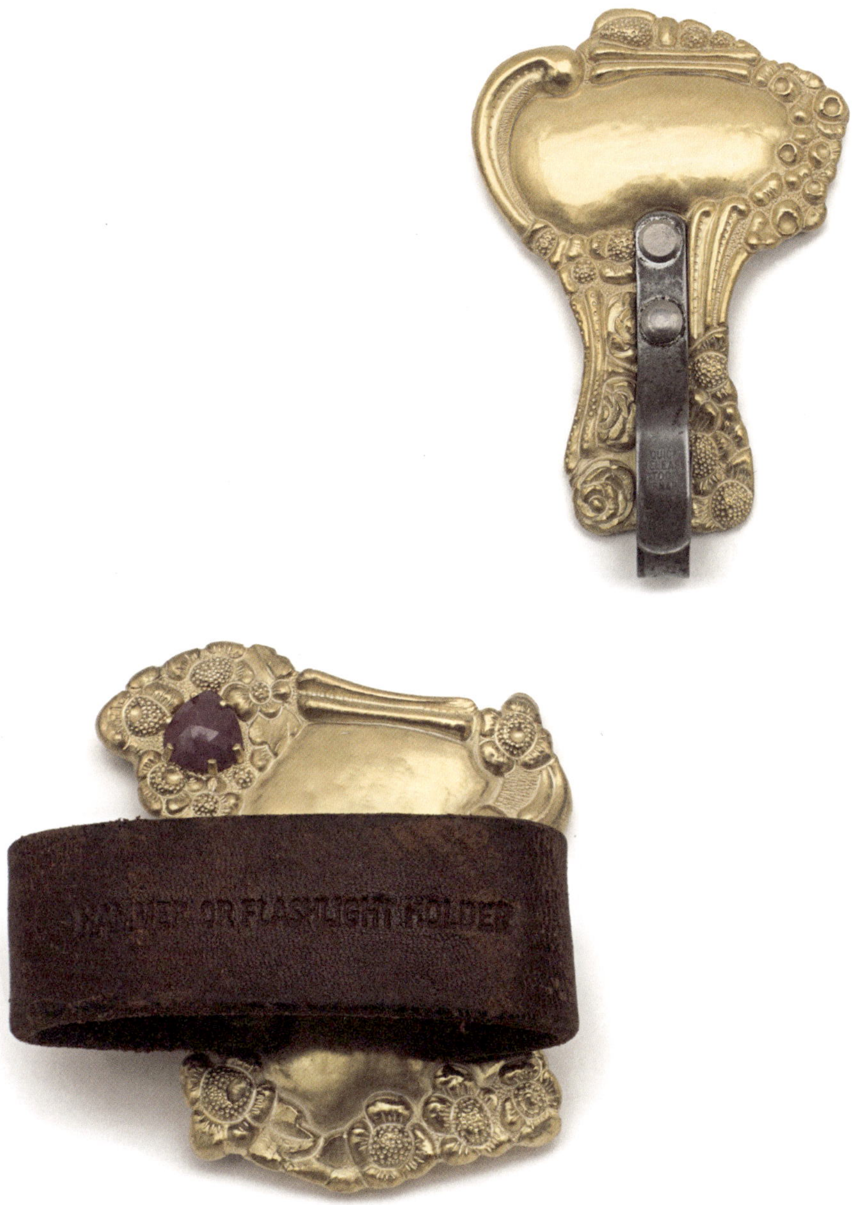

Tobias Alm finds the starting point for his jewelry in a cultural context that predominantly defines masculinity as the opposite of "adorning oneself." He questions whether in the context of misogyny and patriarchal structures tool belts could be described as a kind of vibrant jewelry culture. His works reveal stereotypical masculinity as a normative gender identity and in so doing the pieces shed light on generalized gender roles as well as social power structures. KP

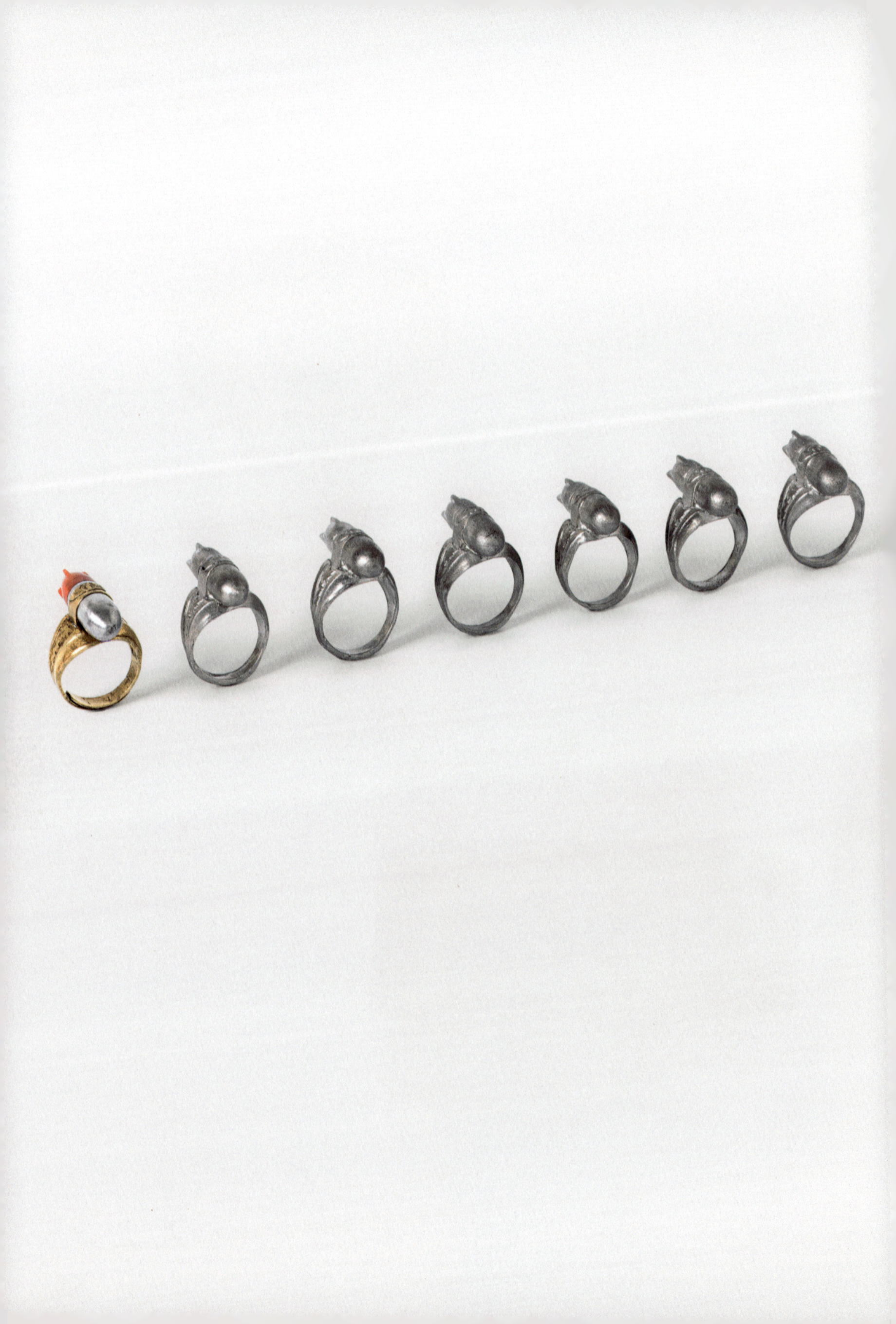

56
Ring I ring "The Lone ranger atomic bomb ring" (original), 1947
Messing, Aluminium, Kunststoff, Polonium-Alpha-Teilchen, Zinksulfid I brass, aluminum, plastic, polonium-alpha particles, zinc sulphide, 3 × 2,5 cm

Ringe I rings "The ring of ignorance" no. 1–10 (replicas), 2018
Zin I tin, 3 x 2,5 cm
Auflagenhöhe: unendlich, max. 1 Million
Edition: endless, max. 1 million

58
Halsschmuck I necklace "Ave Maria", 2008
Kupfer, Eisen I copper, iron, 185 × 3,5 cm
Nordenfjeldske Kunstindustrimuseum, Trondheim, Norwegen I Norway

59
Halsschmuck I necklace "687 Years", 2006
Kunststoff, Kupfer, Eisen I plastic, copper, iron, 71 × 17 cm
Nordenfjeldske Kunstindustrimuseum, Trondheim, Norwegen I Norway

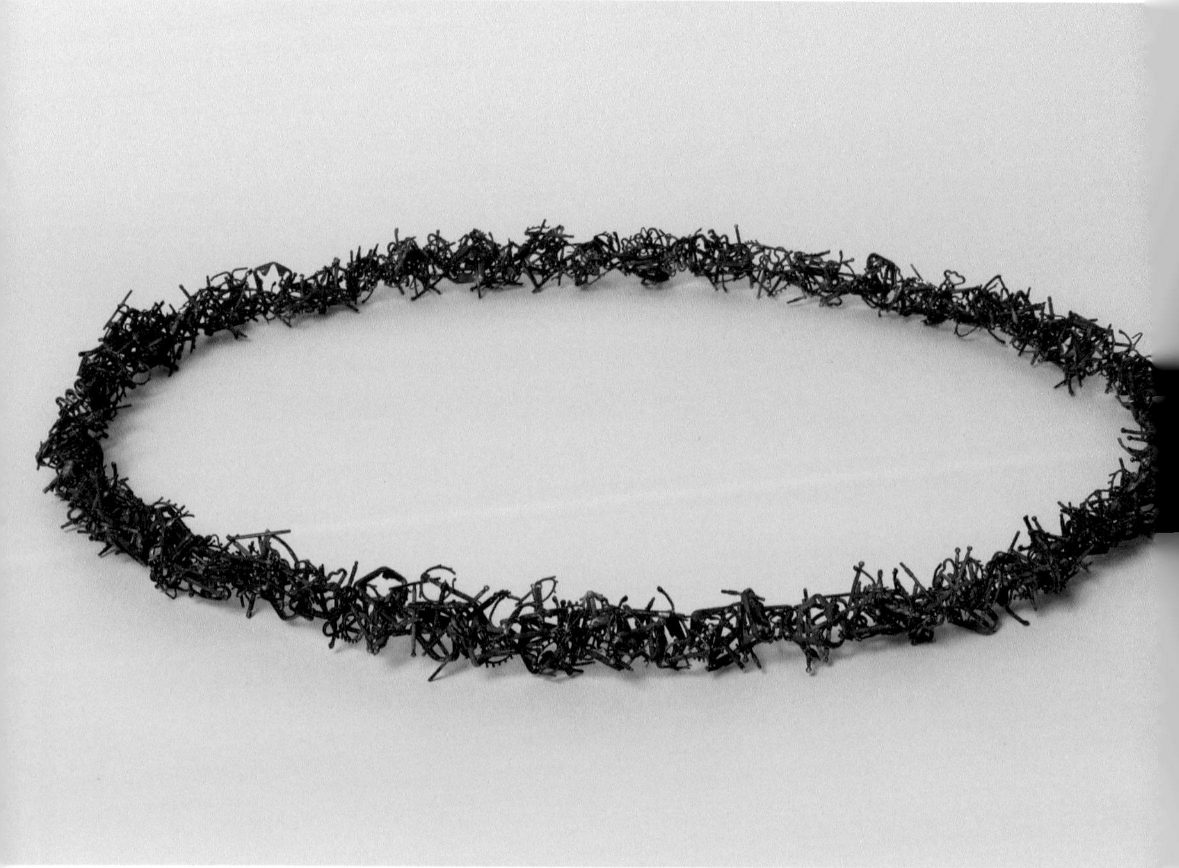

Spiralen sind weltweit das am häufigsten verwendete Verhütungsmittel. Die gebrauchten Verhütungsspiralen, die Nanna Melland in ihrem Werk verarbeitet, waren früher im Einsatz, um ungewollte Schwangerschaften zu vermeiden. In den Schmuckstücken wird die feministische Errungenschaft der Selbstbestimmung in Relation zu stereotypischen Geschlechterrollen untersucht. Dabei wird die Diskrepanz zwischen dem Recht des Einzelnen und den gesellschaftlichen Erwartungen offenbart. KP

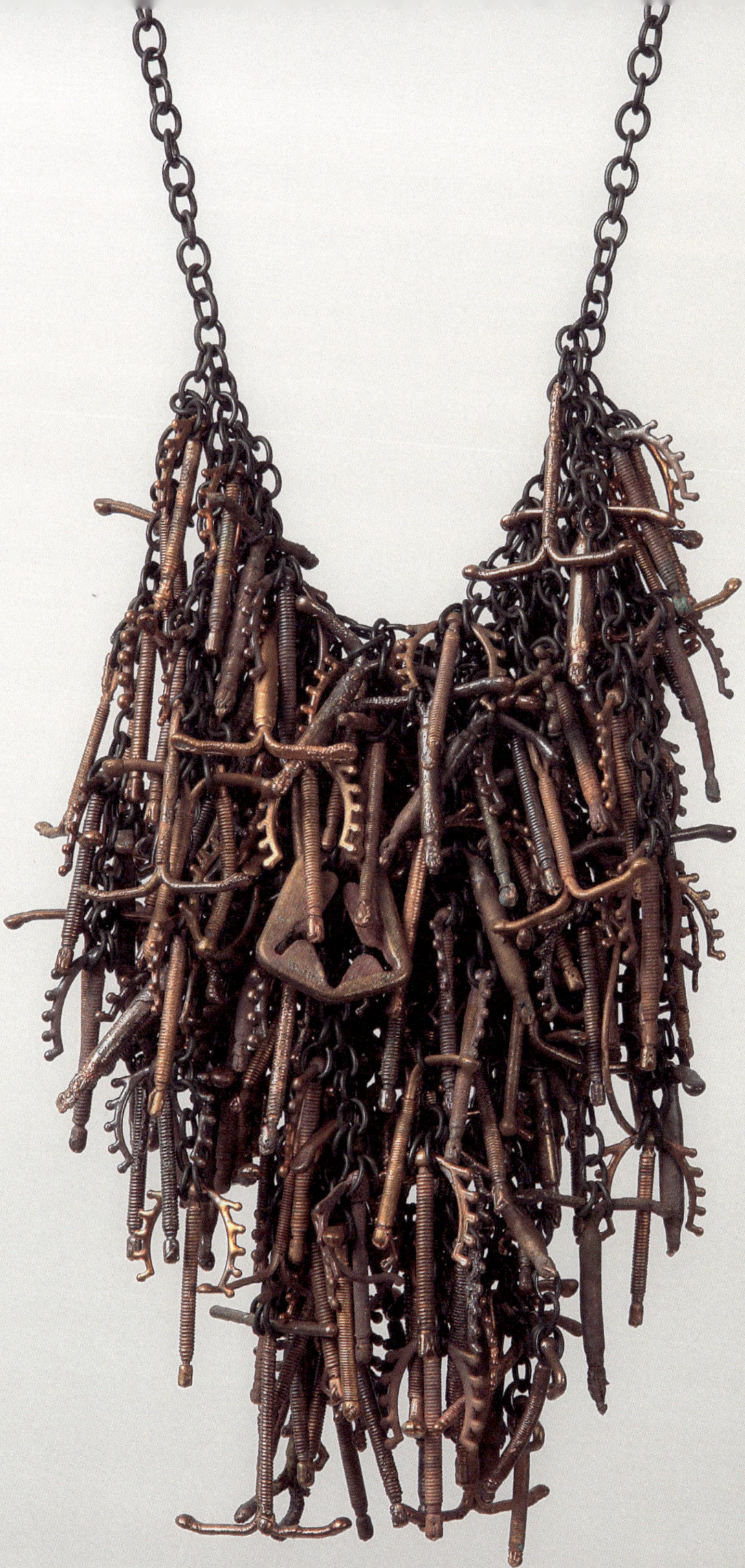

IUDs (Intra Uterine Devices) are the most commonly used contraceptive in the world. The second-hand contraceptive coils Nanna Melland processes in her works were formerly used to prevent unwanted pregnancies. The jewelry explores the feminist achievement of self-determination in relation to stereotypical gender roles. Hereby the discrepancy between individual rights and societal expectations is revealed. KP

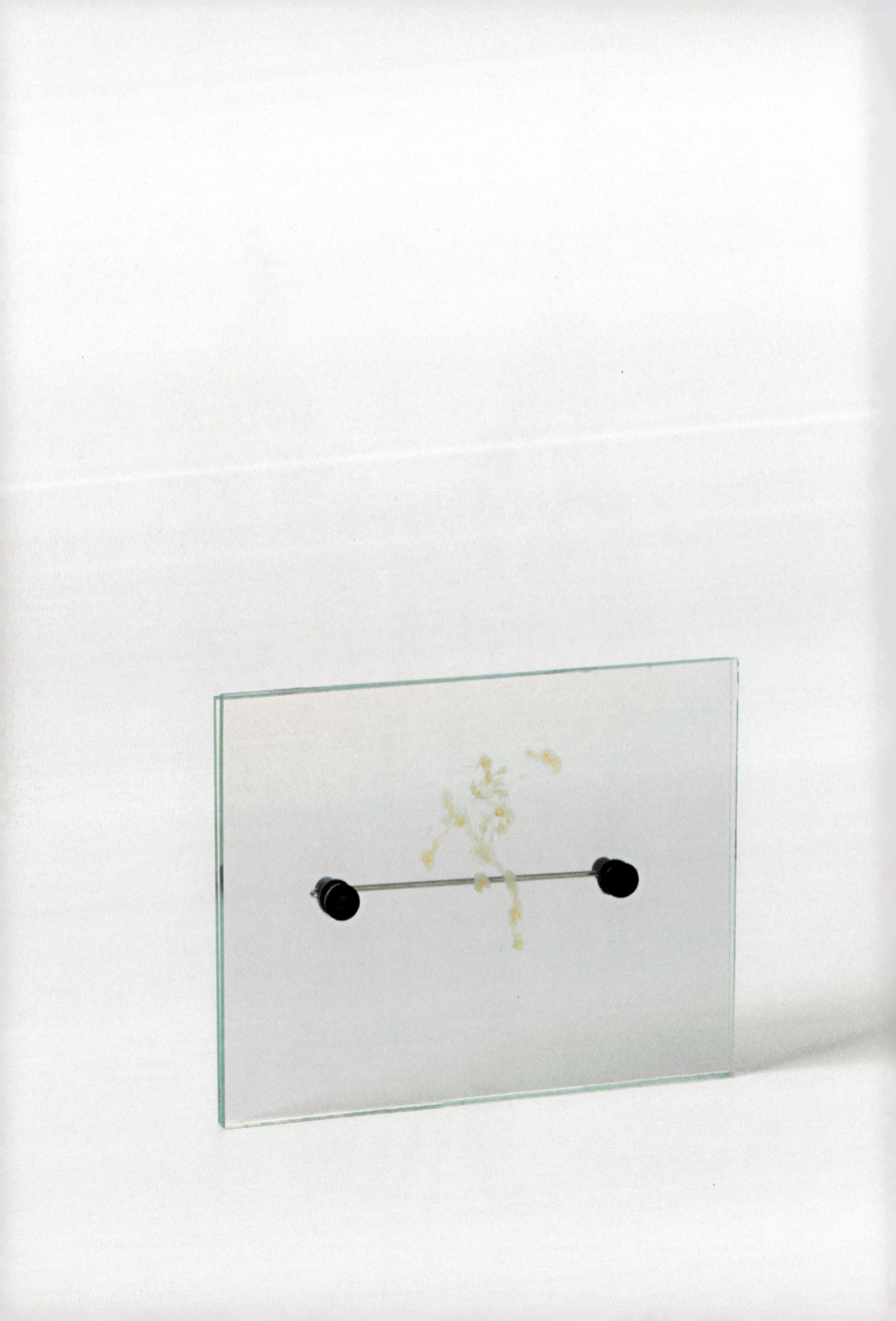

60
Brosche | brooch "The Code", 2016
DNA des Künstlers, Silber, Stahl, Saphirglas
DNA of the artist, silver, steel, sapphire glass
7 × 10 × 0,5 cm

62
Brosche | brooch "Ein Meister Der Selbstbeherrschung Erzählt – Ein Selbstporträt", 2011
400 Schlaftabletten, 50 King Cobra Rot 120 mg Tabletten (Potenzmittel), Gold (Broschierung), Stahl
400 sleeping pills, 50 king cobra red 120 mg pills (potency-enhacing drag), gold (needle), steel
12 × 13 × 5 cm

Brosche | brooch "Ein Meister Der Selbstbeherrschung Erzählt – Ein Selbstporträt", 2011
500 Vital-Tabletten (Anti-Stress), Gold (Broschierung), Stahl
500 vital pills (antistress medicine), gold (needle), steel
12 × 13 × 5 cm

63
Brosche | brooch "Ein Meister Der Selbstbeherrschung Erzählt – Ein Selbstporträt", 2011
500 Schlaftabletten, Gold (Broschierung), Stahl
500 sleeping pills, gold (needle), steel
12 × 13 × 5 cm

Brosche | brooch "Ein Meister Der Selbstbeherrschung Erzählt – Ein Selbstporträt", 2011
500 Viagra-Tabletten, Gold (Broschierung), Stahl
500 viagra pills, gold (needle), steel
12 × 13 × 5 cm
Sammlung | collection Koudijs/Schrijver

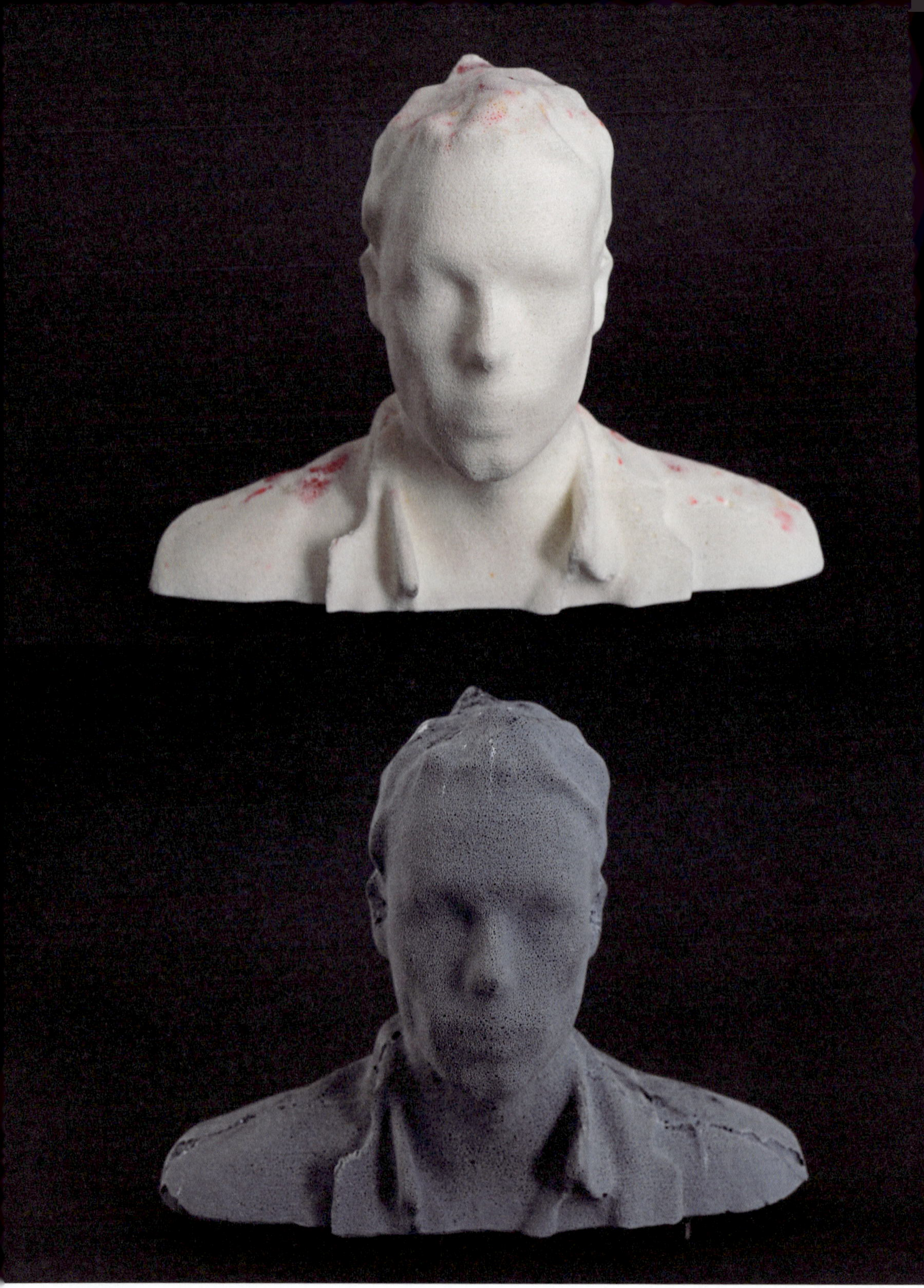

Die Broschen sind in Form von dreidimensionalen Selbstporträts aus Materialien wie Schlaftabletten, Viagra oder Antistress-Medikamenten geschaffen. Hierbei präsentiert Stefan Heuser den Künstler stellvertretend als Teil der kulturellen Egomanie und postmodernen Konsumgesellschaft. Wer letztendlich die hier benutzten Medikamente konsumiert, ist unerheblich. Wichtig ist die Beobachtung von Gebrauch und Missbrauch sowie ein von Kommerz getriebener Bedarf an künstlicher Optimierung. KP

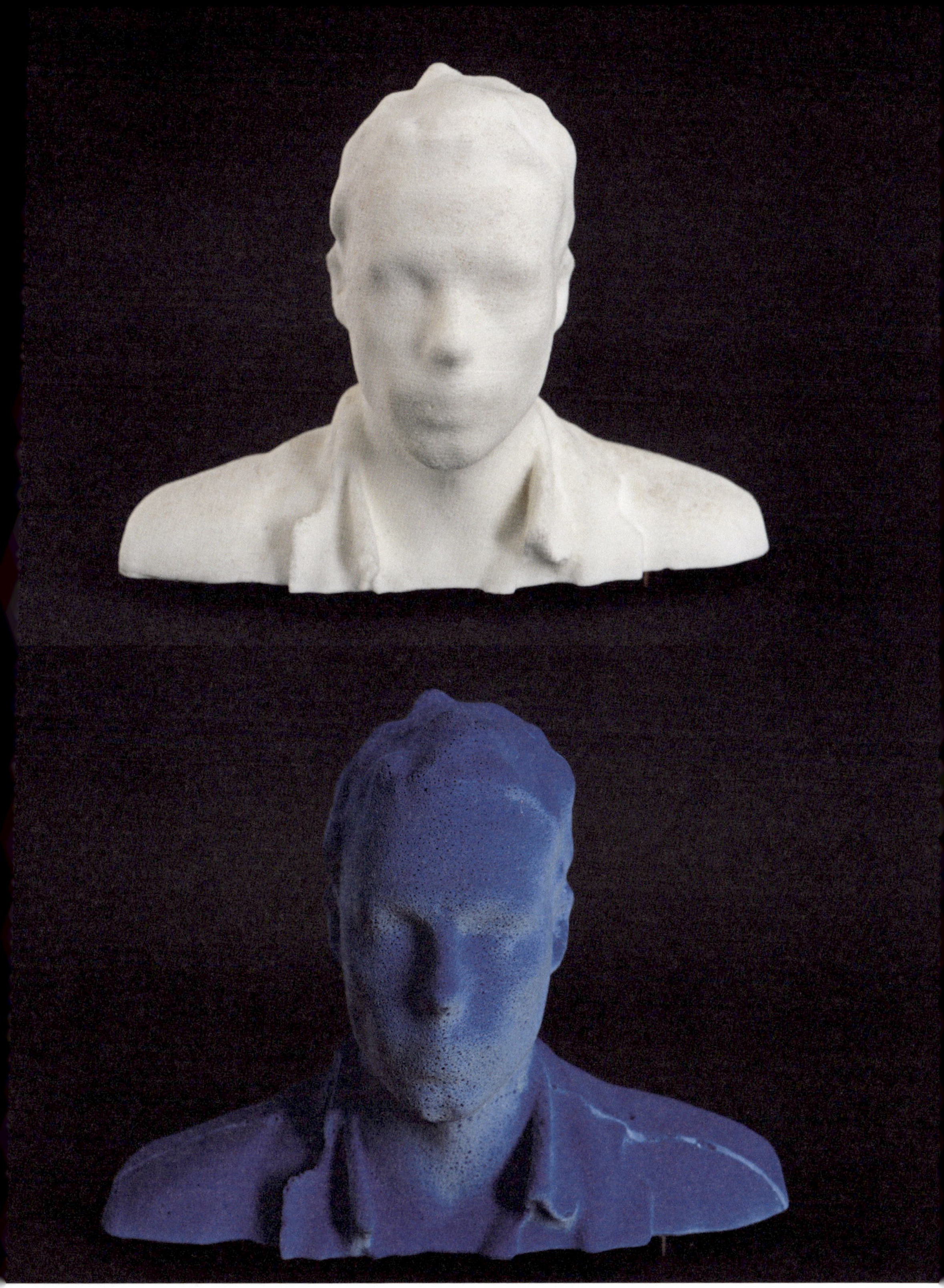

Sleeping pills, Viagra or anti-stress medication provide the material for the brooches in the shape of three-dimensional self-portraits. With them, Stefan Heuser draws an image of the artist as a performer of cultural egomania and postmodern consumer society. Who would ultimately be the consumer of the drugs shown here is irrelevant. Important is the observation of use and abuse as well as of the commercially driven desire for artificial optimization. KP

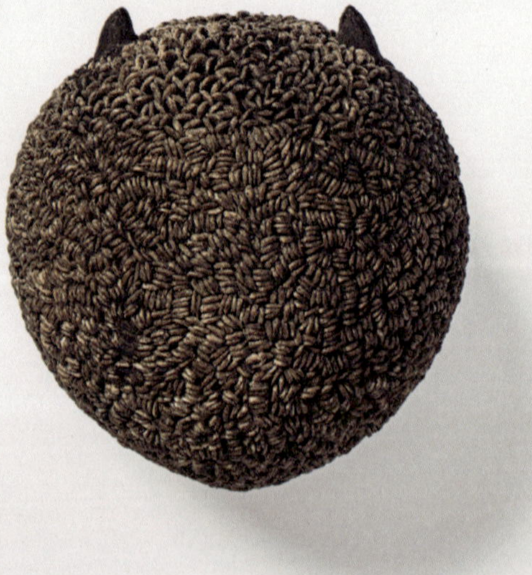

64
Brosche o.T. aus der Installation | brooch untitled from the installation "Zieh Dich aus", 2018
Tomatenkerne, Erde, Holz, Silber
tomato seeds, soil, wood, silver
9 × 8,5 × 6,4 cm

66
Brosche | brooch "Ungefähr Stern", 2018
Brot, Blattgold | bread, gold leaf
12 × 12 × 3 cm

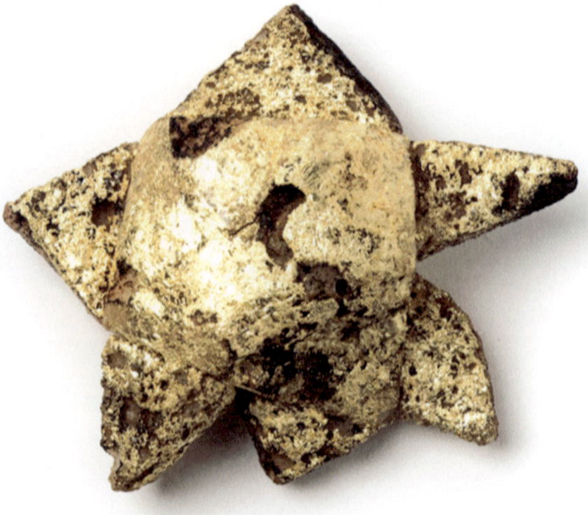

In der Brosche *Ungefähr Stern* von Mari Iwamoto werden gesellschaftliche Erwartungen und Leistungsdruck in ihren Folgen für den Einzelnen untersucht. Die Arbeit ist aus Brot und Gold hergestellt und als eine Art Selbstauszeichnung für enttäuschte Ansprüche konzipiert. Obwohl der Fokus beim Schmuckstück mit einer gewissen Selbstverständlichkeit bei dem/der Träger*in liegt, können weder die sozial- noch die weltpolitischen Bezüge in diesem Stück übersehen werden. Die Nahrung ist vertrocknet und der Glanz des Goldes kann nur Oberfläche sein. KP

The brooch *Ungefähr Stern* by Mari Iwamoto examines social expectations and the pressure to achieve, with a focus on their consequences for the individual. The work is made of bread and gold and is conceived to be a kind of self-award for disappointed expectations. Although it is rather self-explanatory that in jewelry the focus is mostly on the wearer, neither the sociopolitical nor the global-political references in this piece can be overlooked. The nourishment is dried up and the shine of the gold is only surface. KP

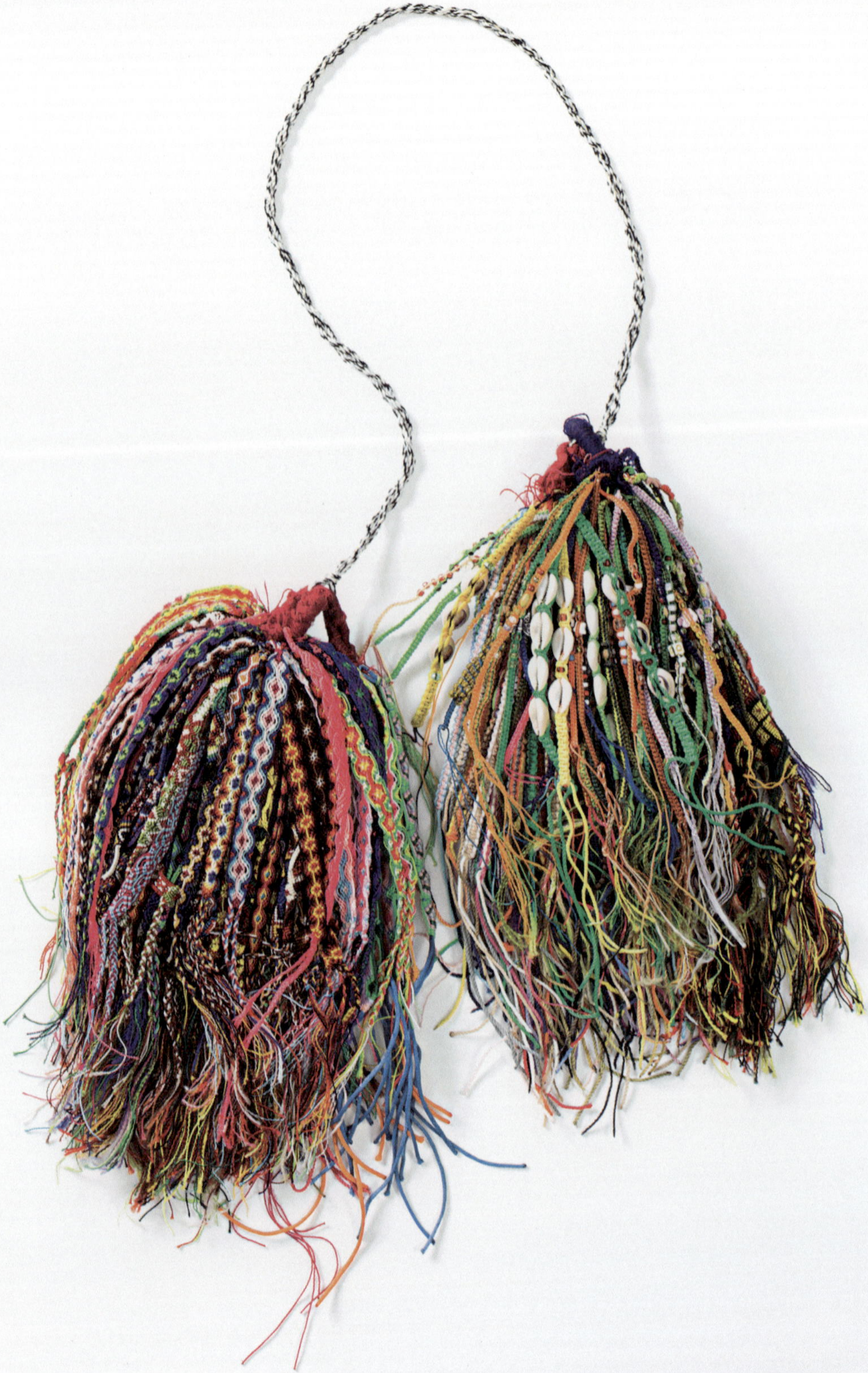

SHACHAR COHEN

68
Halsschmuck | neckpiece "Alma is selling China on the beach of Cancum and I'm buying", 2016
Verkaufsbündel Armbänder aus Mexiko
bundle of bracelets from Mexico
30 × 20 × 10 cm

70
Brosche aus der Serie | brooch from the series "Rated R", 2018, Edelstahl | stainless steel
8 × 12,5 × 2,5 cm
Courtesy Galerie Rob Koudijs

Brosche aus der Serie | brooch from the series "Rated R", 2018, Edelstahl | stainless steel
12,5 × 10,5 × 2,5 cm
Courtesy Galerie Rob Koudijs

71
Brosche aus der Serie | brooch from the series "Rated R", 2018, Edelstahl | stainless steel
12,5 × 10,5 × 2,5 cm
Courtesy Galerie Rob Koudijs

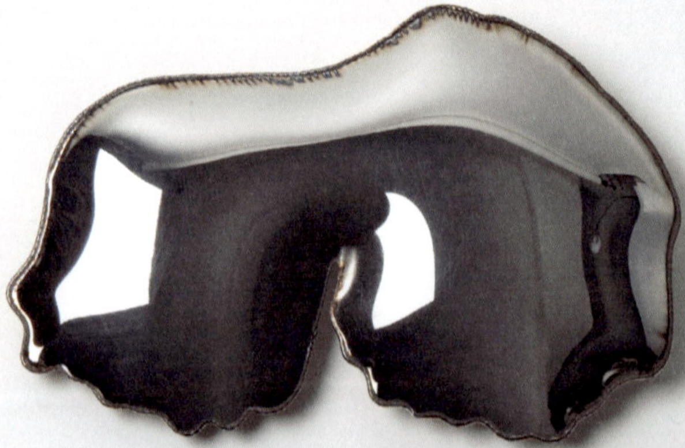

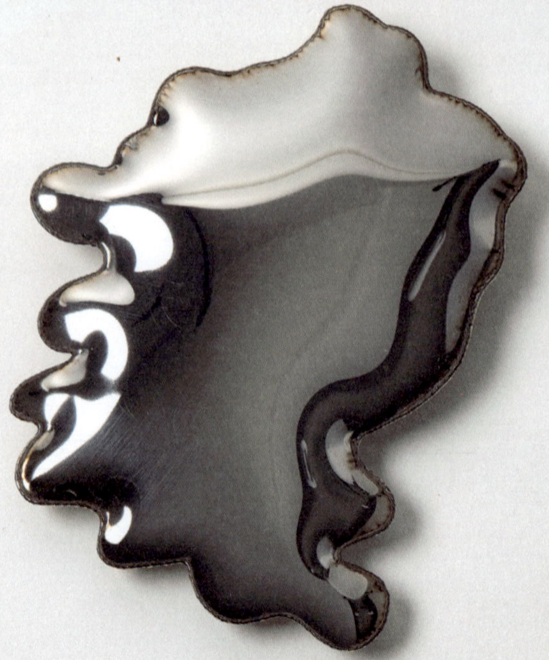

Die spiegel-polierten Oberflächen der Broschen von Shachar Cohen deuten auf die Egozentrik der zeitgenössischen Kultur hin. Die Motive, aus denen die Formen der Broschen entstehen, stammen von gewalttätigen Szenerien aus dem Bereich der Nachrichtenfotografie oder von Computerspielen. Die Motive sind Fragmente größerer Bilder und weisen auf die Wichtigkeit hin, zu hinterfragen, welche Fragmente wir von uns selbst betrachten, wenn wir in einen Spiegel schauen. KP

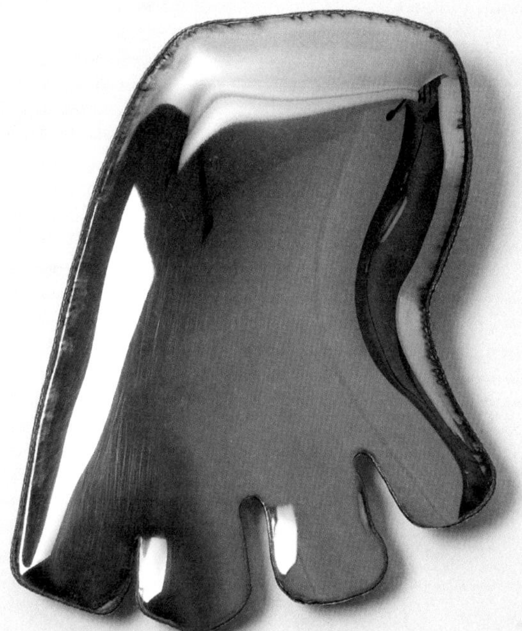

The mirror-polished surfaces of Shachar Cohen's brooches reference the egocentricity of contemporary culture. The brooches' outlines are based on details from violent scenarios, originating from news photography or computer games. The motifs are fragments of larger images and point to the importance of asking ourselves which fragments of our character we are choosing to see when we look in a mirror. KP

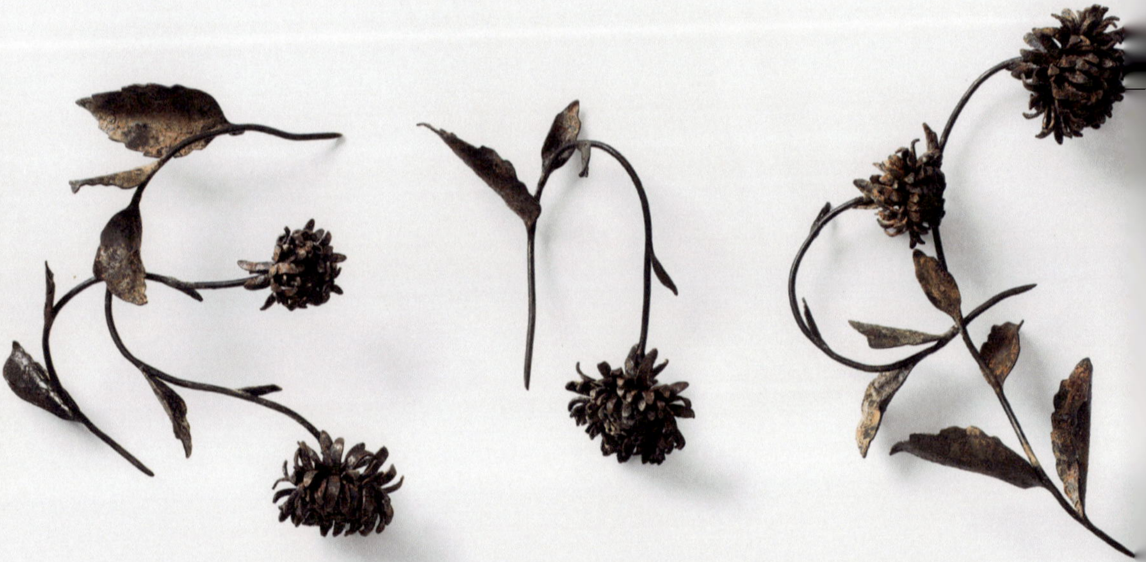

HANNA HEDMAN

72
Anhänger | pendants from the series
"The End-Life After Warming", 2018
Stahl, gerostet; Ruß | steel, rusted; soot
Unterschiedliche Maße | different dimensions

74
Halsschmuck aus der Serie | necklace from the series
"While they Await Extinction", 2011
Silber, z.T. oxidiert; Kupfer, pulverbeschichtet; Farbe
silver, partly oxidized; copper, powder-coated; paint
Anhänger | pendant; 11,5 × 7 (max.) × 2,5 cm
Courtesy Galerie Biro

75
Halsschmuck aus der Serie | necklace from the series
"While they Wwait Extinction", 2011
Silber, z.T. oxidiert; Kupfer, pulverbeschichtet; Farbe
silver, partly oxidized; copper, powder-coated; paint
40 × 18,5 × 7 cm

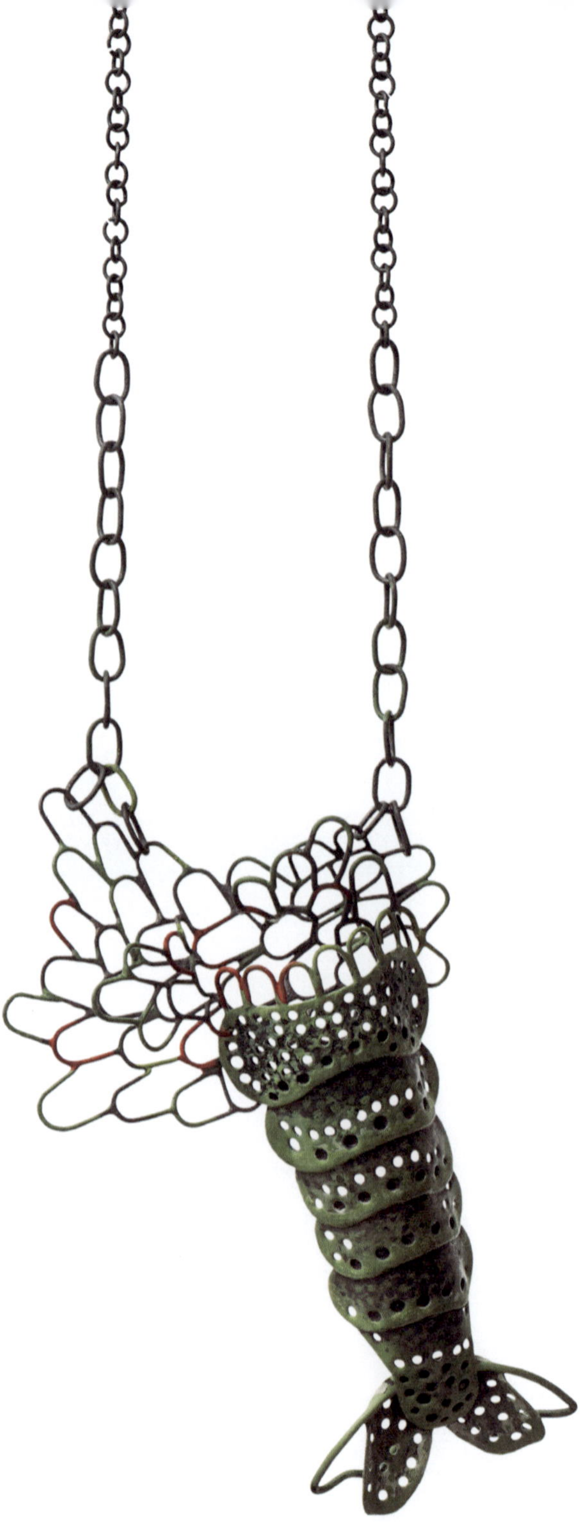

Vom Aussterben bedrohte Tiere und Pflanzen, denen also die Anpassungsfähigkeit fehlt, die in einer menschendominierten Welt benötigt wird, sind das Thema in dem Werk von Hanna Hedman. Der Halsschmuck fordert dazu auf, die Verantwortung wörtlich „zu tragen" und sich mit dem Konflikt zwischen einer kulturellen Romantisierung der Natur und der Realität der Zerstörung auseinanderzusetzen. KP

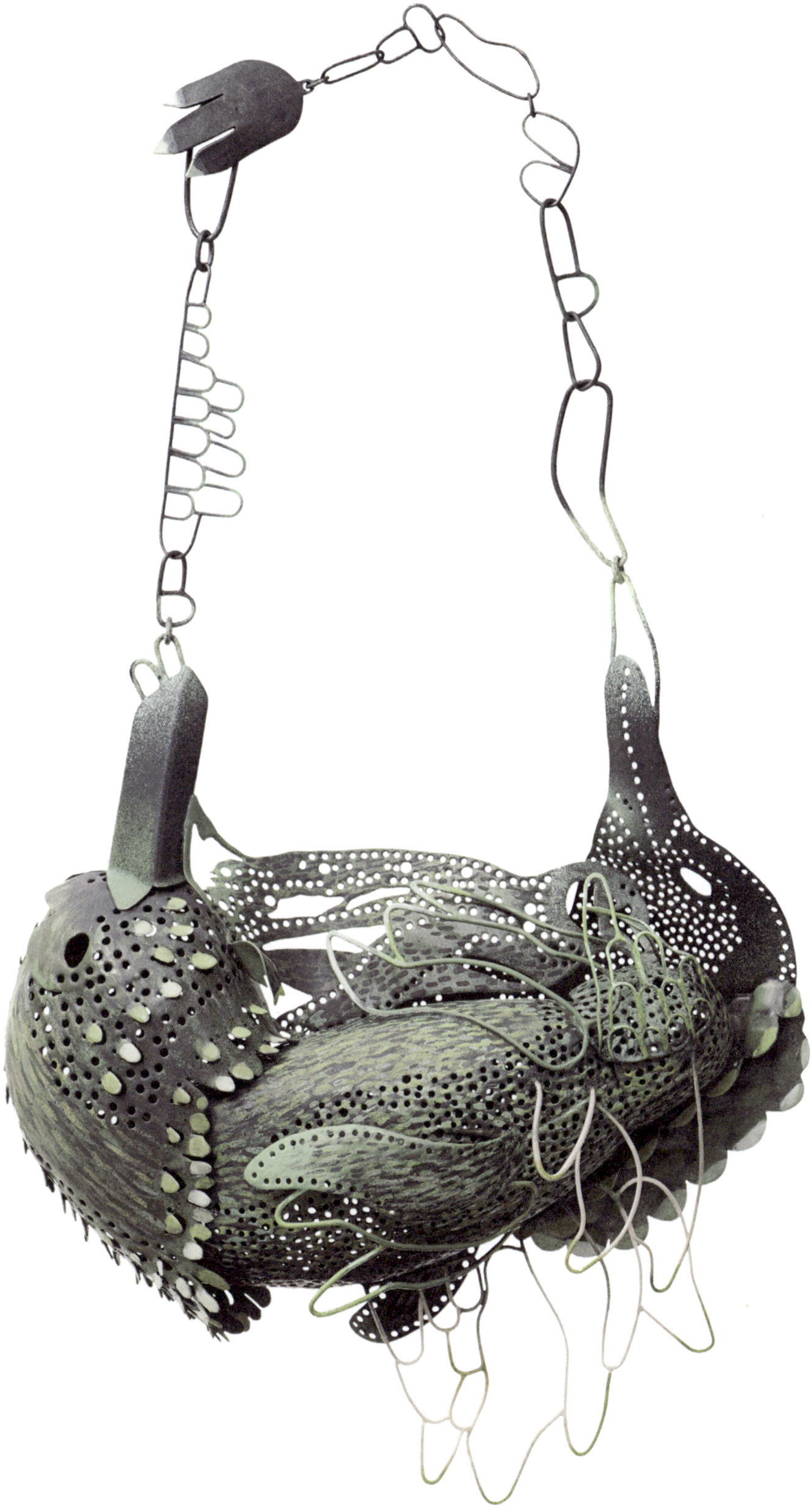

Hanna Hedman's work looks at endangered animals and plants, and thus at lifeforms unable to adapt to a human-dominated world. The necklaces call for literally "bearing the responsibility" and for facing the conflict between a predominant cultural reflex of romanticizing nature and the reality of the destruction. KP

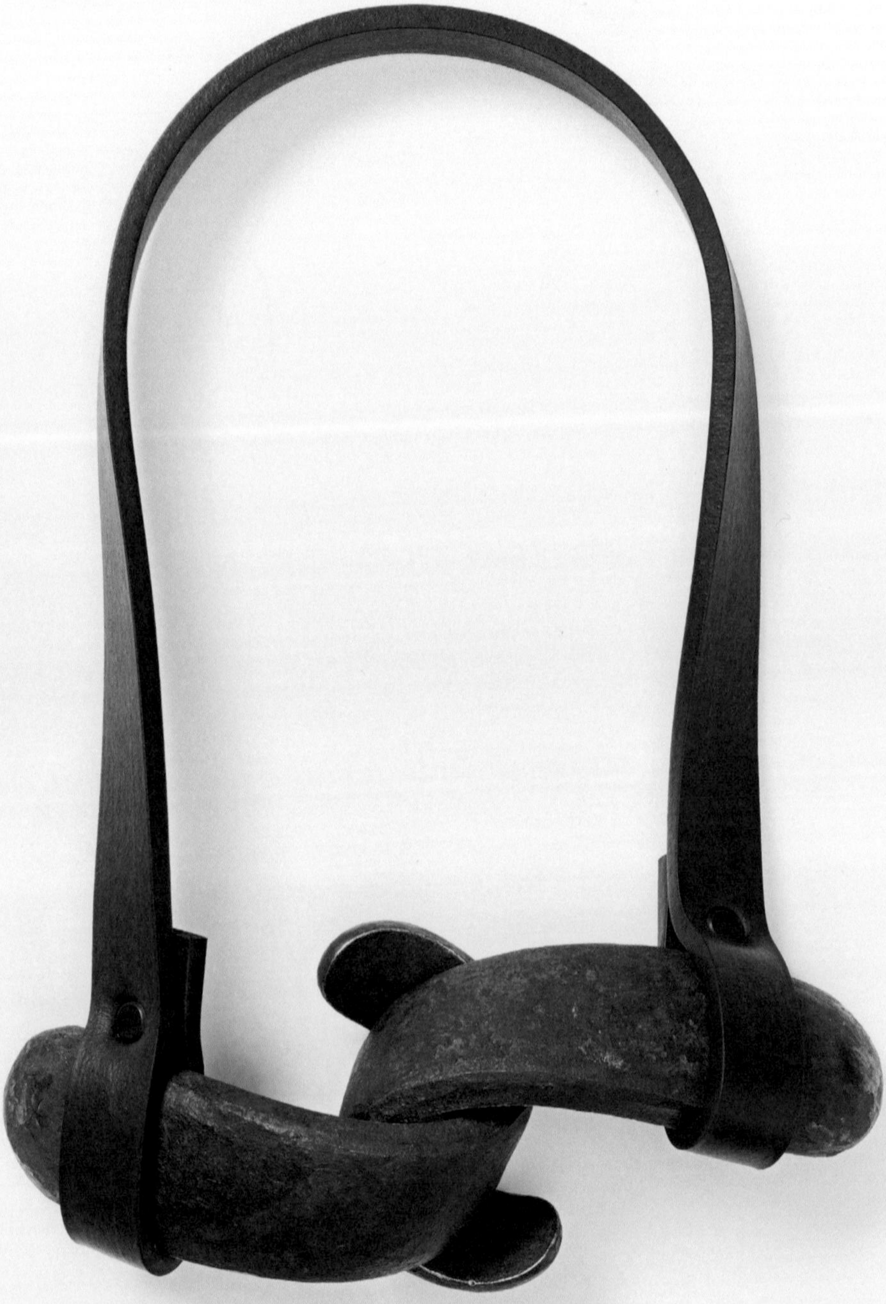

76
Halsschmuck | necklace "French Kiss", 2012
Eisen, Leder | pur iron, leather
L. | l. 29,8 cm

78
Armschmuck „TRAP“ aus der Serie | bracelet "TRAP" from the series "FERS – IRONS (as chains or fetters)", 2009–2013
Eisen, geschmiedet | wrought pur iron
5,5 × 7,5 × 5 cm

79
Armschmuck „TRAP“ aus der Serie | bracelet "TRAP" from the series "FERS – IRONS (as chains or fetters)", 2009
Eisen, geschmiedet | wrought pur iron
5 × 11,5 × 5,5 cm

Armschmuck „TRAP“ aus der Serie | bracelet "TRAP" from the series "FERS – IRONS (as chains or fetters)", 2009
Eisen, geschmiedet | wrought pur iron
3,5 × 10,5 × 6 cm

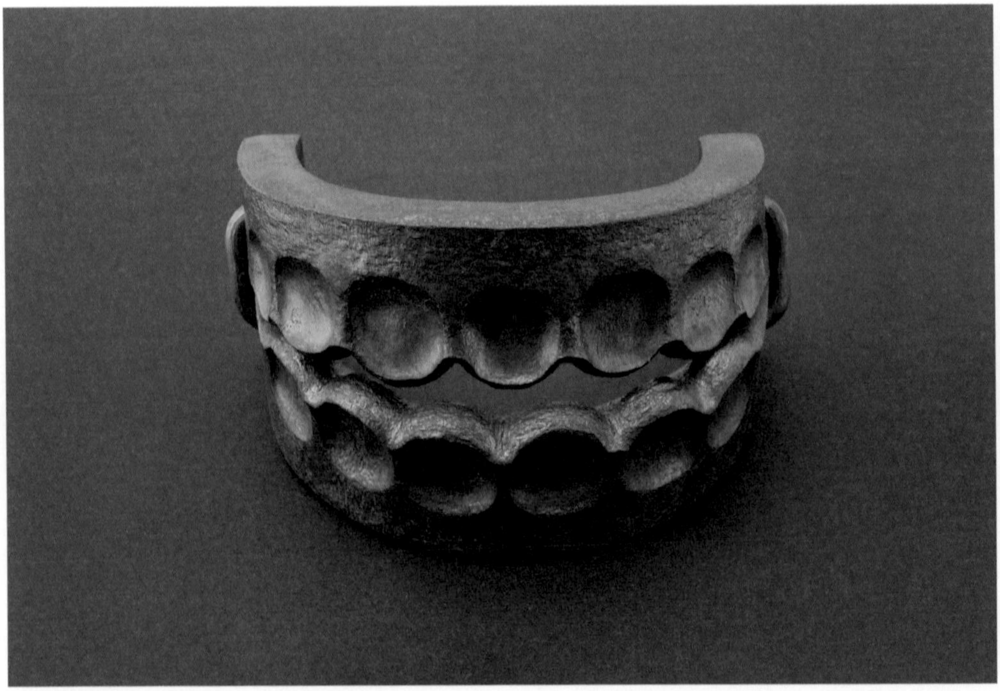

Die Armbänder *TRAP* von Sofie Hanagarth sind aus Eisen geschmiedet. Wie historische Abzugeisen bestehen sie aus zwei „gezähnten" Bügeln, allerdings ohne den Federmechanismus, der die Tierfallen tödlich werden lässt. Die „Bezahnung" der Armbänder bezieht sich auf die menschliche Anatomie, wodurch ein verstörender Querverweis zu historischen und zeitgenössischen Machtstrukturen entsteht, die Mensch wie Tier in Ketten legen. KP

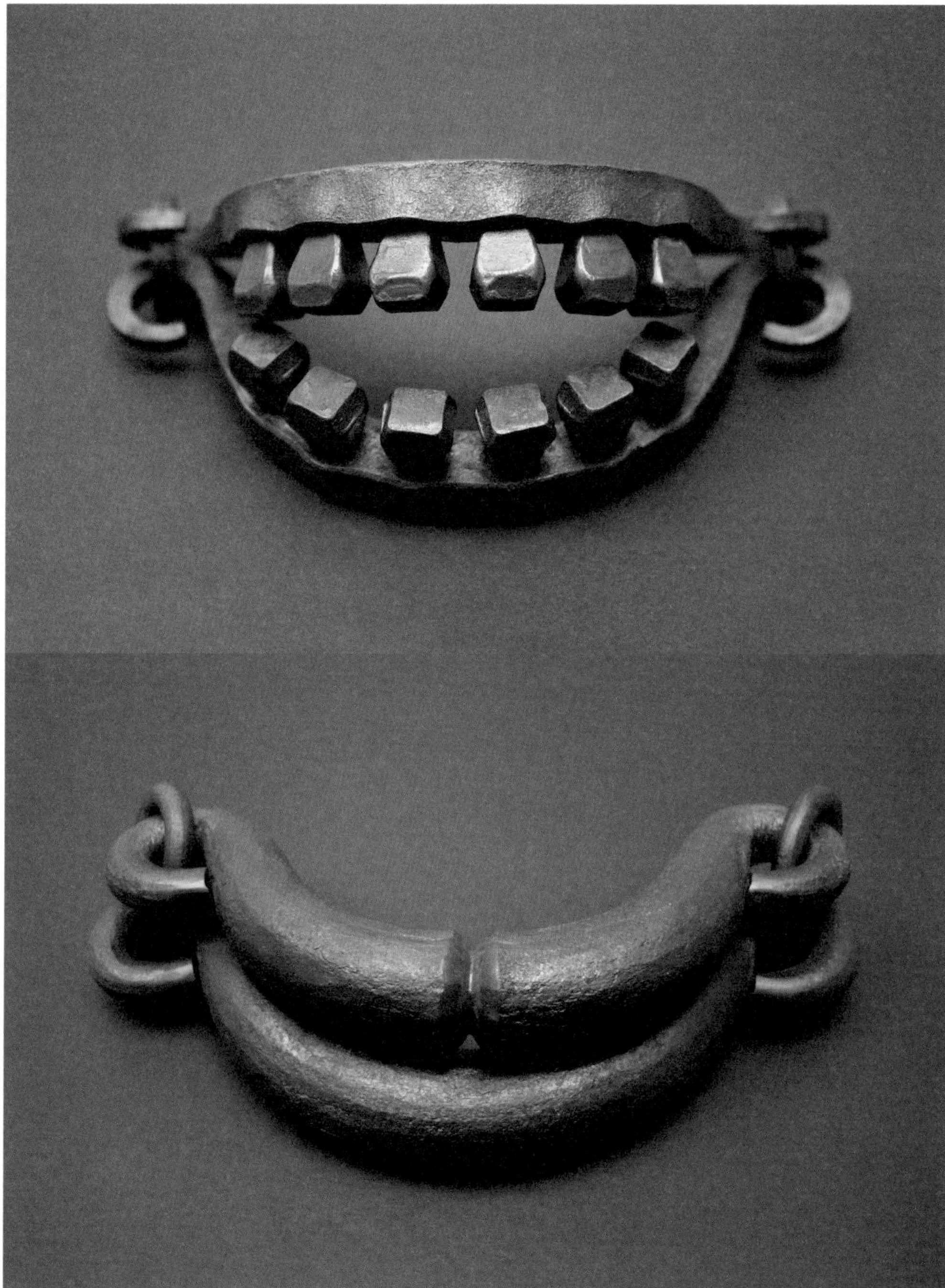

Sofie Hanagarth's *TRAP* bracelets are forged from iron. Similar to historical animal traps, they consist of two "toothed" clamps, but without the spring mechanism that makes these traps lethal. The "dentition" of the bracelets relates to the human anatomy, creating a disturbing cross-reference to historical and contemporary power structures that have placed both humans and animals in chains. KP

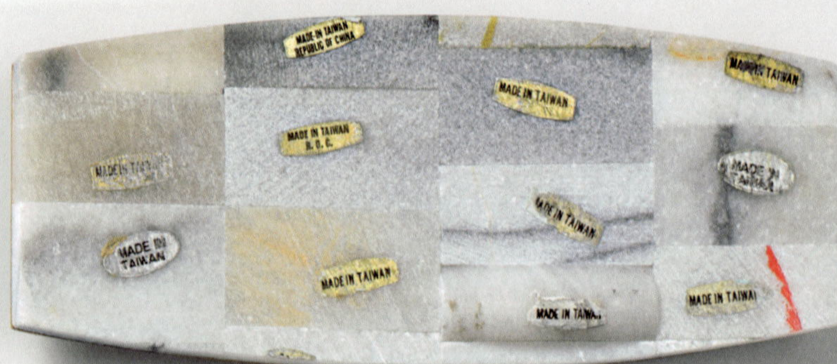
MADE IN TAIWAN
REPUBLIC OF CHINA
MADE IN TAIWAN
MADE IN TAIWAN
R.O.C.
MADE IN
TAIWAN
MADE IN TAIWAN
MADE IN TAIWAN
MADE IN TAIWAN

80
Brosche | brooch “Made in Taiwan II”, 2017
Marmorgeschirr (alt), Messing
marble tableware (vintage), brass
5 × 12 × 0,7 cm
Courtesy Gallery Marzee

82
Brosche aus der Serie | brooch from the series
“Notions of Skill”, 2013
Marmorgeschirr (alt), Velours, Messing
marble tableware (vintage), velour, brass
15 × 16 × 3 cm

83
Brosche aus der Serie | brooch from the series
“Notions of Skill”, 2013
Marmorgeschirr (alt), Messing
marble tableware (vintage), brass
16 × 6 × 1 cm

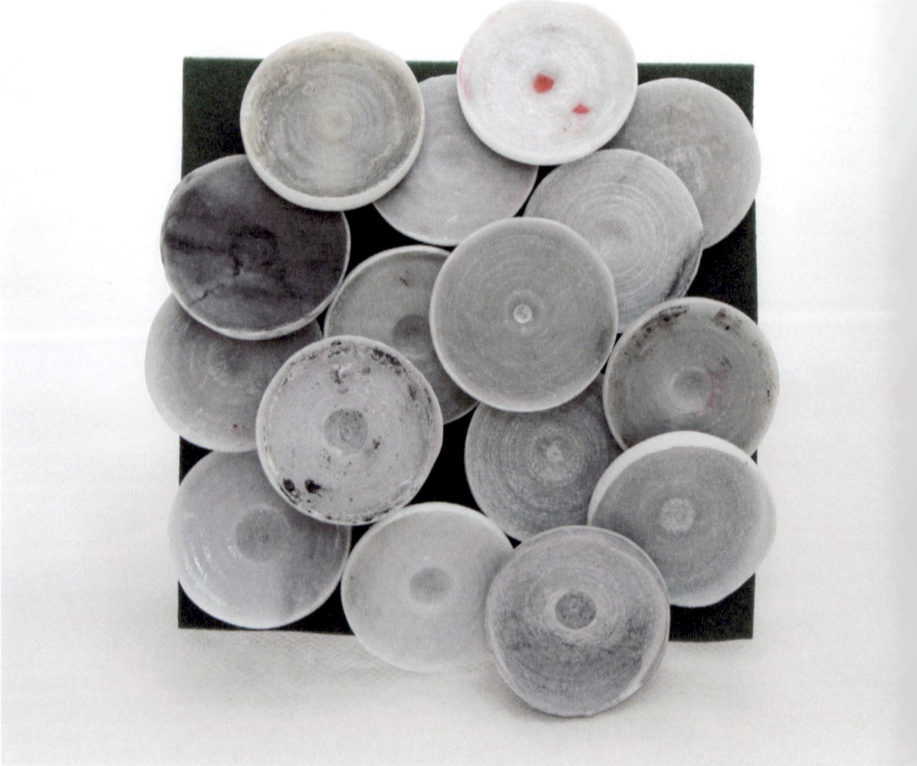

Die Marmorgegenstände, die Tarja Tuupanen als Material für ihren Schmuck dienen, wurden in Asien als Massenware produziert mit der Zielsetzung, dem skandinavischen Durchschnittsgeschmack zu entsprechen. Im Bewusstsein um ihre fragwürdigen Ursprünge und ästhetischen Mängel werden die zu verarbeitenden Objekte sorgfältig von der Künstlerin ausgesucht. Bei der künstlerischen Rekonstruktion bleiben Spuren der ursprünglichen Gegenstände lesbar, aber durch den radikalen Umbau der Objekte wird die Authentizität von kultureller Herkunft in einer postkolonialen Konsumgesellschaft hinterfragt. KP

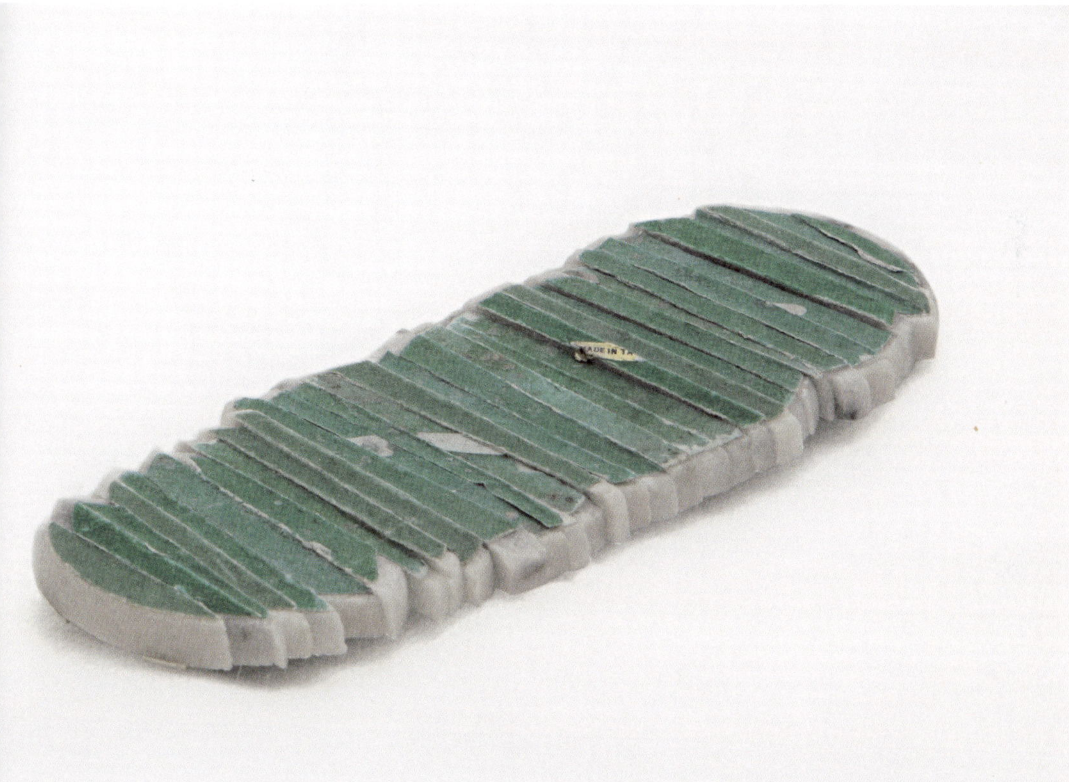

The marble objects that serve as raw materials for Tarja Tuupanen's jewelry were mass-produced in Asia with the aim of matching the average Scandinavian taste. Conscious of their aesthetic defects and questionable origins, the artist selected the objects to be processed with great care. Traces of the original object remain recognizable in the artistic reconstruction, yet the radical reforming of the marble objects also raises questions as to the authenticity of cultural origin in a postcolonial consumer society. KP

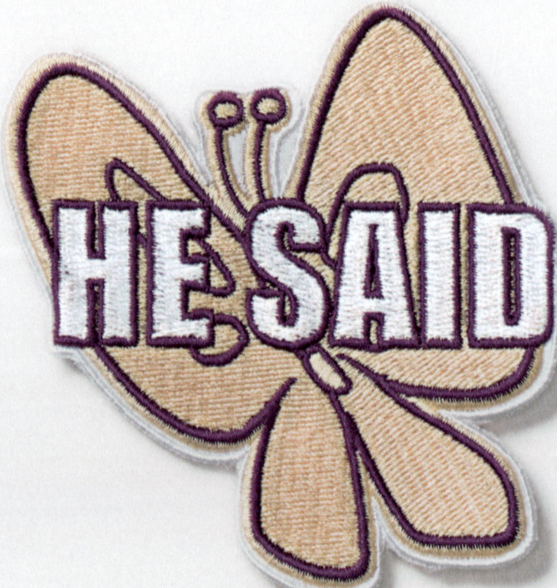
HE SAID

84
Objekt o.T. (Muster) | object untitled (sample), 2019
Polyesterfaden | polyester thread
8,4 × 8,8 cm

86/87
Brosche | brooch "Manifest (Thank God)", 2008
Siebdruck auf Mylar (Polyesterfolie); Stahl, vergoldet
screenprinting on Mylar (polyester foil); steel, gilded
Ø 5,6 cm

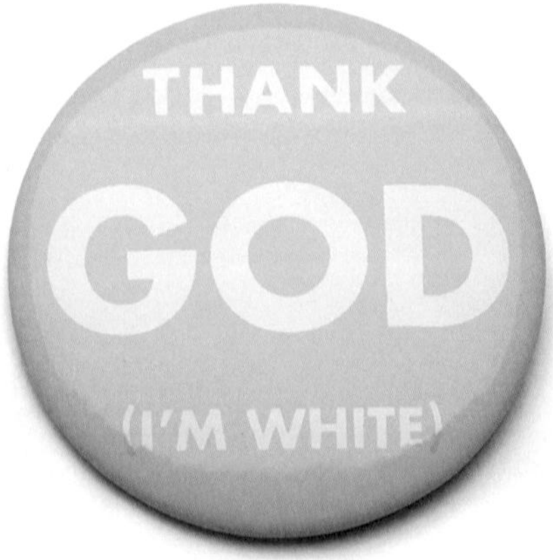

Thank God (I'm White) ist die vordergründige und provokante Aussage der Brosche. In der heutigen Zeit bestehen leider etliche Gründe dafür dankbar zu sein, als privilegierter Weißer geboren zu werden. Aber das dürfte kaum die Aussage der Brosche sein. Benjamin Lignel weist zwar auf dieses Privileg hin, aber noch mehr verweist er auf den verborgenen Rassismus, der in der westlichen Welt schlummert. Indem er aus dem oben genannten Satz eine Brosche macht, entsteht die Fragestellung, wer sie tragen sollte. Die Brosche verdeutlicht die Problematik des postreligiösen Menschen, der durch soziale Interaktion und Selbstreflexion moralische Richtlinien finden muss. Und es zeigt den schmucktragenden Menschen als sozialen Akteur, der Angst hat, mehr als eine angepasste Oberfläche von sich preiszugeben. KP

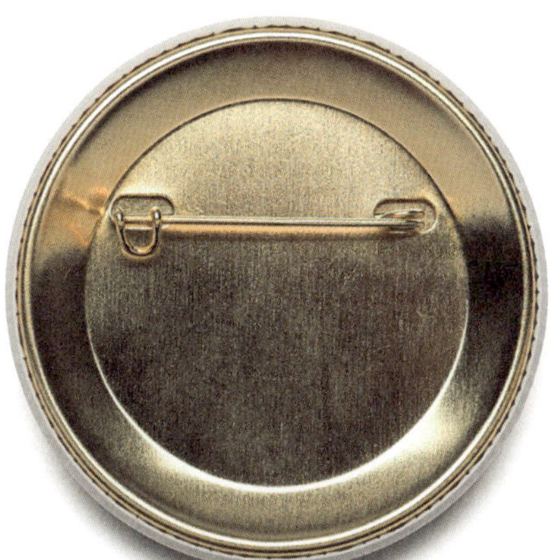

The ostensible and provocative statement of the brooch reads "Thank God (I'm White)". Unfortunately, there are many reasons in current times to be grateful for being born a privileged white man. Yet that is unlikely to be the brooch's true message. Although Benjamin Lignel points to this privilege, he points even more to the hidden racism that is dormant in the Western world. By creating a brooch that bears the sentence, he raises the question as to who should wear it. The brooch illustrates the difficulties post-religious human beings face as they look to create moral guidelines based on social interaction and self-reflection. It also reveals the adorned human being as a social actor fearful of showing more than a customized surface of him or herself. KP

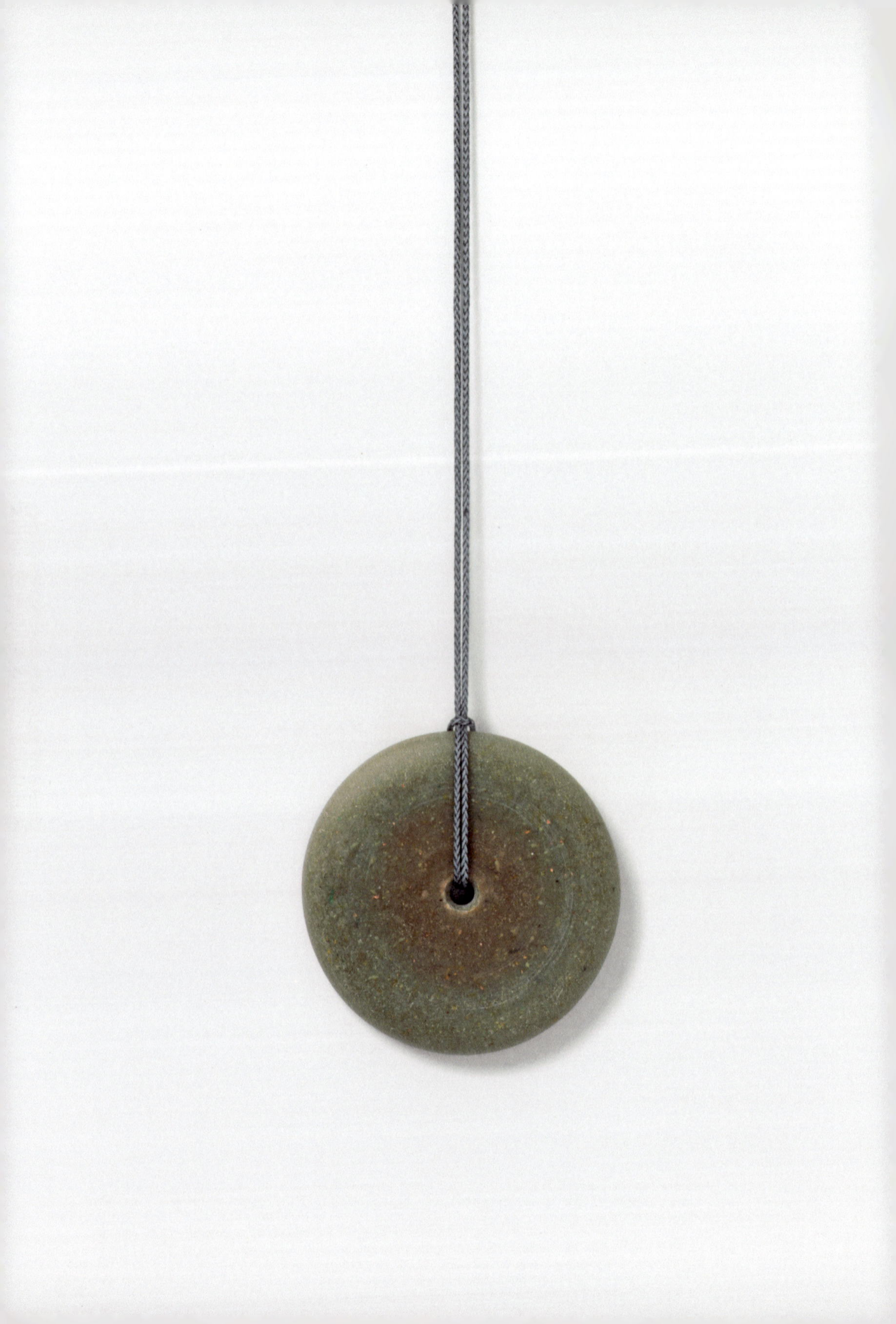

88
Anhänger o.T. aus der Serie I pendant untitled
from the series "Nu Jade", 2018
Elektroabfälle (CPU-Karten, Kupfer, Feingold),
reflektierender Faden I e-waste (CPU boards, copper,
fine gold), reflective thread, Ø 6 cm

90
Anhänger o.T. aus der Serie I pendant untitled
from the series "Conversation Piece", 2016
Gold, Silber, Quarzkristall, reflektierender Faden
gold, silver, quartz crystal, reflective thread, 50 × 6 × 6 cm
Courtesy Galerie Ellen Maurer-Zilioli

91
Brosche o.T. (brooch 00) aus der Serie I brooch untitled
(brooch 00) from the series "Kino", 2014
Optische Folie eines Smartphones, Gold, Tantal, Quarzkristall
optical film from a smart phone, gold, tantalum, quartz
crystal, 8,6 × 5,2 × 1,3 cm
Die Neue Sammlung – The Design Museum
Dauerleihgabe der Danner-Stiftung, München
Permanent Loan from the Danner Foundation, Munich

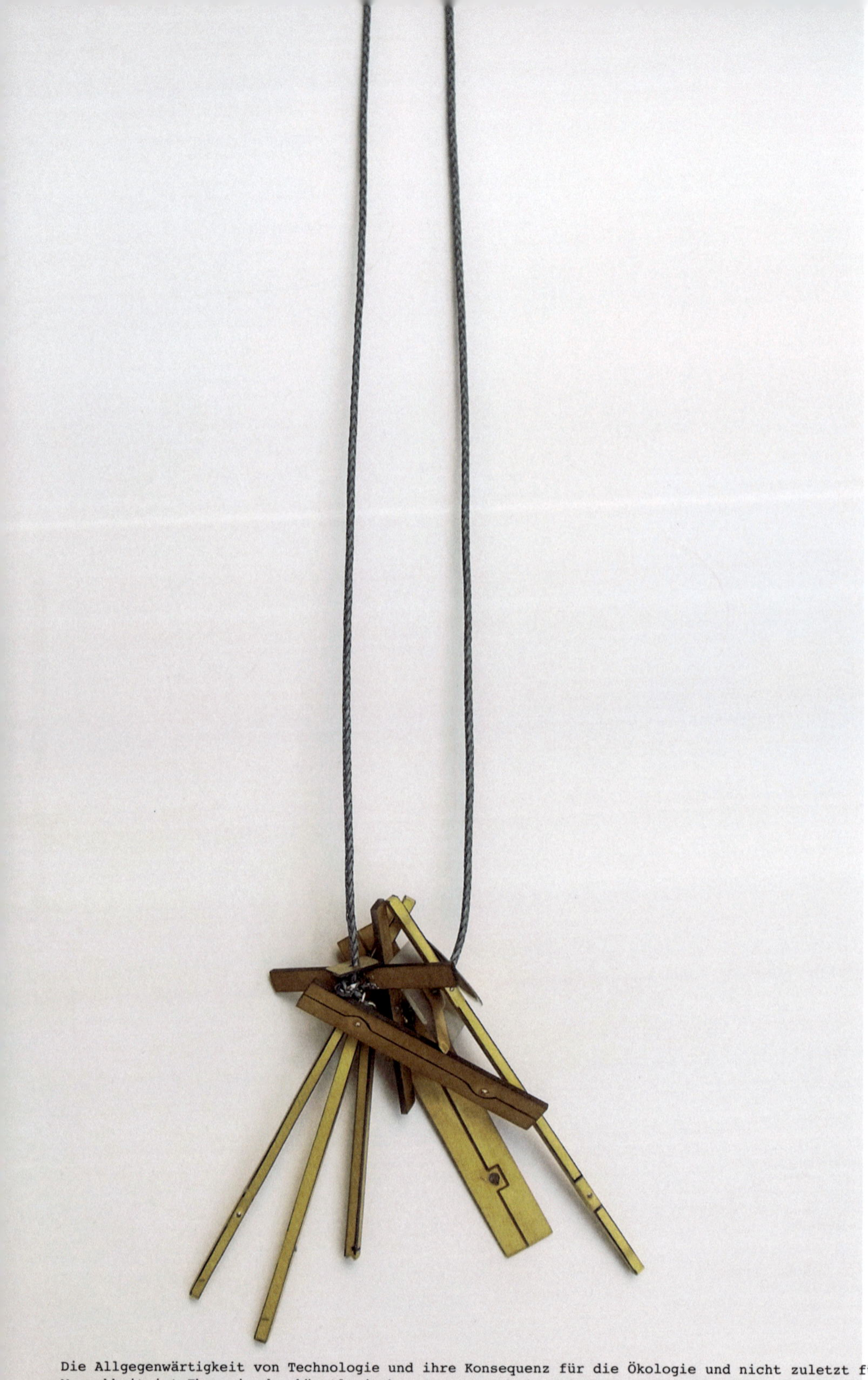

Die Allgegenwärtigkeit von Technologie und ihre Konsequenz für die Ökologie und nicht zuletzt für die Menschheit ist Thema in der künstlerischen Zusammenarbeit zwischen Beatrice Brovia und Nicolas Cheng. Durch das Benutzen von Materialien aus gebrauchten High-Tech-Geräten wie dem Konfliktmineral Tantal oder dem aus Elektroschrott gewonnenen Gold weisen sie auf die globale Wirkung der konsumsüchtigen Gesellschaft hin. Dabei stellen sie gleichzeitig einen Bezug zur Geschichte ihres eigenen Mediums her – dem Schmuck. KP

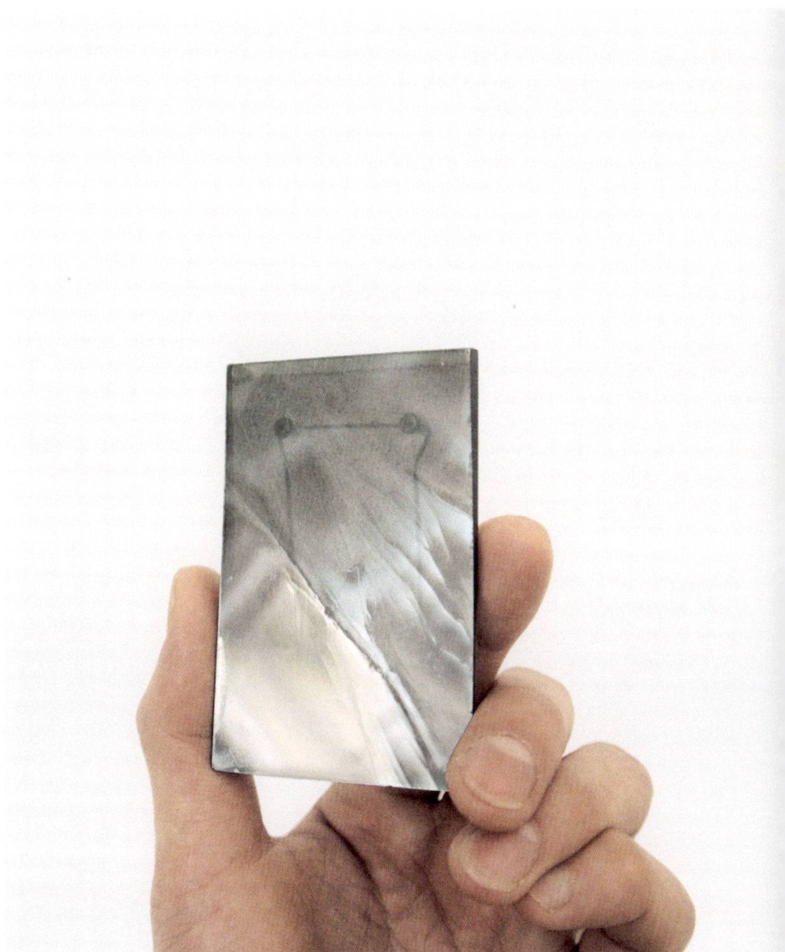

The artistic collaboration between Beatrice Brovia and Nicolas Cheng revolves around the omnipresence of technology and its consequences for ecology, and not least humanity. By re-using materials from second-hand high-tech equipment such as the conflict mineral tantalum or gold extracted from e-waste, they call attention to the global impact of a consumption-driven society. At the same time, they also make reference to the history of their own medium – jewelry. KP

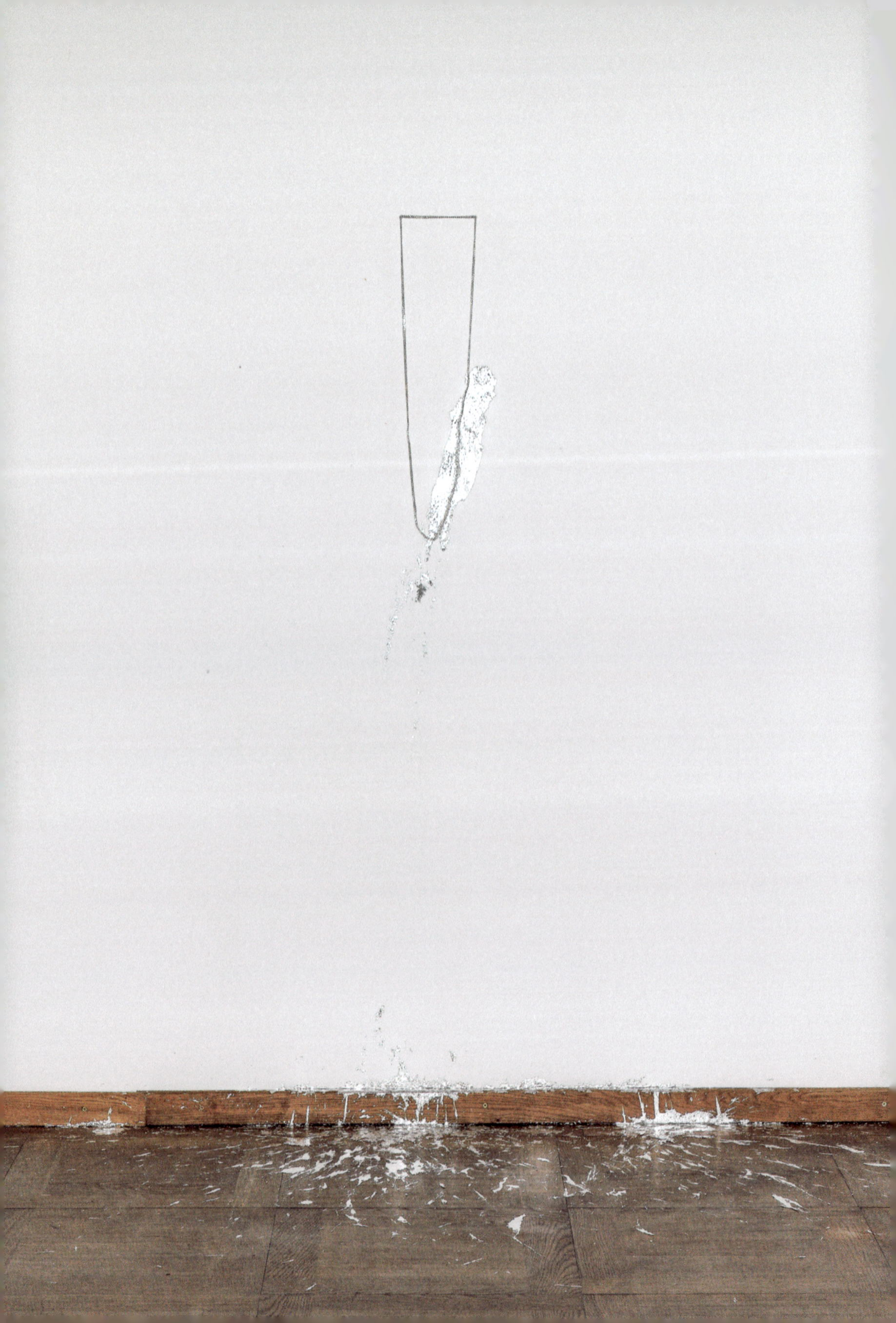

NADINE KUFFNER

92
Objekt o.T. | object untitled, 2018
Zinn, Silber | tin, silver

94
Halsschmuck o.T. | necklace untitled, 2018
Zinn | tin, 35 × 21 × 0,5 cm

95
Halsschmuck | necklace "A Jeweller's Anarchy", 2017
Zinn, Schnur | tin, string, 40 × 16 × 0,5 cm

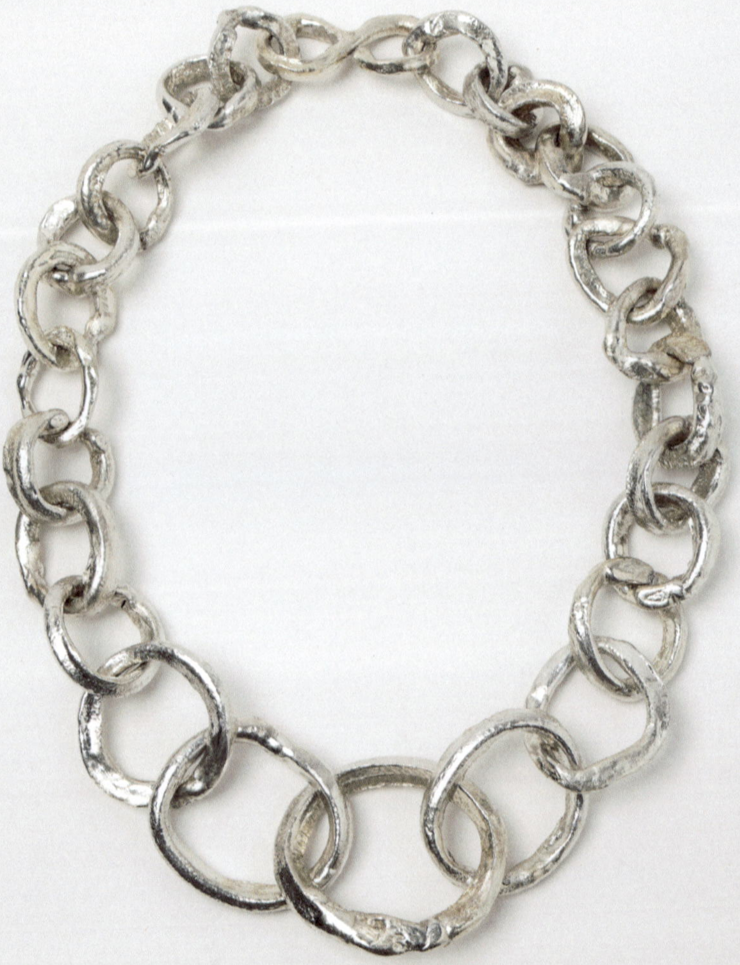

Nadine Kuffner untergräbt bewusst die allgemein vorherrschenden Erwartungen an handwerkliche Methodik. Ihre Werke wurden mit geschmolzenem Zinn „gemalt". Hierbei entstehen Arbeiten, die sowohl das Handwerk als ein gesellschaftliches Phänomen hinterfragen wie auch die üblichen Zuteilungen von Herstellungsmethodik in den verschiedenen Kunstgattungen. Dadurch wird aus einer Auseinandersetzung mit Handwerk eine Reflexion über gesellschaftliche Wertesysteme, und die üblichen Qualitätsfaktoren Zeit, Können und Materialwert werden zum Diskurs gestellt. KP

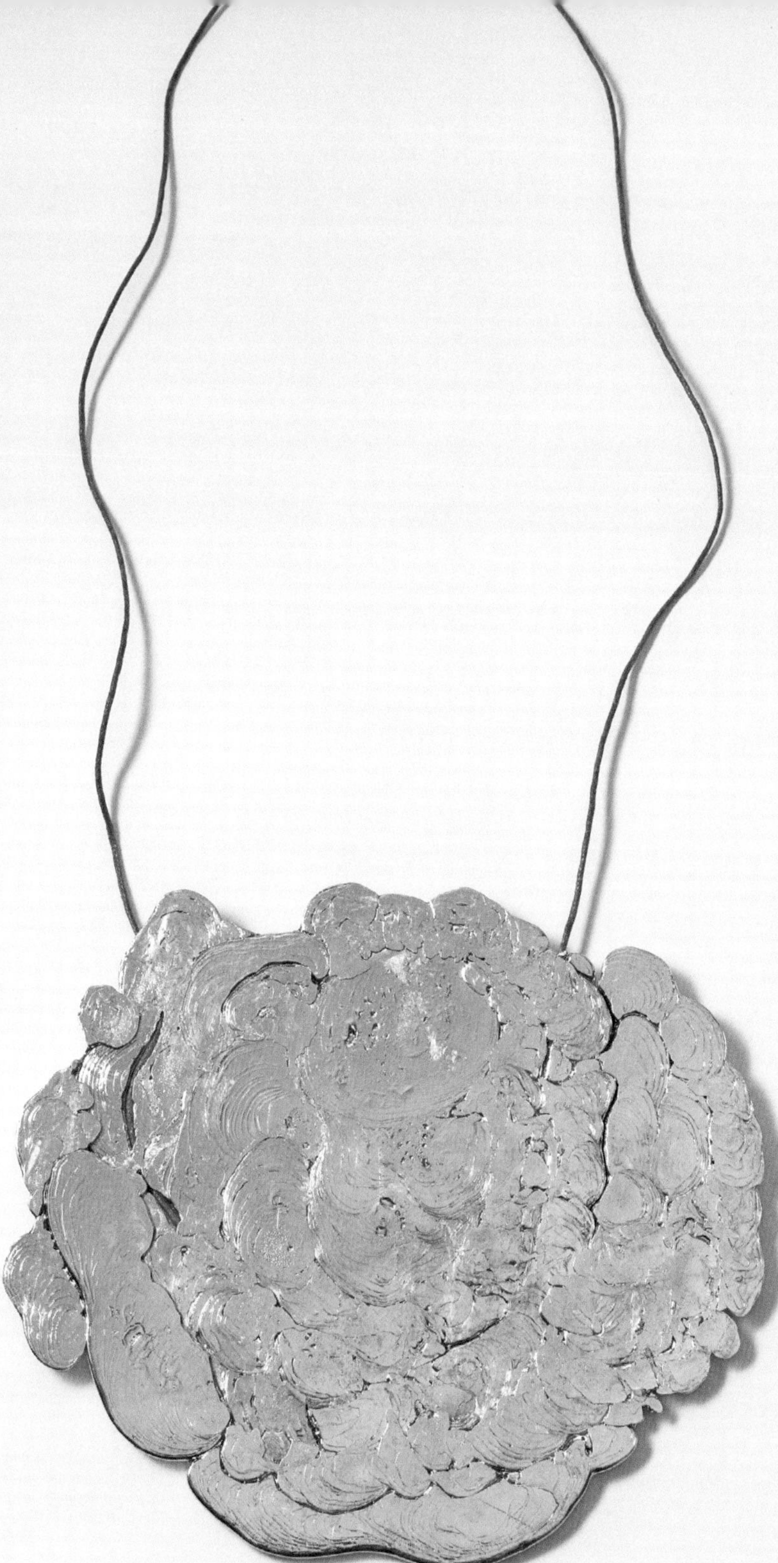

Nadine Kuffner deliberately undermines the expectations generally held of craft methodology. Her pieces are "painted" using melted tin. In this way she creates jewelry that challenges craftsmanship as a societal phenomenon, but also the customary classifications of production methodology in various art forms. As a result, the examination of craft becomes a reflection on social value systems, and the usual measurements of quality, such as time, skill, and material value, are put up for discussion. KP

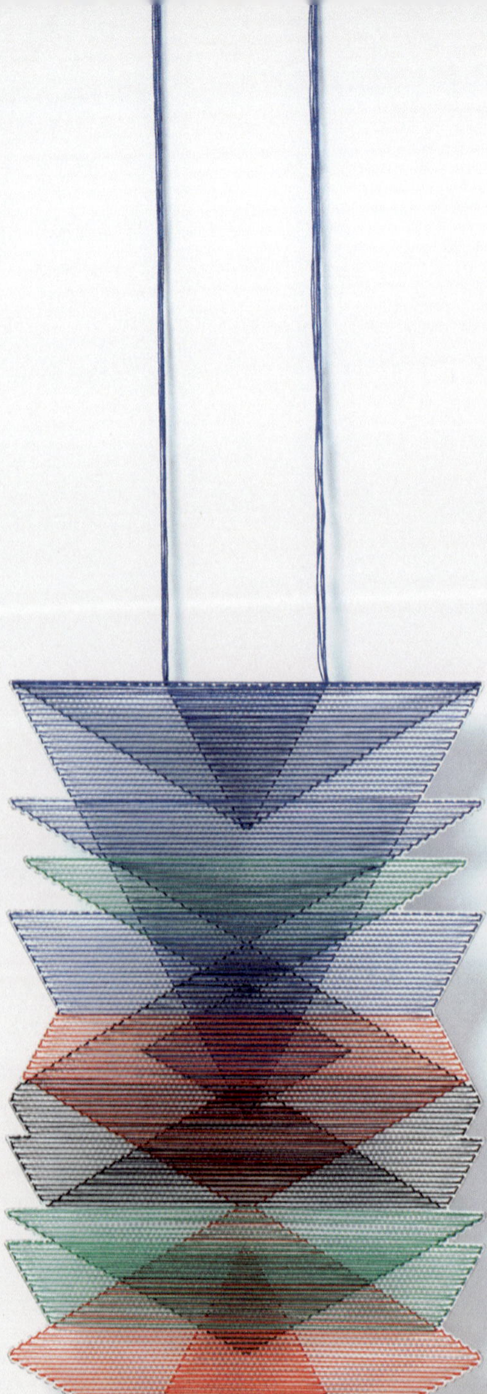

DANA HAKIM

96
Halsschmuck o.T. | neckpiece untitled, 2019
Vorgefertigtes Eisennetz, Polsterfäden | prefabricated iron mesh, upholstery threads
59 × 14 × 2 cm

98
Halsschmuck o.T. aus der Serie | neckpiece untitled from the series "My Four Guardian Angels – Blue Series", 2012
Vorgefertigtes Eisennetz, Ketten, Christbaumkugel, reflektierende Fäden, Baumwolle, Farbe, Lack
prefabricated iron mesh, chains, Christmas bauble, reflective threads, cotton, paint, lacquer, 29 × 24 × 7 cm

99
Halsschmuck o.T. | neckpiece untitled, 2013
Vorgefertigtes Eisennetz, Ketten, Aluminiumgitter, Fäden, Lack | prefabricated iron mesh, chains, aluminum mesh, threads, lacquer, 48 × 16,5 × 3 cm

Halsschmuck „Alter Ego" aus der Serie | neckpiece "Alter Ego" from the series "My Four Guardian Angels – Blue Series", 2010
Vorgefertigtes Eisennetz, Ketten, Kunststoff, Fäden, Farbe, Lack | prefabricated iron mesh, chains, plastic, threads, paint, lacquer , 42 × 20 × 2 cm
Privatsammlung, Niederlande | private collection, Netherlands

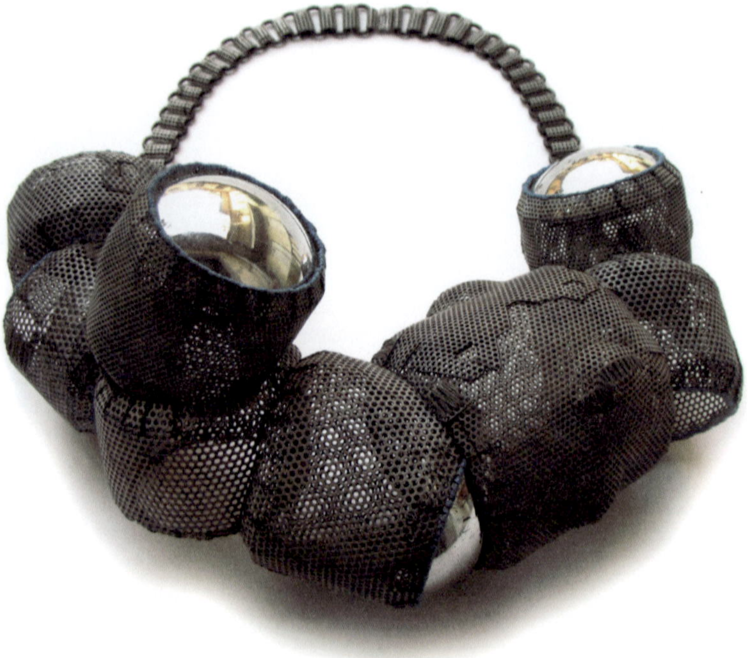

Bei Amuletten entsteht die Schutzfunktion oft durch eine Aneignung des Zeichens oder Materials von etwas, gegen das man sich schützen möchte. Amulette sowie zeitgenössische Materialien und technoide Formen einer allgegenwärtigen Überwachungsgesellschaft stellen für Dana Hakims Werk die Rahmenbedingungen. Mit diesem Ausgangspunkt untersucht sie das Phänomen der Ausgrenzung und Verdächtigung von Menschen in einer zunehmend digitalen Welt. KP

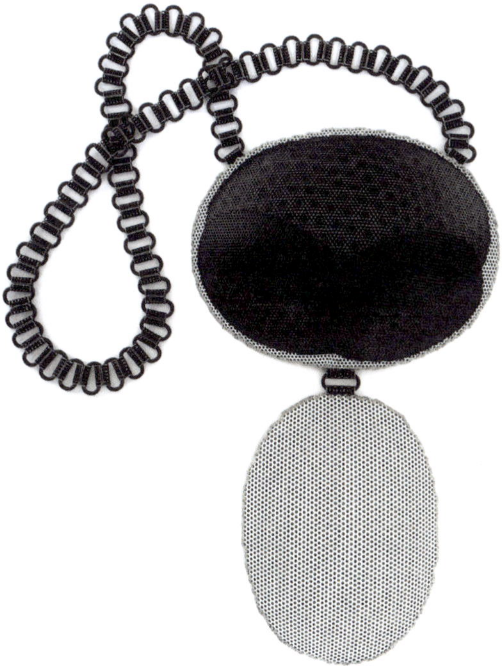

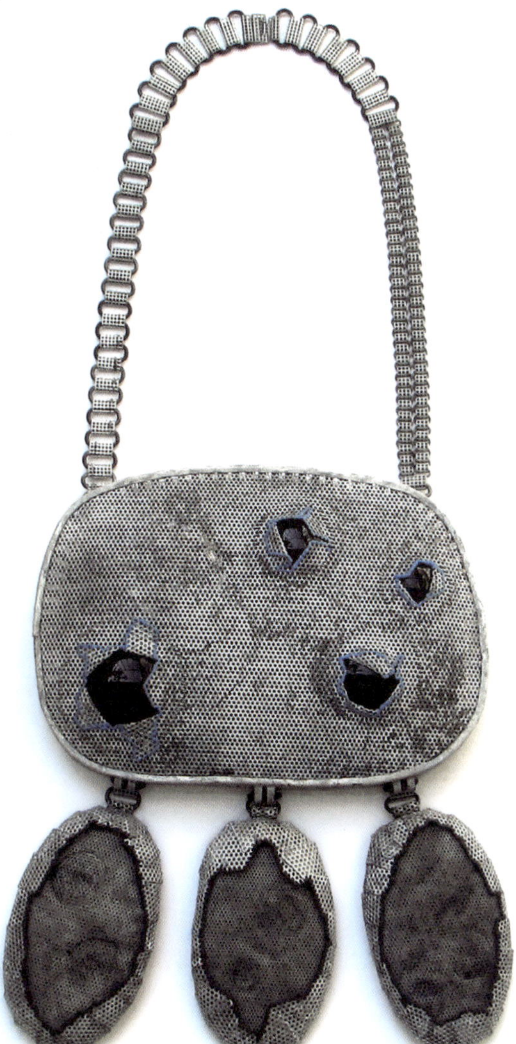

In amulets, the protective function is often created by appropriation of a sign or material from something against which the protection is needed. Amulets, as well as contemporary materials and the technoid formal language of a pervasive surveillance society, provide the framework for Dana Hakim's jewelry. From this starting point she explores the phenomenon of the exclusion and suspicion of individuals in an increasingly digitized world. KP

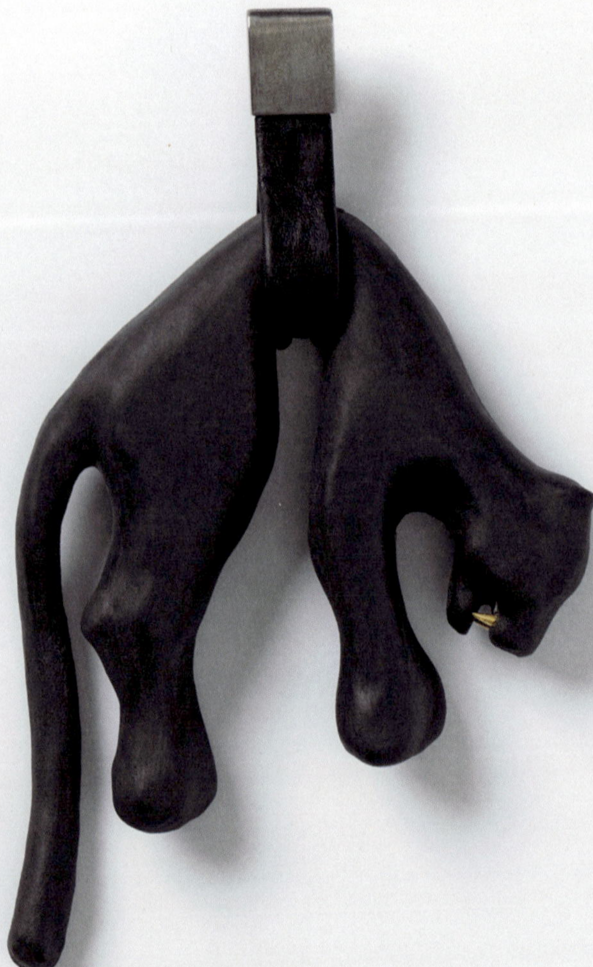

YASAR AYDIN

100
Brosche „Noir“ | brooch “Noir”, 2018
Porzellan, Leder, Gold, Silber | porcelain, leather, gold, silver
14,5 (max.) × 8,7 × 1,5 cm

102
Brosche aus der Serie | brooch from the series
“Layers of Pink”, 2011
Eisen, Leder, Speckstein | iron, leather, soap stone
13 × 6 cm

103
Brosche aus der Serie | brooch from the series
“Layers of Pink”, 2011
Eisen, Leder, Glas | iron, leather, glass
14 × 9 cm

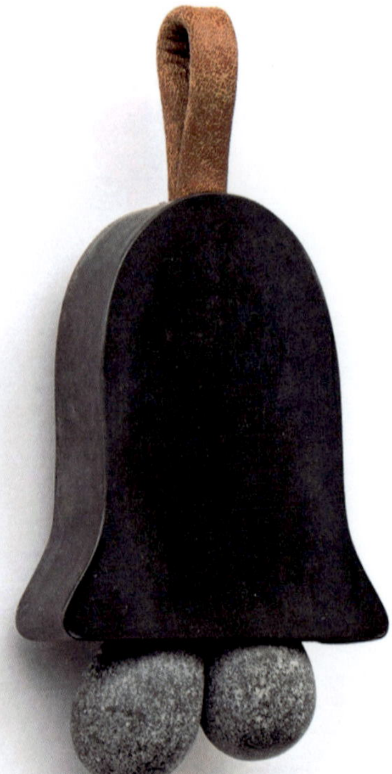

Die Broschen von Yasar Aydin beschäftigen sich mit homosexueller Identitätsbildung. Durch die eigene sexuelle Orientierung außerhalb der Normen einer Gesellschaftsstruktur zu sein, bedeutet nicht, einen Freiraum zu erhalten, sondern eher, sich in einem noch engeren Identitätsraster zu befinden. Hierbei wird die sexuelle Orientierung zur sozialen Identität. Dass die Werke von Yasar Aydin offensichtliche sexuelle Konnotationen beinhalten, ist deswegen nicht ein Ausdruck von persönlichen Vorlieben, sondern eine Reflexion des gesellschaftlichen Umgangs mit homosexuellen Identitäten. KP

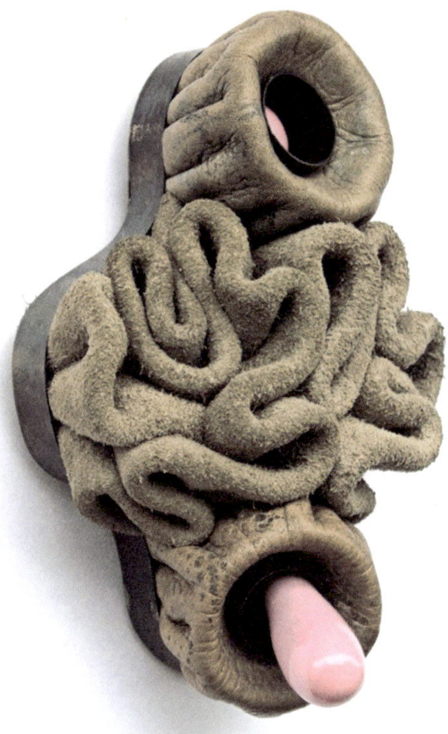

Yasar Aydin's brooches examine homosexual identity formation. Not fitting into the normative structures of society due to one's sexual orientation does not mean that one is free of social conventions: Instead, one tends to find oneself in an even narrower identity grid. Sexual orientation then becomes a person's social identity. That Yasar Aydin's works contain obvious sexual connotations is therefore not an expression of a personal preference, but a reflection on how homosexual identities are treated in society. KP

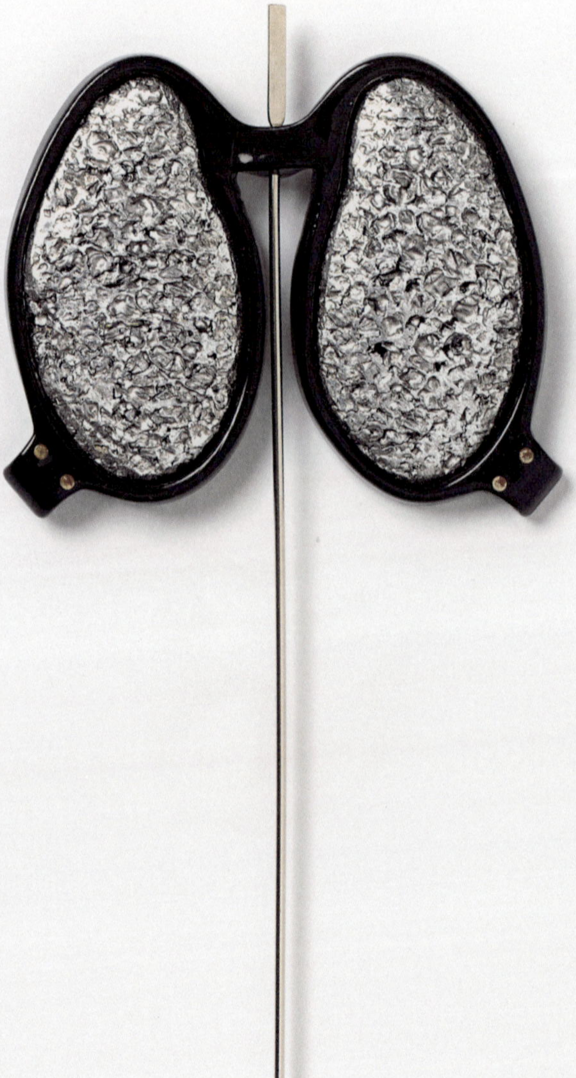

104
Dovile Bernadisiute / Lee Kuczewski
Brosche | brooch "Warped V_1.03", 2018
Zelluloseacetat (Brillengestell), Aluminium (offenporig), Nickel
cellulose acetate (glasses frame), open-cell aluminum,
nickel core, 15 × 7 × 2 cm

106
Halsschmuck | necklace "Traces of a Floor", 2015
Aluminiumschaum, Titan, Baumwollband
aluminum foam, titanium, cotton ribbon
10 × 7 × 1,5 cm

107
Brosche | brooch "Found Plastic Object", 2015
Aluminiumschaum, Edelstahl, Gummi
aluminum foam, stainless steel, rubber
Ø 10 cm, H. | h. 1 cm

Brosche | brooch "Found Wooden Object", 2015
Aluminiumschaum, Edelstahl
aluminum foam, stainless steel
7 × 8 × 2 cm

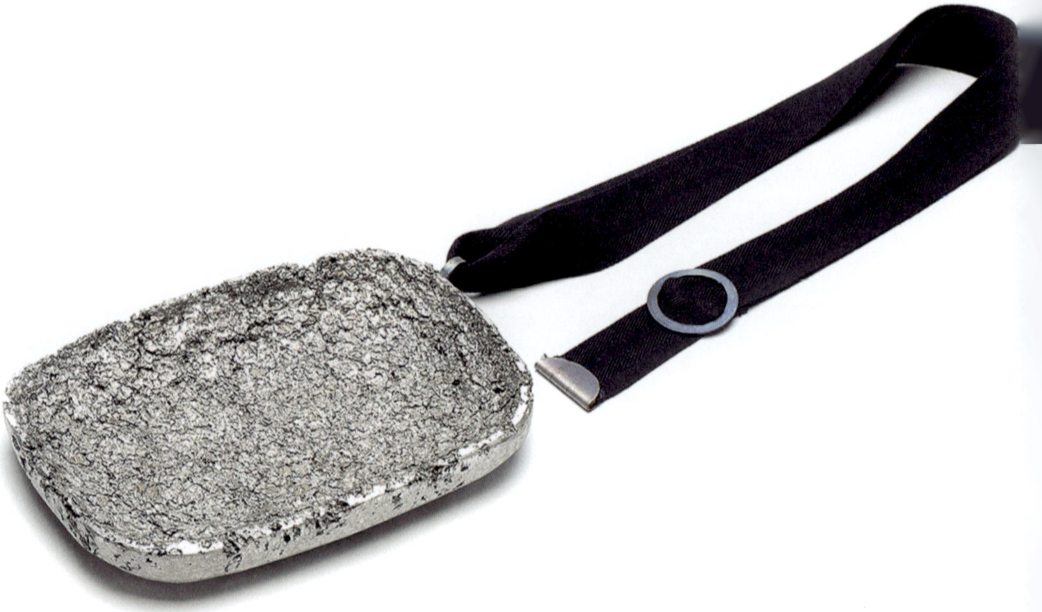

Die Werke von Dovile Bernadisiute bestehen aus Abdrücken der Oberflächen von jenen urbanen Orten, die hauptsächlich als Übergänge oder als Zwischenorte genutzt werden. Die Schmuckstücke beschreiben die Diskrepanz zwischen einem privaten und einem öffentlichen Bereich und die Entfremdung, die solche „Nichtorte" in Menschen auslösen können. Sich durch Schmuck oder anderweitig einen öffentlichen Raum anzueignen, steht hierbei am Anfang eines Protestes. KP

Dovile Bernadisiute's works consist of surface imprints taken from urban spaces primarily characterized by transition or intermediate areas. The items of jewelry point to the discrepancy between the private and public sphere and to the emotional alienation that such "non-places" can trigger in people. Appropriating a public space, through jewelry or otherwise, here marks the beginning of protest. KP

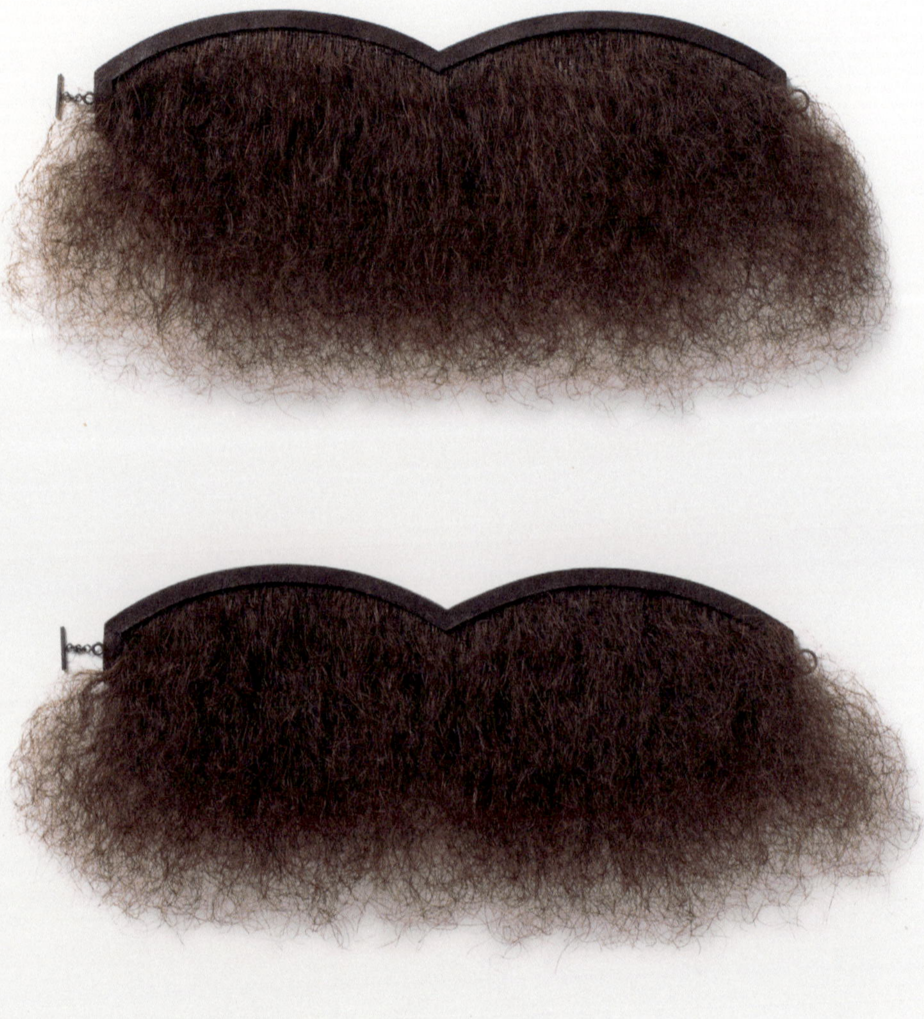

CARLA CASTIAJO

108
Objekte | objects "Fetischismus", 2018
Menschliches Haar, Leder, Stoff, Silber
human hair, leather, fabrics, silver
9,5 × 17 × 1 cm

110
Brosche aus der Serie | brooch from the series
"Martyrs – Heroes in Paradise", 2006
Kopf einer Barbie-Puppe (Gummi), Gold, menschliches Haar
head of a Barbie (rubber), gold, human hair
13 × 13 × 2,3 cm

111
Brosche aus der Serie | brooch from the series
"Martyrs – Heroes in Paradise", 2006
Puppenkopf (Gummi), Gold, menschliches Haar
doll head (rubber), gold, human hair
9,3 × 7,2 × 5,4 cm

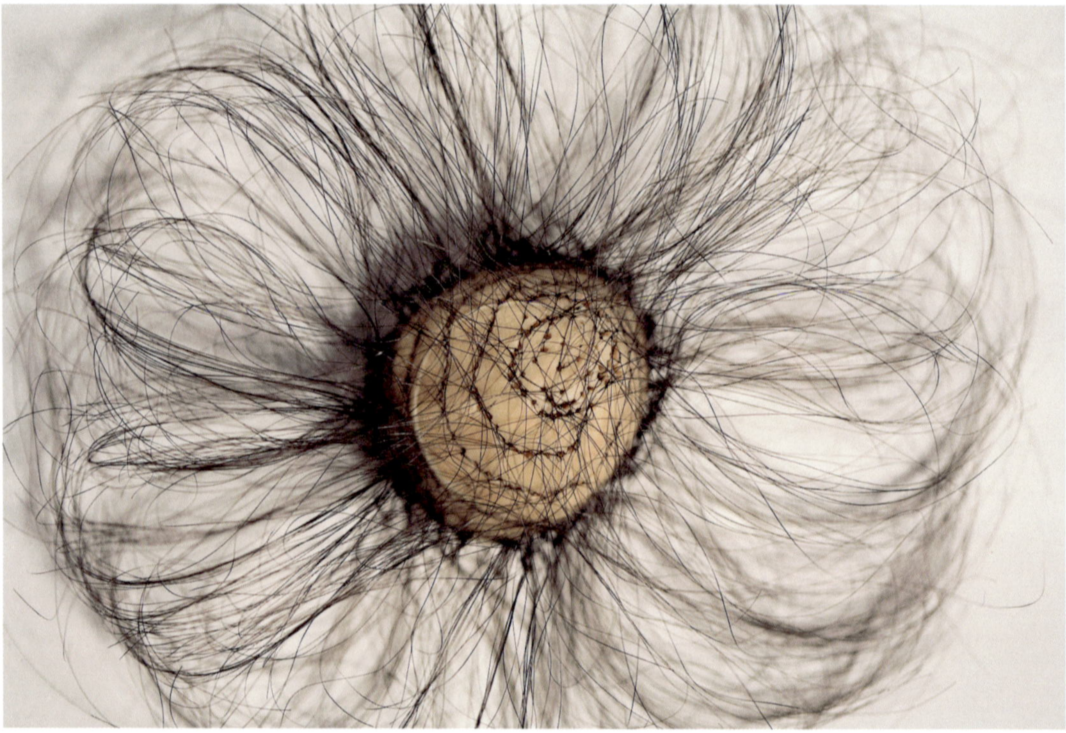

Die Broschen von Carla Castiajo sind aus Puppenköpfen, Gold und menschlichem Haar hergestellt. Im Titel nehmen sie Bezug zu Märtyrern. Die Herstellungsweise der Broschen erinnert an die Art von obsessiver Handarbeit (von Frauen), die oft im sakralen Kunsthandwerk beobachtet werden kann. Puppensammeln, Handarbeit und Haargestaltung sind Tätigkeiten, die stereotypisch mit Weiblichkeit verbunden werden. In den Werken von Carla Castiajo erhalten sie aber etwas Verstörendes – Puppen sind Objekte, die auch zur Aneignung von normativen Geschlechterrollen dienen, aber hier sind sie geköpft, und die Gestaltung der Haare entspricht nicht den gängigen Schönheitsvorstellungen. KP

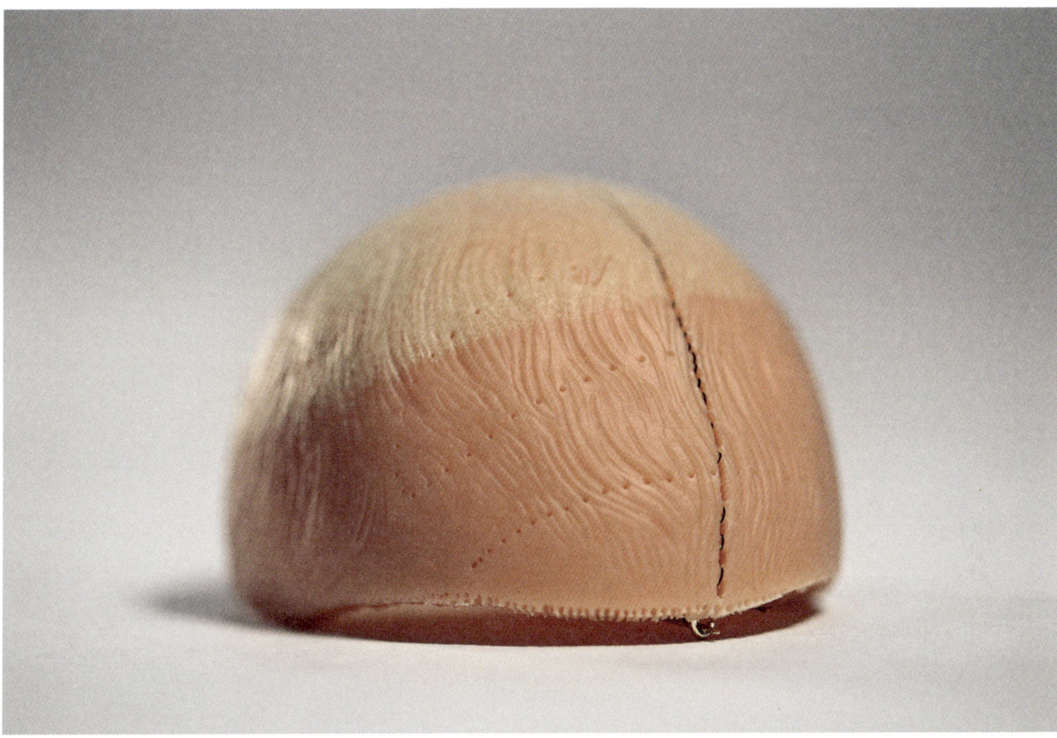

Carla Castiajo's brooches are made from dolls' heads, gold and human hair. Their titles refer to martyrs, and the way in which the brooches are made is also reminiscent of the kind of obsessive manual work (by women) that can be observed in the sacral arts and crafts. Doll collecting, handicraft and hair-styling are activities stereotypically associated with femininity. However, in Carla Castiajo's works they gain a disturbing quality – dolls are objects also used in the cultivation of normative gender roles, yet here they are beheaded and the design of their hair does not correspond with commonly held concepts of beauty. KP

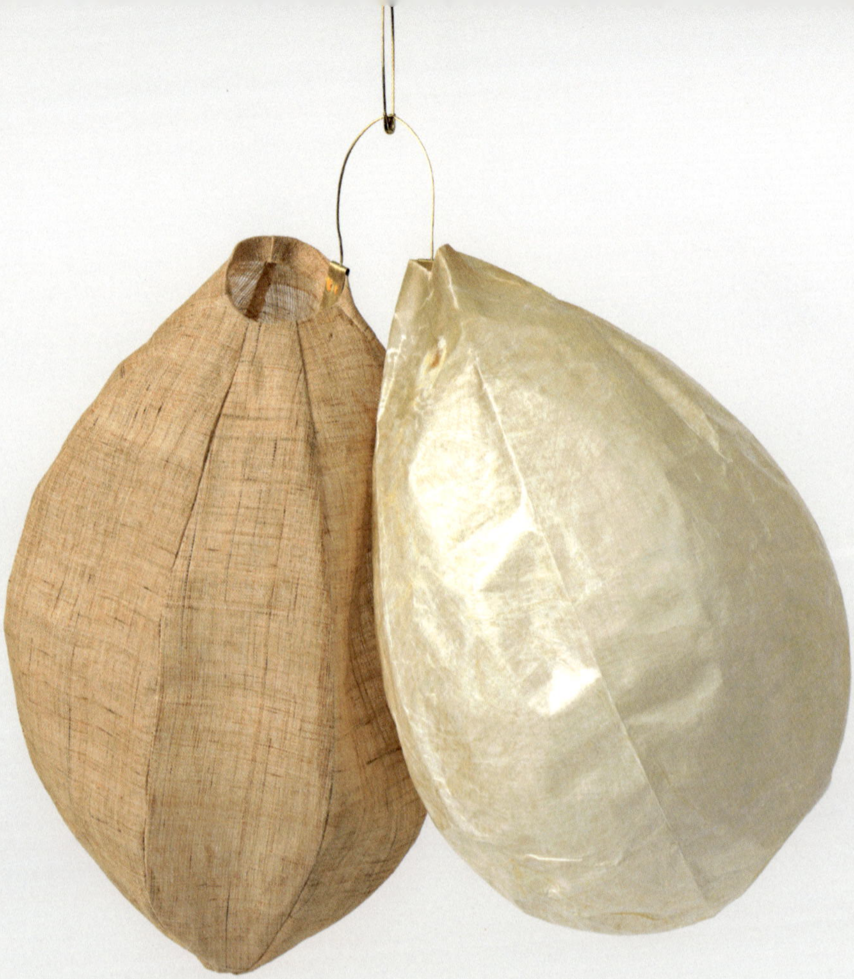

IRIS EICHENBERG

112
Brosche o.T. | brooch untitled, 2018
Leinen, Messing, Schweineblase | linen, brass, pig bladder
60 × 30 × 18 cm

115
Anhänger | necklace "years later", 2009
Nylonstrümpfe, Spiegel, Silber | nylons, mirror, silver
11 × 3 × 4 cm

Der weibliche Körper, der in dem Werk von Iris Eichenberg untersucht wird, kann einerseits als individueller Erfahrungsbereich von Frauen und anderseits als ein gesellschaftliches Konstrukt gelesen werden. Die Schmuckstücke drücken ein Gefühl von Befremdung gegenüber dem eigenen Körper aus, das oft noch durch die vorherrschenden patriarchalischen Gesellschaftsstrukturen verstärkt wird. Dabei weisen die Arbeiten auf die Problematik hin, sich innerhalb genormter Geschlechterrollen mit dem eigenen Körper zu identifizieren. KP

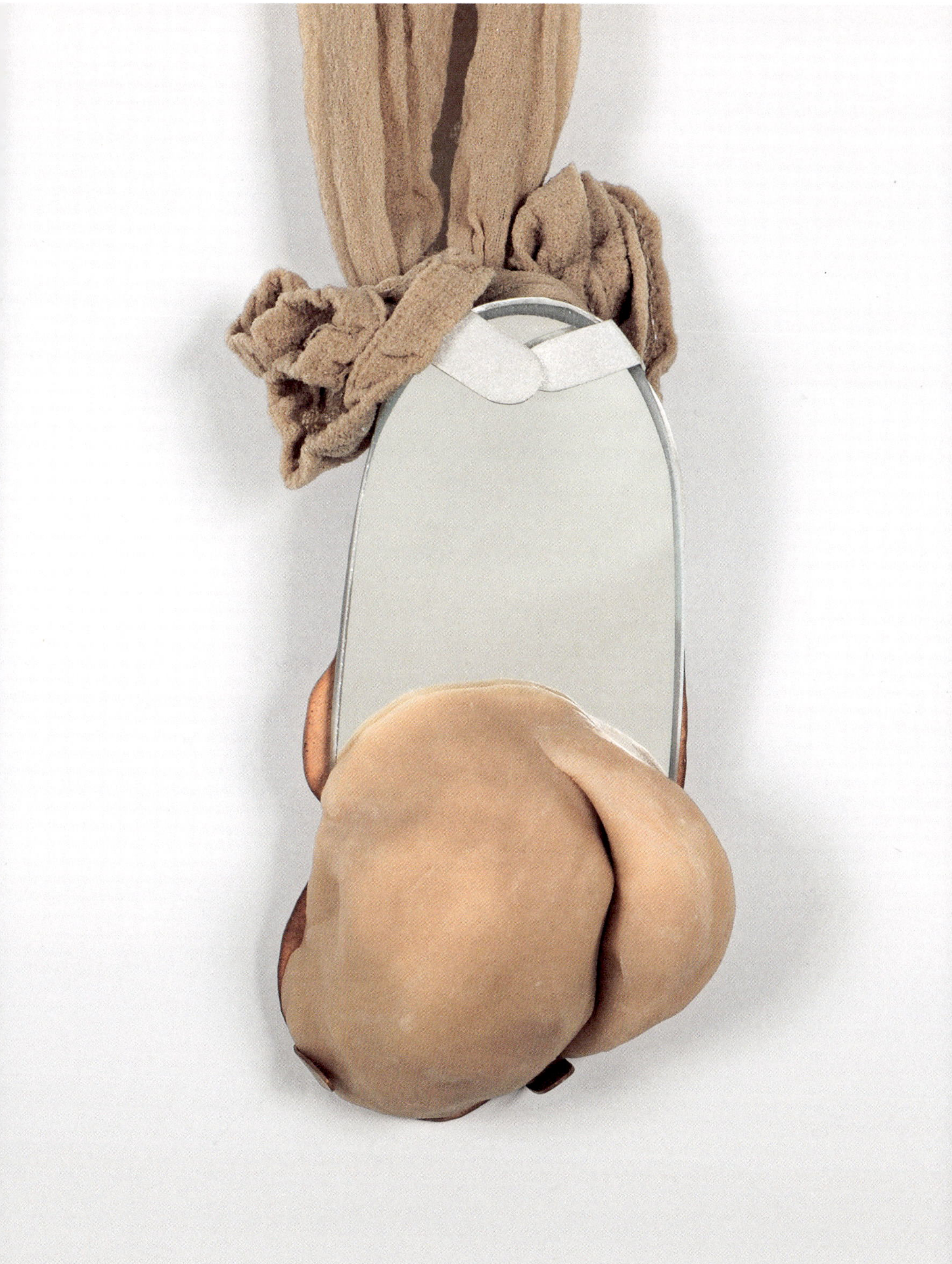

Iris Eichenberg’s work examined the female body, both in terms of its being a realm of individual female experiences and as a societal construction. The jewelry expresses a feeling of alienation towards one's own body, something that is often reinforced by the prevailing patriarchal social structures. As such, the pieces problematize the construction of self-identification with the body in the context of normative gender patterns. KP

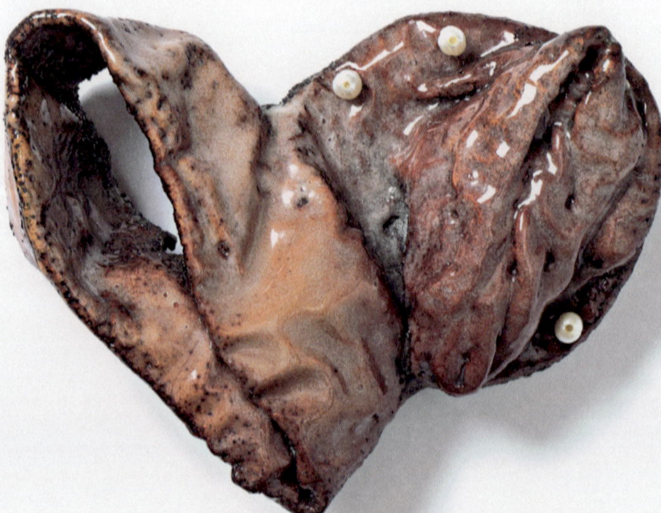

CAROLINA GIMENO

116
Brosche | brooch "Portable Pleasure, when Intimacy become Public. No 37", 2018
Elektogeformte Socken, Kupfer, Email, Messing, Perlen
electro-formed socks, copper, vitreous enamel, brass, pearls
12 × 14,5 × 5,5 cm

119
Brosche | brooch "Portable Pleasure, when Intimacy become Public. No 11", 2014
Elektrogeformte Socken, Kupfer, Email, Silber
electro-formed socks, copper, vitreous enamel, silver
6 × 7 × 5 cm

Brosche | brooch "Portable Pleasure, when Intimacy become Public. No 4", 2014
Elektrogeformte Socken, Kupfer, Email, Silber
electro-formed socks, copper, vitreous enamel, silver
16 × 7,5 × 5 cm

Brosche | brooch "Portable Pleasure, when Intimacy become Public. No 16", 2015
Elektrogeformte Socken, Kupfer, Email, Baumwolle, Nylon, Kunststoff, Kristalle, Silber | electro-formed socks, copper, vitreous enamel, cotton, nylon, plastics, crystals, silver
12 × 14 × 4 cm

Aus gesammelten „verwaisten" Socken wurden die Formen gefaltet, die für die Broschen von Carolina Gimeno die Grundlage geben. Die hierbei entstandene Konnotation zum weiblichen Körper ist unübersehbar und bildet eine provokative Grundlage, um die Zurschaustellung von Körpern in der Öffentlichkeit zu reflektieren. Die Intimität von Körpern ist gleichzeitig als etwas Privates und etwas Politisches anzusehen, da das äußere Erscheinungsbild fortwährend gesellschaftlich reguliert wird. KP

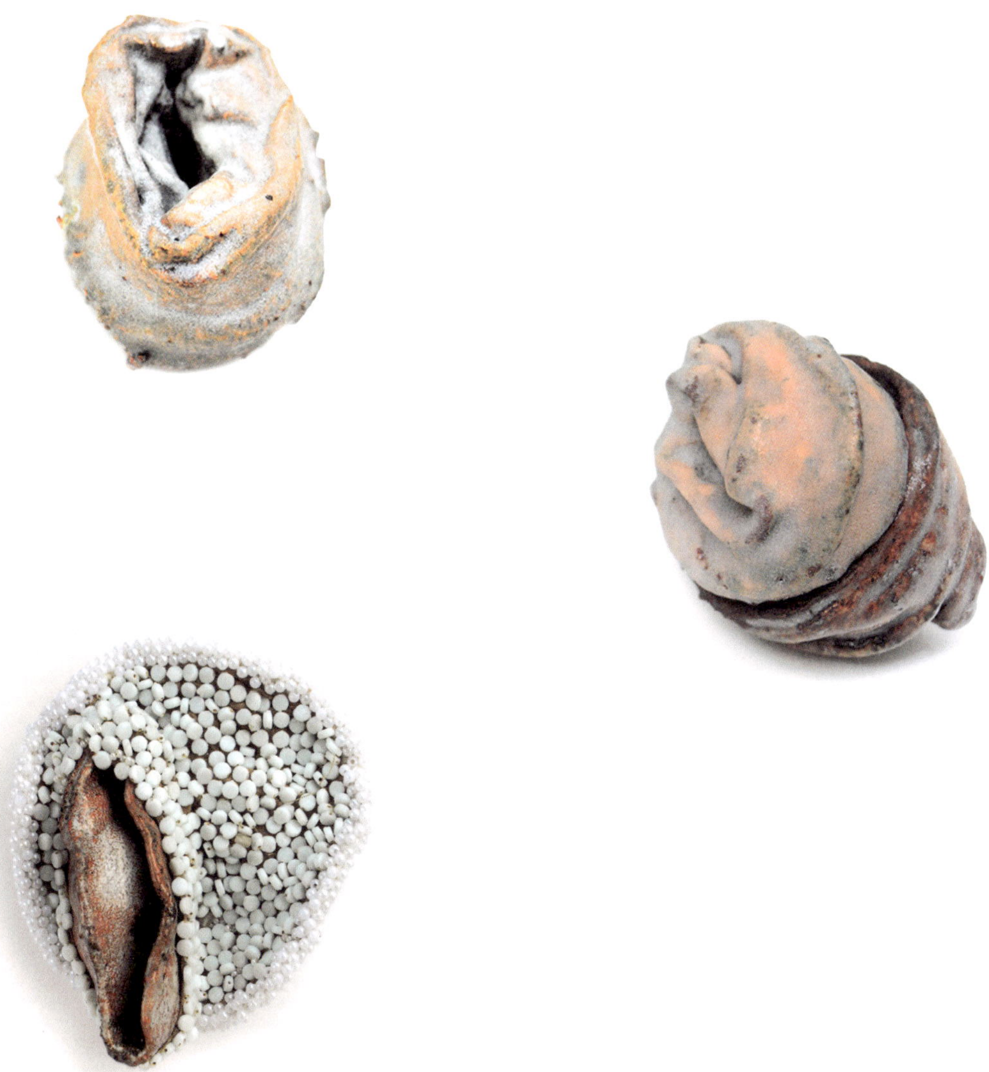

Carolina Gimeno folds the shapes that form the starting point of her brooches from collected "orphaned" socks. The resulting quite obvious reference to the female body provides a provocative basis on which to reflect upon the display of bodies in the public sphere. The intimacy of bodies must be considered something simultaneously private and political, since the outward appearance of bodies is perpetually regulated by society. KP

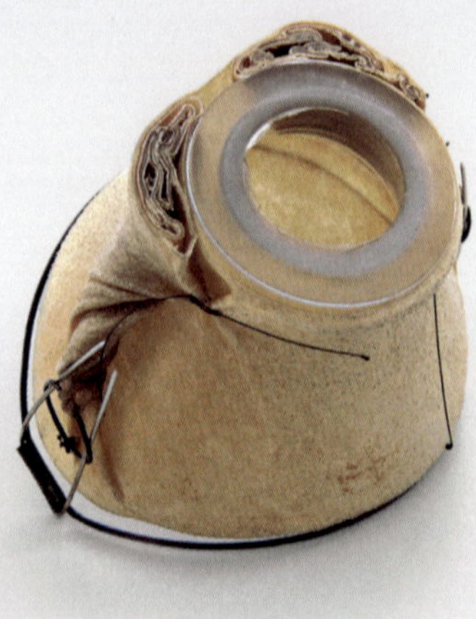

120
Brosche | brooch "Hurt Body #1", 2006–2007
Pergament, Kunststoff, Edelstahl, Eisen, Nylon
vellum, plastic, stainless steel, iron, nylon
5,5 × 6,6 × 5,8 cm

122
Brosche | brooch "Study of an Organ / Imprint (Counterpart I)", 2013
Gamsleder, Eisen, Stahl, Faden, Speckstein, Wachs
chamois leather, iron, steel, thread, soapstone, wax
14 × 6 × 4 cm

123
Anhänger–Brosche–Objekt | pendant–brooch–object "Cura Posterior IV (Ni Dieu, ni maître)", 2011
Süßkartoffel, Pergament, Eisen, Stahl, Nylon, Tusche
yam, vellum, iron, steel, nylon, India ink
19,5 × 7 × 3,5 cm

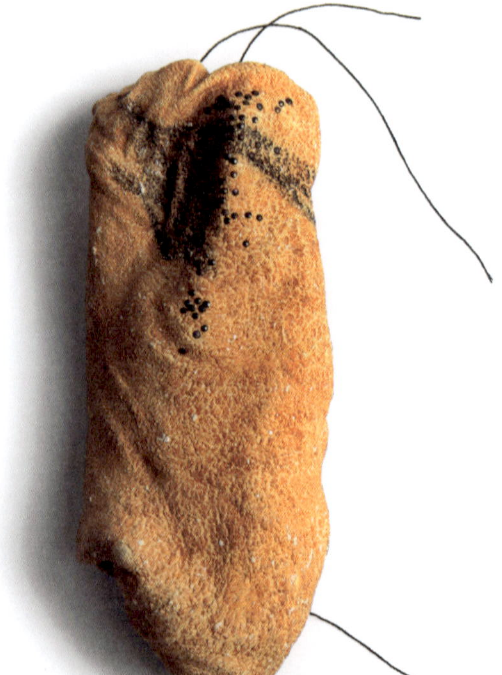

Die Arbeiten von Hannah Joris hinterfragen die gängige Vorstellung, dass ein Mensch wichtiger ist als ein Tier, jung fast immer besser ist als alt, und dass manche menschlichen Körper wertvoller sind als andere. Hannah Joris nutzt sowohl die kulturelle Bedeutungsebene von Materialien wie auch ihre physikalischen Eigenschaften, um Narrative zu vermitteln. Ihre Materialwahl beinhaltet u.a. Tierhaut, Wurzelgemüse und Stahlnägel. Die Eigenschaft eines Materials zu vertrocknen und zu schrumpfen, dient während des Herstellungsprozesses zur Gestaltung der Arbeiten. Der Ausdruck der Broschen ist beunruhigend körperlich und weist auf die unterschiedlichen Bewertungen von Körpern in der Gesellschaft hin. KP

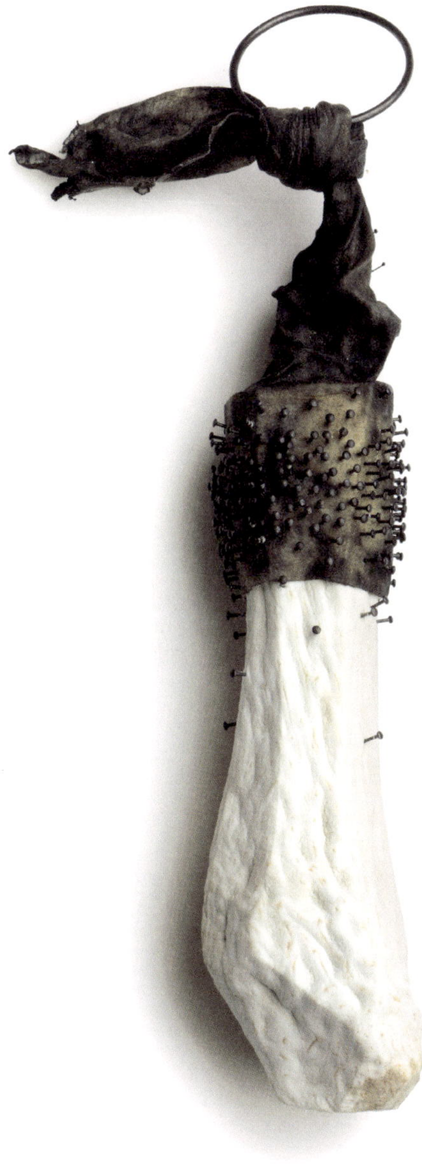

Hannah Joris' work challenges the common notion that human beings are more important than animals, the young most often are considered better than the old, and that some human bodies are more valuable than others. Hannah Joris uses both the cultural meaning of her materials as well as their physical properties to convey narratives. Among others, her choice of materials includes animal skin, root vegetables and steel nails. Many of her materials wither and shrink during the work process, and this characteristic trait dictates the form of her pieces. The expression of the brooches is disconcertingly physical, and points to the different valuations of bodies in society. KP

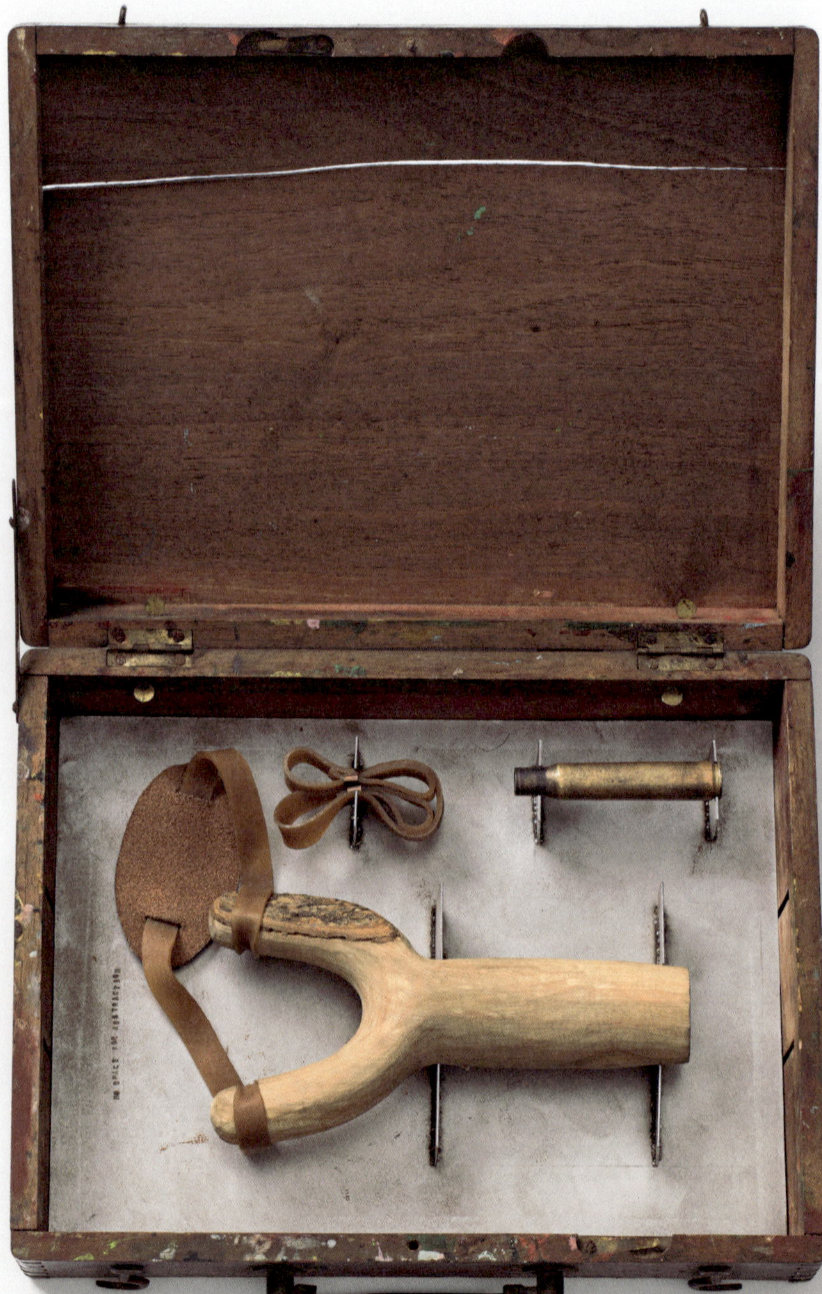

124
Objekt | object "No Space for Abstraction", 2018
Olivenholz, Eisen, Gummi, Leder, Messing
olive wood, iron, rubber, leather, brass
18,5 × 24 × 6,6 cm (Kasten | case)

126
Brosche | brooch "In Conflict", 2018
Holz, Eisen, Silber | wood, iron, silver
9,5 × 9 × 5 cm

127
Brosche | brooch "In Conflict", 2018
Holz, Eisen, Silber | wood, iron, silver
9,5 × 9 × 5 cm

Brosche | brooch "In Conflict", 2018
Holz, Eisen, Silber | wood, iron, silver
9,5 × 9 × 5 cm

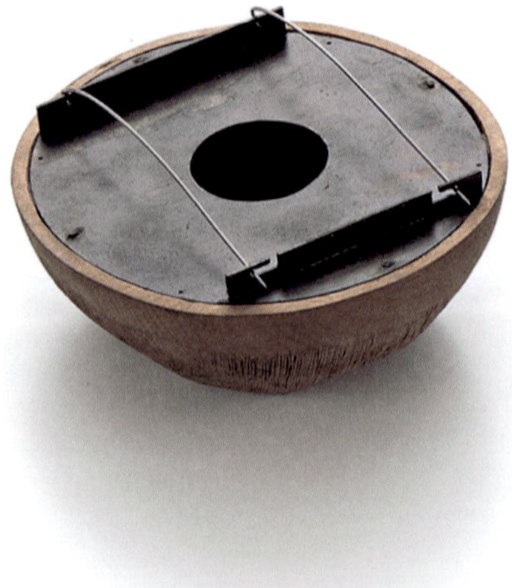

Kuppeln krönen Gebäude. Es ist nicht zufällig, dass diese Formen auf religiösen Bauwerken und Regierungsgebäuden vorkommen. Sie symbolisieren Macht, sowohl wirtschaftliche wie religiöse. In den Werken von Sanaa Khalil dienen Holzkuppeln als Grundform. Diese werden bis zur Erschöpfung mit Feuer, Säuren, Hämmern und Messern bearbeitet. Dadurch wird die Herstellungsweise der Broschen zu einem wesentlichen Narrativ innerhalb der Arbeiten und zeigt das Gefühl von Verwundbarkeit und Machtlosigkeit des Einzelnen in einer konfliktbeladenen Welt. KP

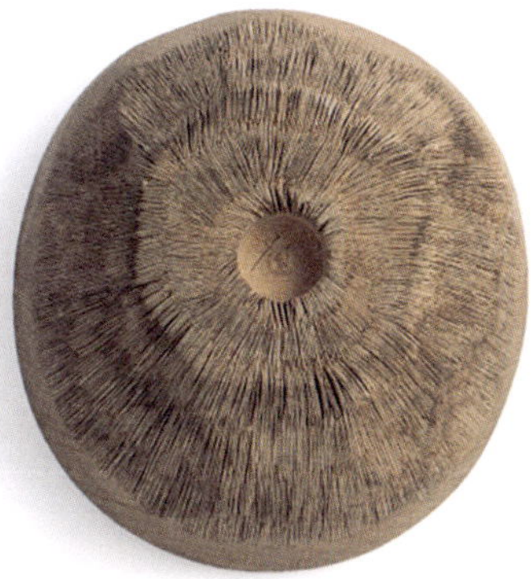

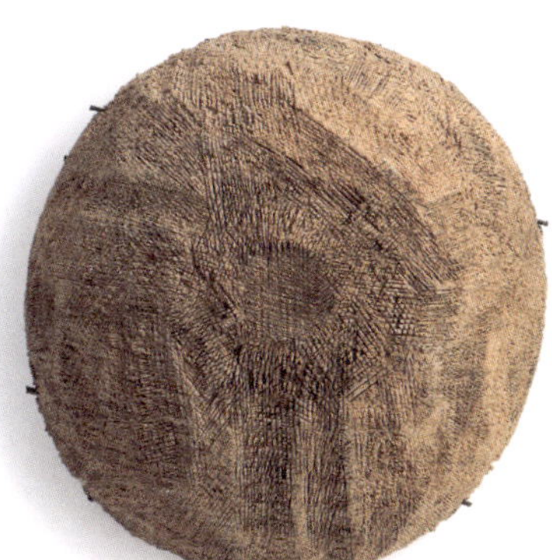

Domes crown buildings. It is not by accident that these forms occur in religious and governmental architecture. They symbolize power, both economic and religious. In the work of Sanaa Khalil, wooden domes serve as a basic form. These are processed to the point of exhaustion, using fire, acids, hammers or knives. Hereby the production of the brooches becomes an essential narrative within the work, and it illuminates the feeling of individual vulnerability and powerlessness in a conflict-laden world. KP

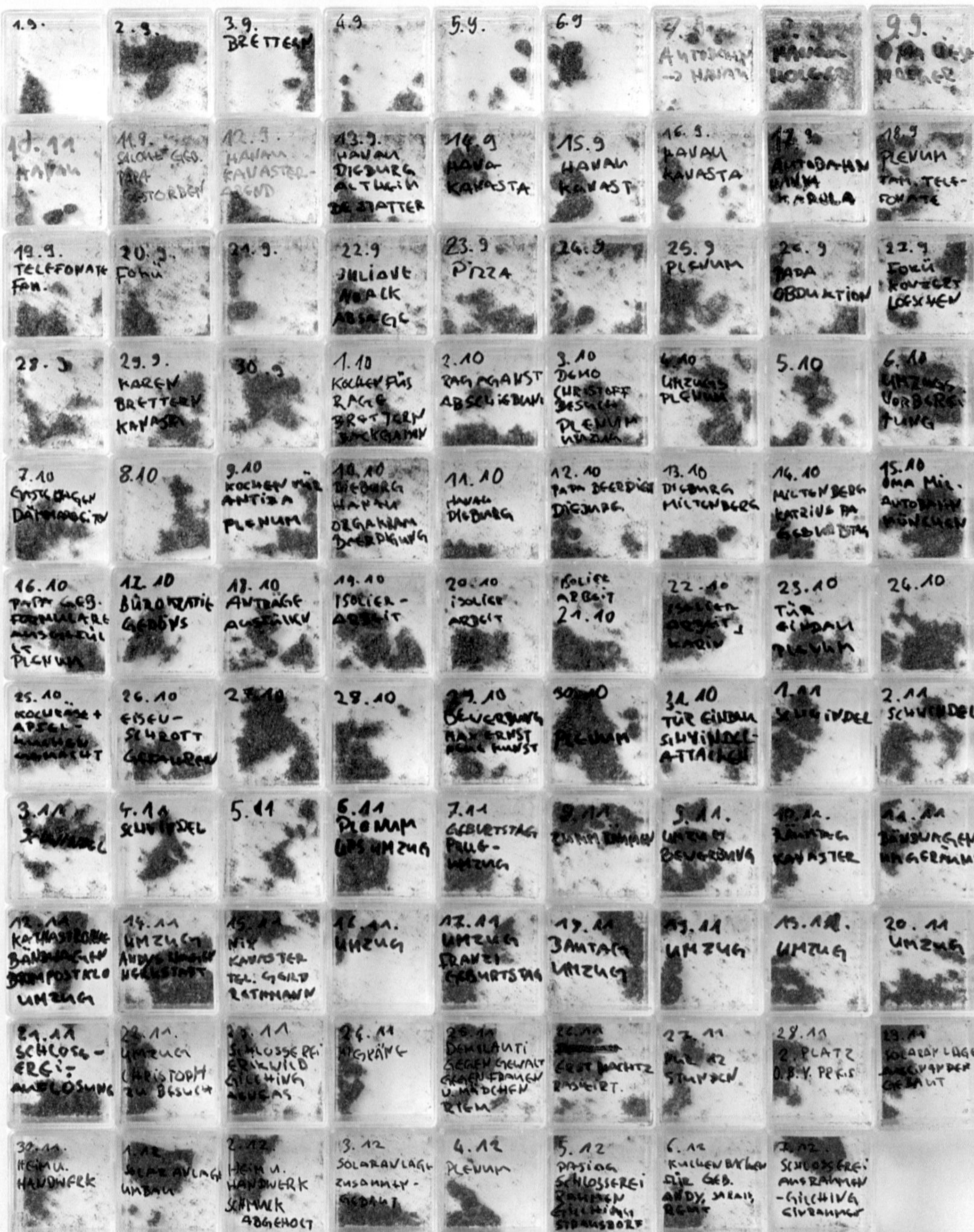

1.9.
2.9.
3.9. BRETTERN
4.9.
5.9.
6.9
9.9.
11.9.
12.9.
13.9. HANAU DIEBURG
14.9
15.9 HANAU KANAST
16.9. HANAU KANASTA
18.9 PLENUM
19.9. TELEFONATE
20.9.
21.9.
22.9
23.9 PIZZA
24.9
25.9 PLENUM
26.9
27.9
28.9
29.9. KAREN BRETTERN
30.9
1.10
2.10
3.10 DEMO
4.10
5.10
6.10
7.10
8.10
9.10 PLENUM
10.10 DIEBURG
11.10 HANAU DIEBURG
12.10
13.10 DIEBURG
14.10
15.10
16.10 PLENUM
17.10
18.10
19.10
20.10
21.10
22.10
23.10
24.10
25.10
26.10 EISEN-SCHROTT
28.10
29.10
30.10 PLENUM
31.10
1.11
2.11 SCHWINDEL
3.11
4.11
5.11
6.11 PLENUM
7.11
19.11
21.11
25.11
26.11
27.11
28.11 2. PLATZ
29.11
30.11 HEIM U. HANDWERK
1.12
2.12. HEIM U. HANDWERK
3.12
4.12 PLENUM
5.12
6.12
7.12

128
Broschen „Haartagebuch" | brooches "hair diary", 2018
Kopfrasur eines Tages seit September 2018
head shave of one day since September 2018
2,8 × 2,8 × 1,7 cm (98 Kästchen | 98 cases)

130
Brosche o.T. | brooch untitled, 2018
Haare (Merlin Klein), Silber, Stahl, Epoxy
hair (Merlin Klein), silver, steel, epoxy
4,4 × 4,1 cm

131
Anhänger | pendant "Bohrkern aus einer Treppenstufe der Akademie der Bildenden Künste München", 2018
Bohrkern (Stein), Kaugummi, Drahtseil
drill core (stone), chewing gum, wire robe
6 × 4 cm

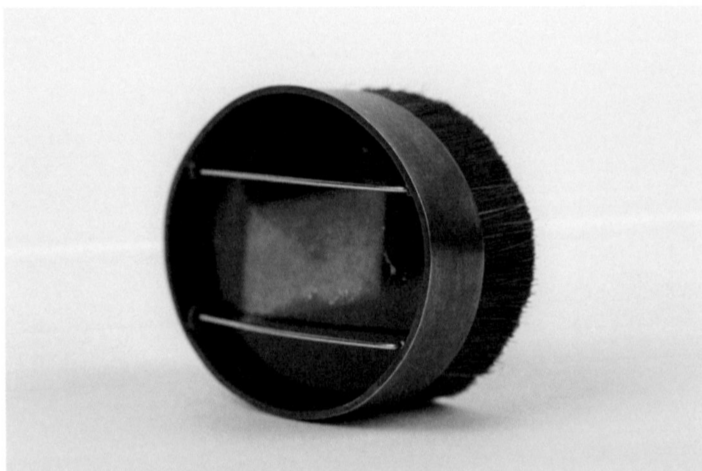

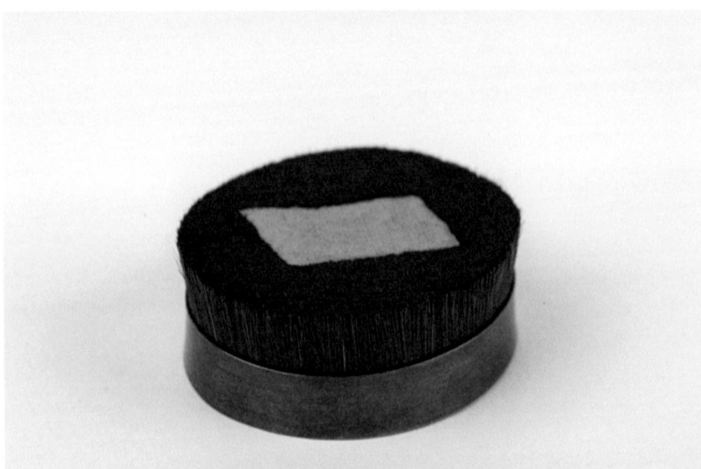

Aus den ehrwürdigen und denkmalgeschützen Stufen einer öffentlichen Institution in München hat Merlin Klein, rund um ein abgetretenes Kaugummi, ein Stück Stein herausgearbeitet. Der daraus entstandene Halsschmuck hat Gewicht und wirft Fragen auf bezüglich des Verhältnisses zwischen Individuum und sozialpolitischen Strukturen. Die Radikalität dieser Arbeit spiegelt nicht nur eine künstlerische Geste wider, sondern beleuchtet die unterschiedlichen Stufen des Unwillens und/oder der Resignation gegenüber den Institutionen der Macht in einer als ungerecht empfundenen Gesellschaft. KP

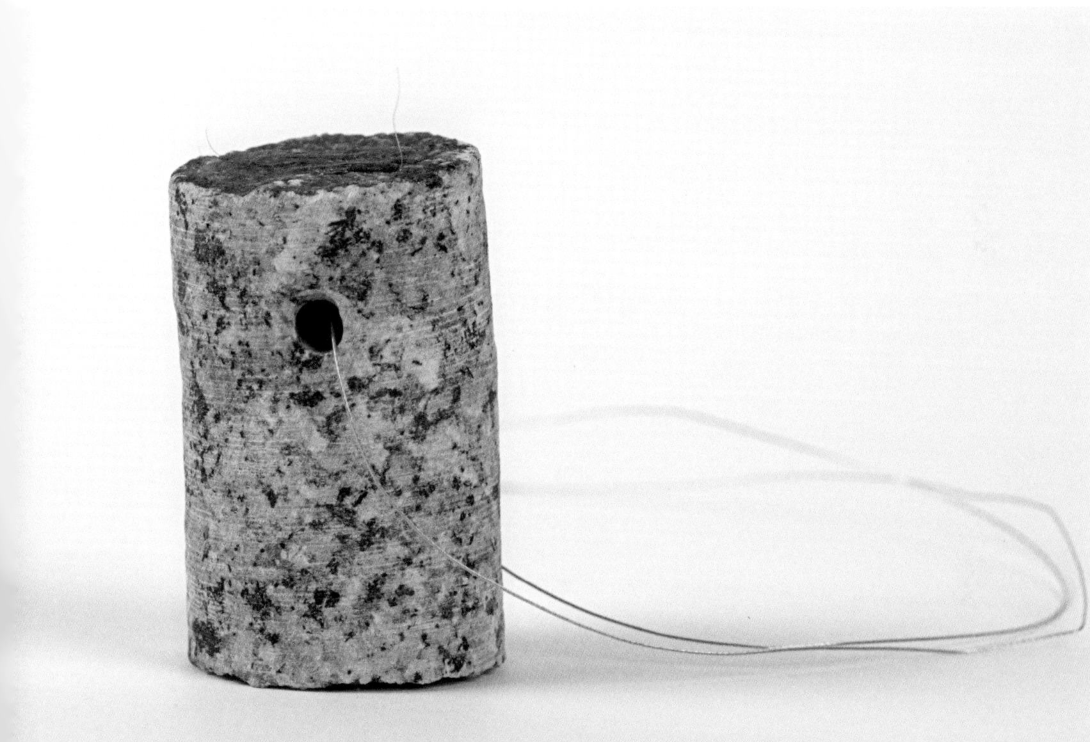

From an awe-inspiring listed staircase of a public institution in Munich, Merlin Klein has worked out a piece of stone around a trampled piece of chewing gum. The resulting, weighty necklace raises questions of the relationship between the individual and sociopolitical structures. The radical nature of this work not only reflects an artistic gesture, but also sheds light on the different levels of indignation and/or resignation towards the institutions of power within a society perceived as unequal. KP

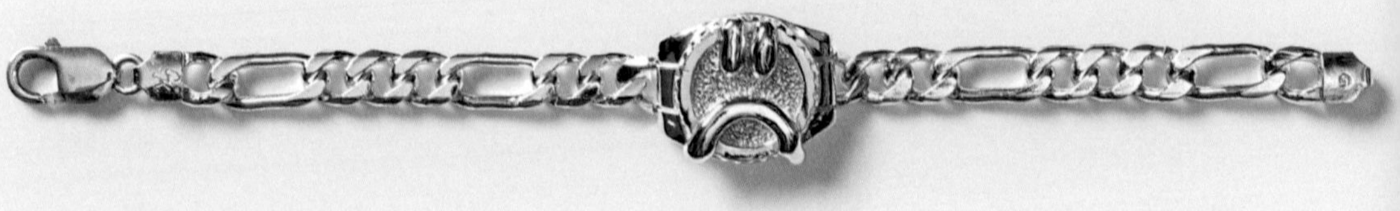

132
Armschmuck | bracelet “Sad Times”, 2019
Silber | silver
10,5 × 9,5 × 2,5 cm

134
Armschmuck | bracelet “Replica Five”, 2010
Messing, vergoldet; Edelstahl
brass, gilded; stainless steel
6 × 6 × 4,5 cm

135
Armschmuck | bracelet “Replica One”, 2010
Messing, vergoldet; Edelstahl
brass, gilded; stainless steel
6 × 6 × 3,8 cm

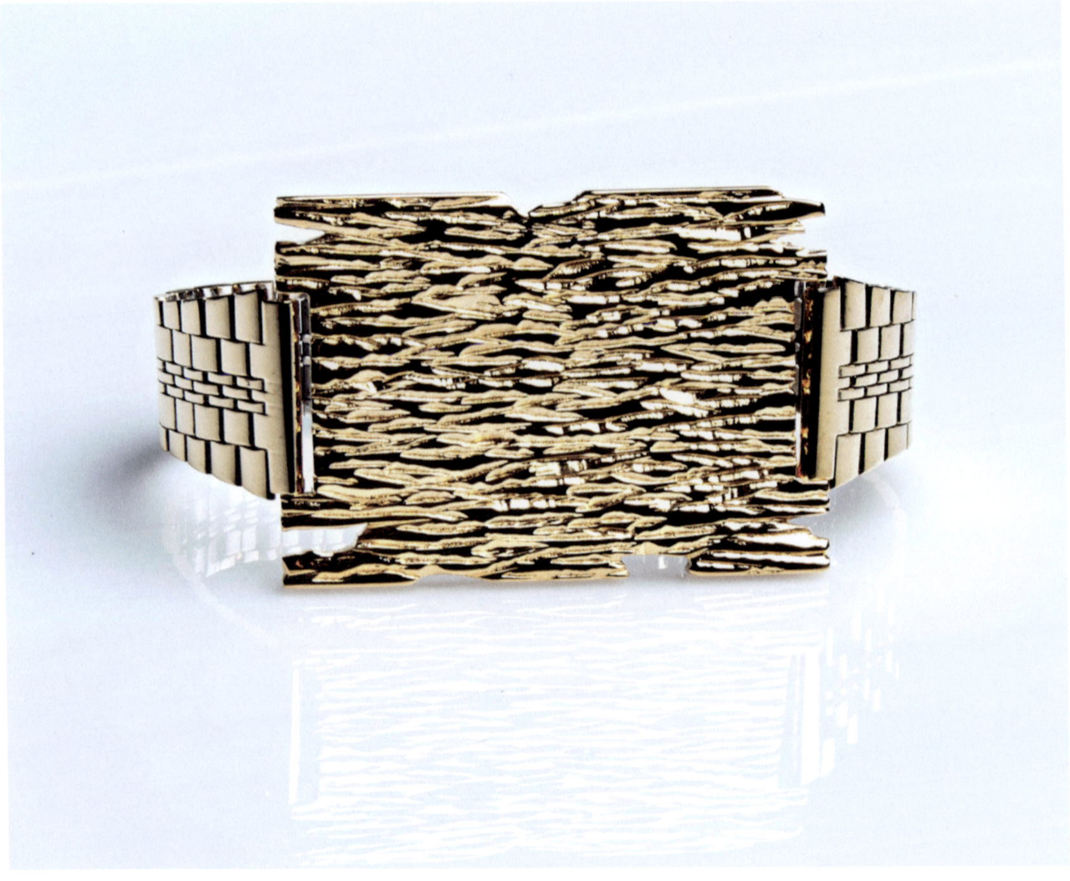

Die Werke von Göran Kling scheinen ein Widerspruch zu dem sparsam vorhandenen, aber technikaffinen Herrenschmuck des 19. Jahrhunderts darzustellen. Opulent präsentieren sich die Armbanduhren ohne Zeitangaben. Dabei ist Zeit mehr denn je als kulturelle Währung und Statussymbol der westlichen Welt zu verstehen. Göran Klings Arbeiten imitieren eine konsumgesellschaftliche Ästhetik, deren Fassade er hauptsächlich nutzt, um gängige kulturelle Währungen ins Absurde zu führen. KP

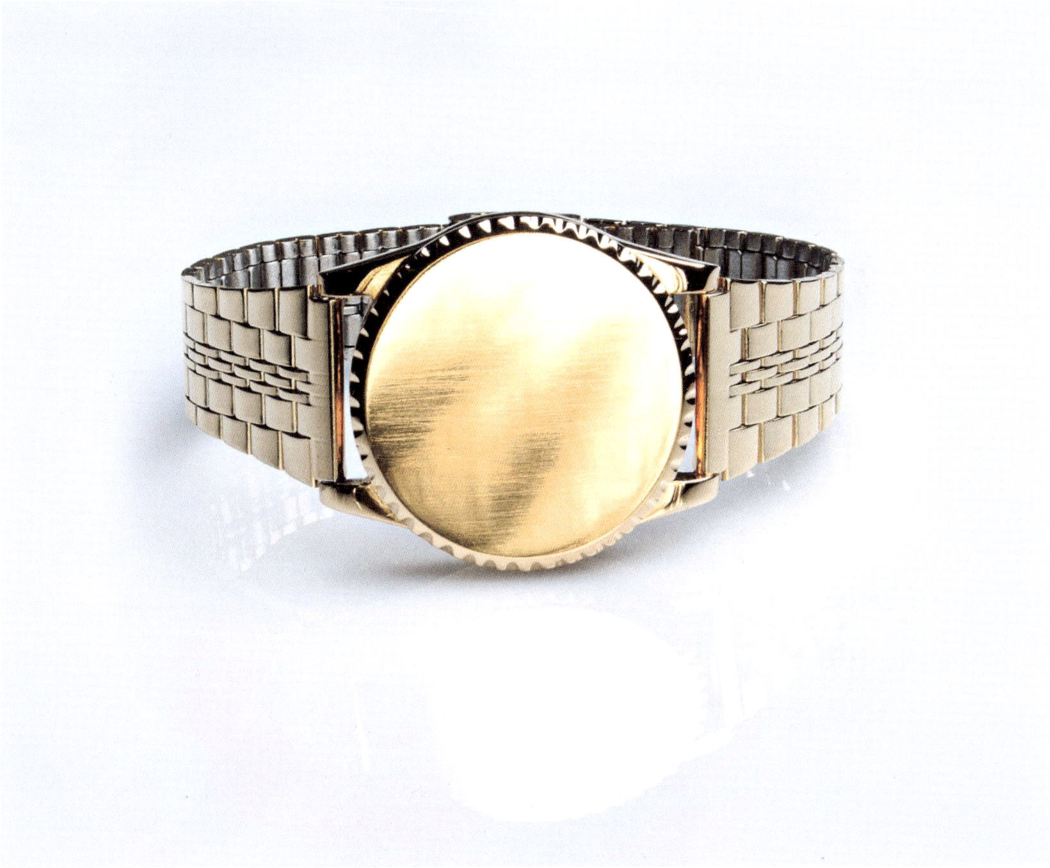

When seen alongside the sparingly worn, technically oriented men's jewelry of the 19th century, Göran Kling's works appear contradictory. His wristwatches are opulent but provide no information as regards the time. Yet now more than ever, time must be perceived as a cultural currency and status symbol in the Western world. Göran Kling's pieces imitate the typical aesthetics of consumer society, but this is a façade, created primarily for taking common cultural currencies to the absurd. KP

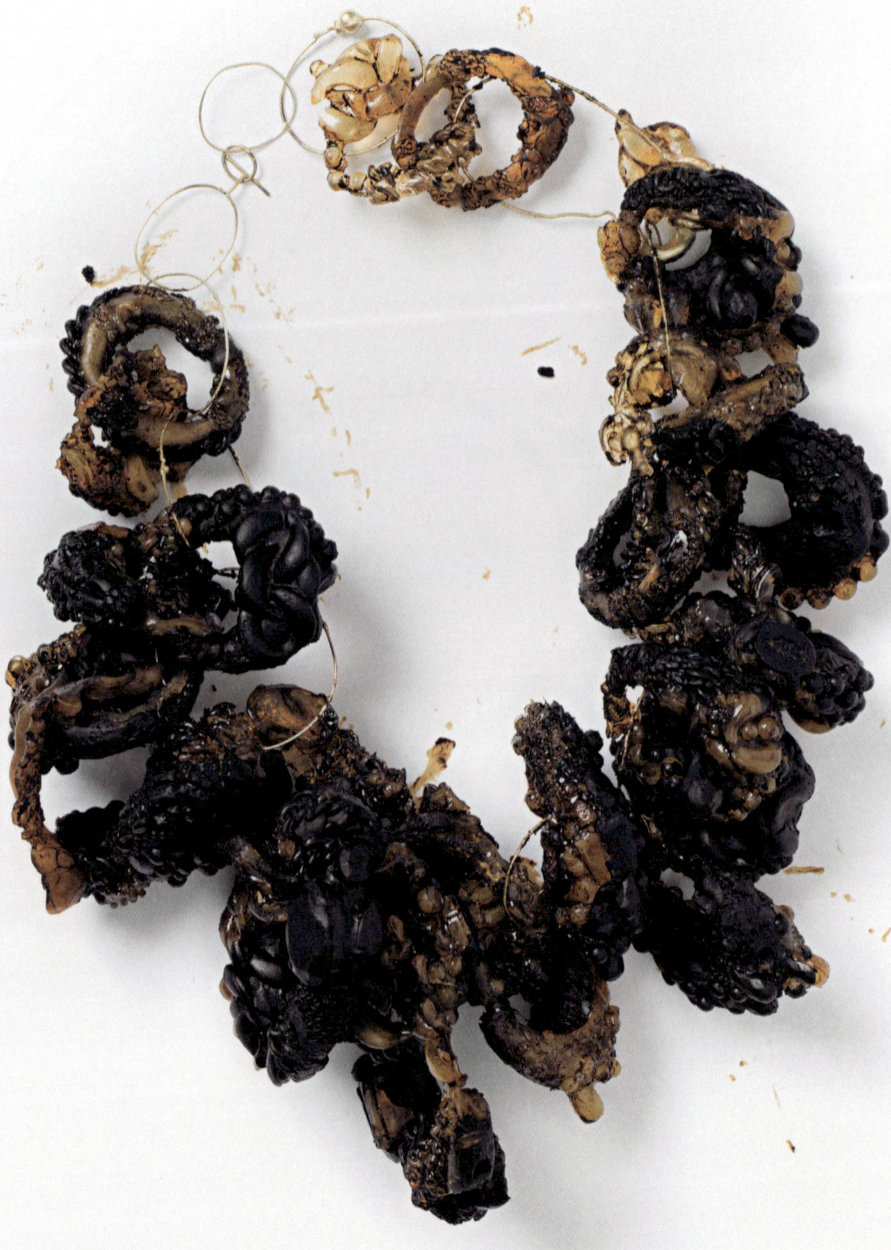

KATRIN SPRANGER

136
Halsschmuck aus der Serie I necklace from the series
"Best Before", 2018
Erdöl, Erdölerzeugnisse (Polymere), Gold
crude oil, crude oil products (polymers), gold
L. I l. 36 cm

138
Anhänger aus der Serie I pendant from the series
"Best Before", 2012
Silber, Blattgold, Erdöl, Erdölerzeugnisse (Polymere)
silver, leaf gold, crude oil, crude oil products (polymers)
20 × 25 × 70 cm

139
Anhänger aus der Serie I pendant from the series
"Best Before", 2012
Anhänger (alt), oxidiert; Erdöl; Erdölerzeugnisse
(Polymere); Silber I pendant (vintage), oxidised; crude oil;
crude oil products (polymers); silver
15 × 10 × 70 cm

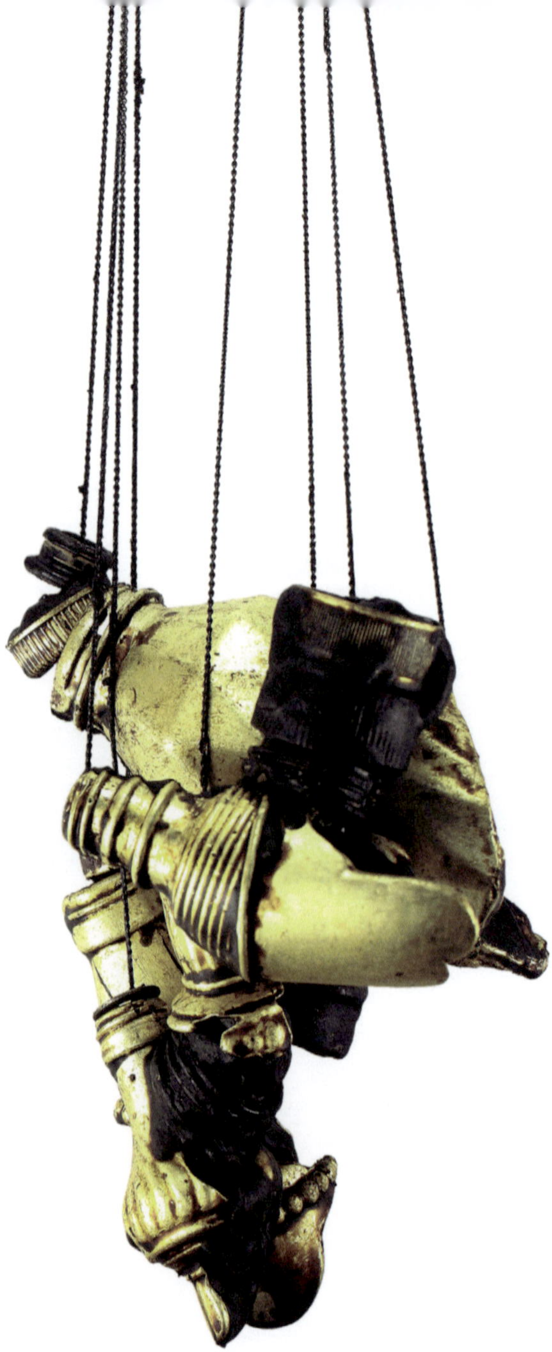

Die etwas abstrakte, aber unmittelbar bevorstehende Bedrohung durch die Erschöpfung des Erdöls, die eine Gefährdung der westlichen Zivilisation darstellt, ist Thema der Werke von Katrin Spranger. Dies wird der Beschmutzung von Kleidung und Körper eines einzelnen Menschen beim Tragen gegenüber gestellt. Dabei werden die Problemstellungen von Ökologie, Globalisierung und Konsumgesellschaften als eine politische wie auch persönliche Angelegenheit offenbart. KP

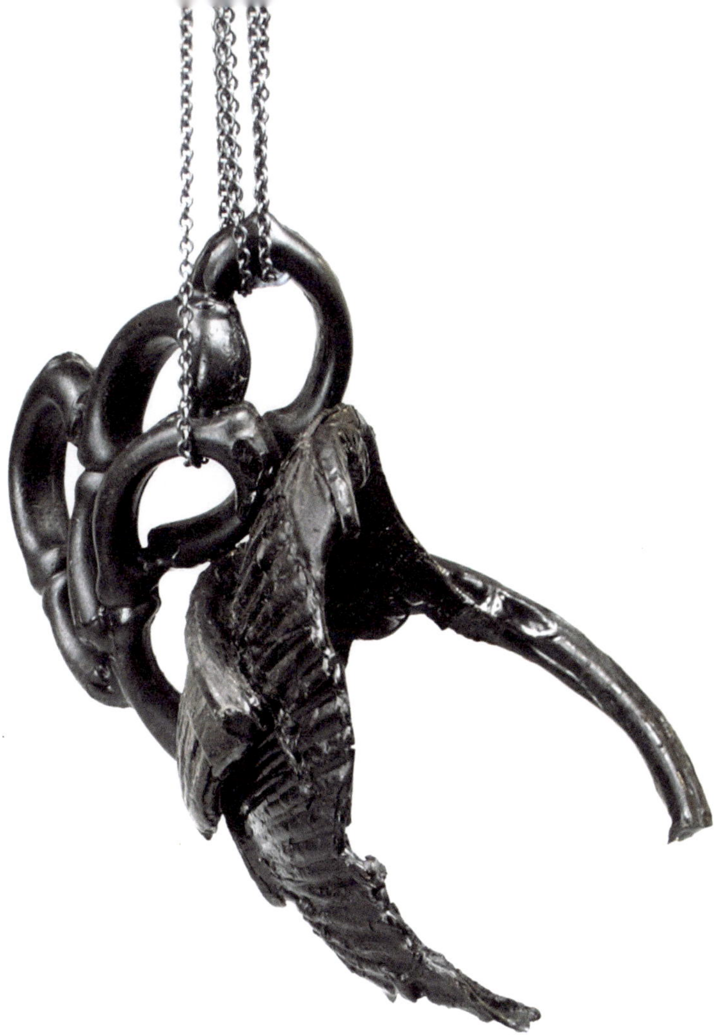

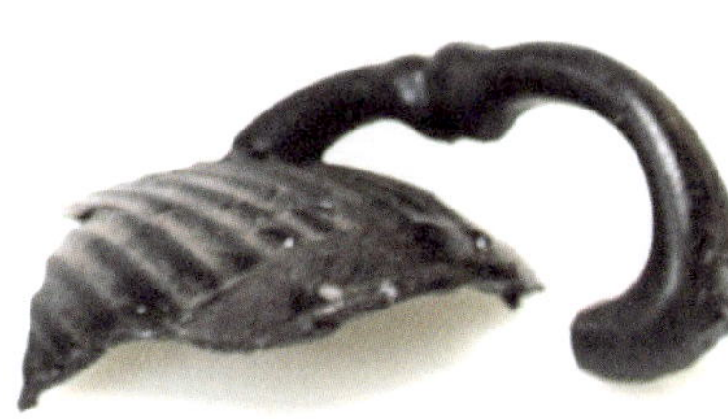

The somewhat abstract but imminent threat of crude oil depletion, which poses a threat to Western civilization, is the subject of Katrin Spranger's work. This is contrasted, when the pieces are worn, with the soiling of an individual's clothing and body. The issues of ecology, globalization and consumer societies are thus revealed to be of political as well as of personal concern. KP

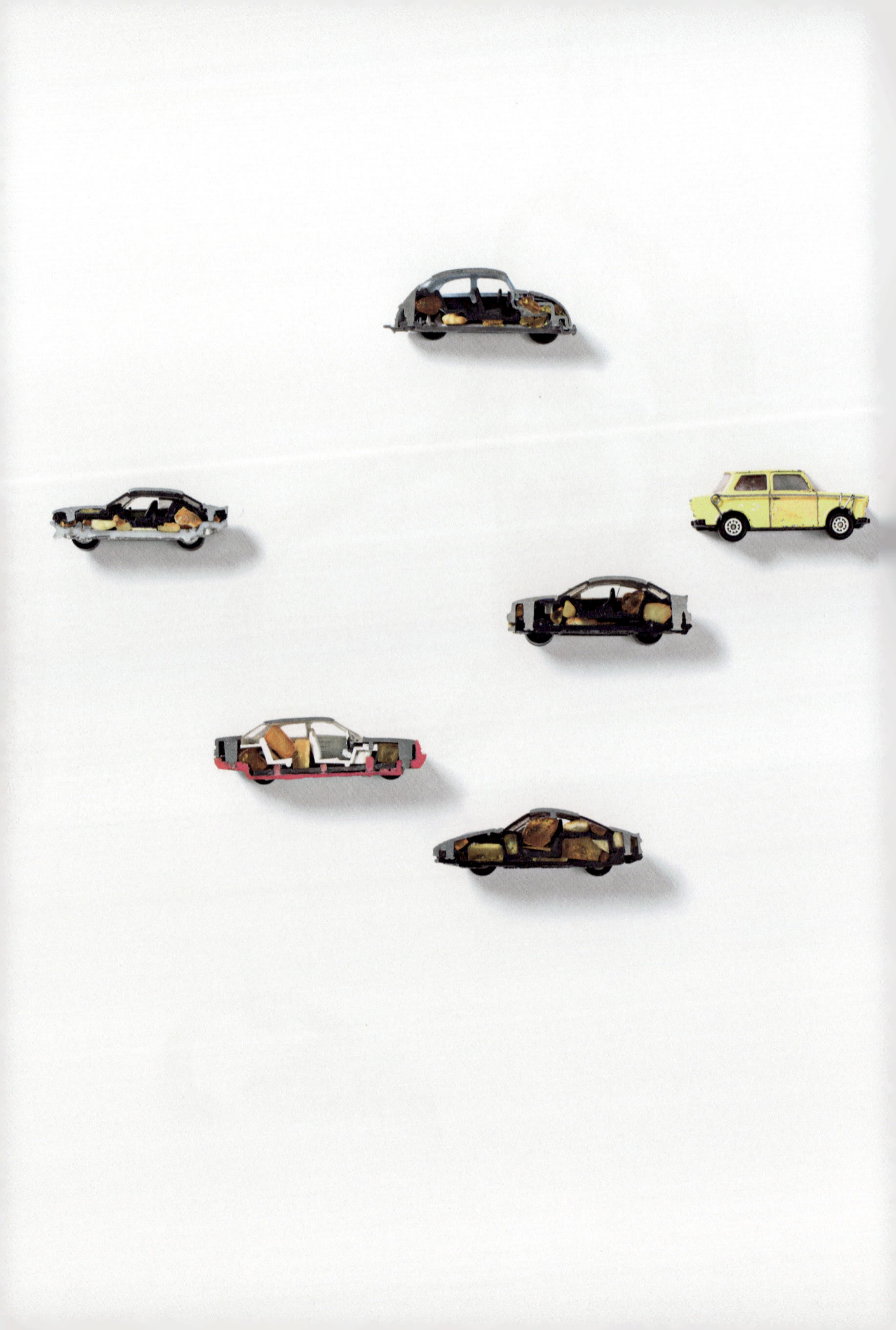

GISBERT STACH

140
Broschen aus der Serie | brooches from the series
"Smuggler", 2017–2019
Spielzeugautos, Bernstein, Kleber, Stahldraht
toy cars, amber, glue, steel wire
Unterschiedliche Maße | different dimensions

142
Brosche | brooch "BY-Schnitzel", 2016
Bernstein, Silikon, Stahldraht | amber, silicone, steel wire
15 × 15 × 1,8 cm

143
Brosche | brooch "DE-Schnitzel", 2015
Bernstein, Silikon, Stahldraht | amber, silicone, steel wire
17,5 × 10 × 1,8 cm

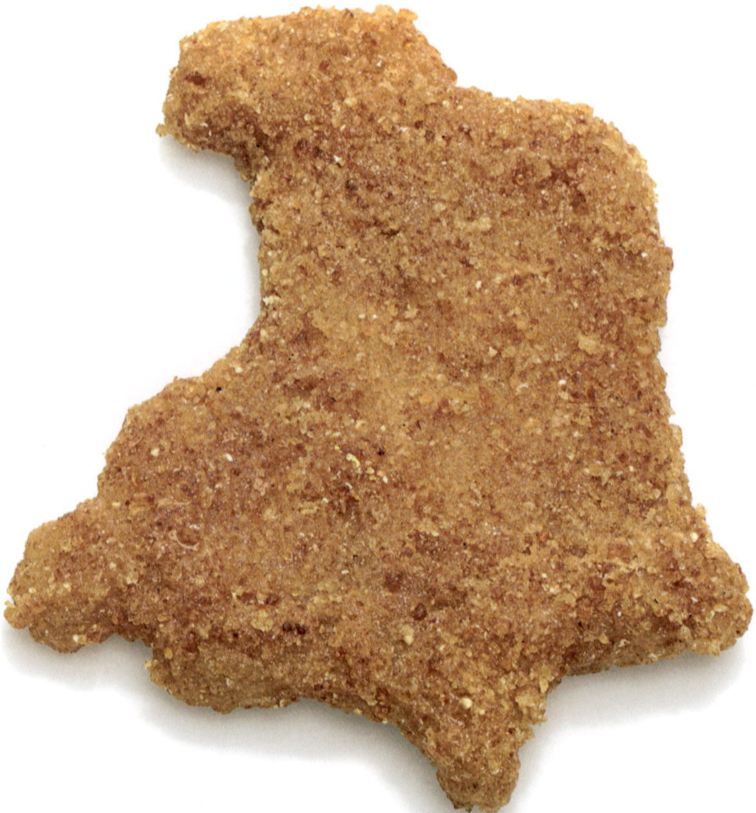

Aus zerkleinertem Bernstein hergestellt und in den Formen von Bayern, Deutschland und dem europäischen Kontinent täuschen die Broschen von Gisbert Stach vor, ein Schnitzel zu sein. Durch den radikalen Umgang mit dem traditionsbehafteten Material Bernstein, aber auch durch die Anspielung an eine von Überfluss, Fastfood und Essstörung gekennzeichnete Gesellschaft, wird der Umgang mit Privilegien innerhalb der mitteleuropäischen Kulturen hinterfragt. KP

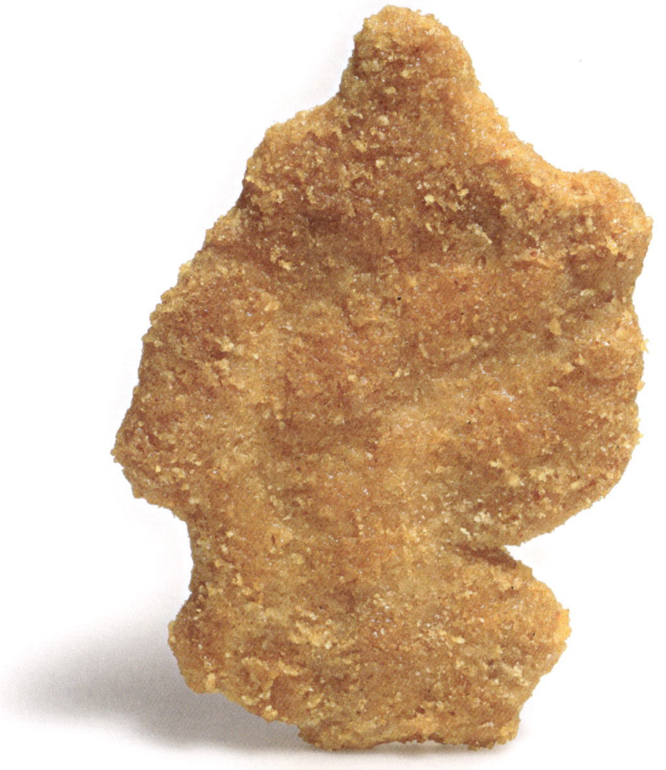

Gisbert Stach's brooches are shaped like Bavaria, Germany and the European continent, while the material used – crushed amber – creates the illusion that these are schnitzels. The artist questions the handling of privileges in Central European cultures through the radical manipulation of the tradition-bound material amber, but also through the reference to a society characterized by abundance, fast food and eating disorders. KP

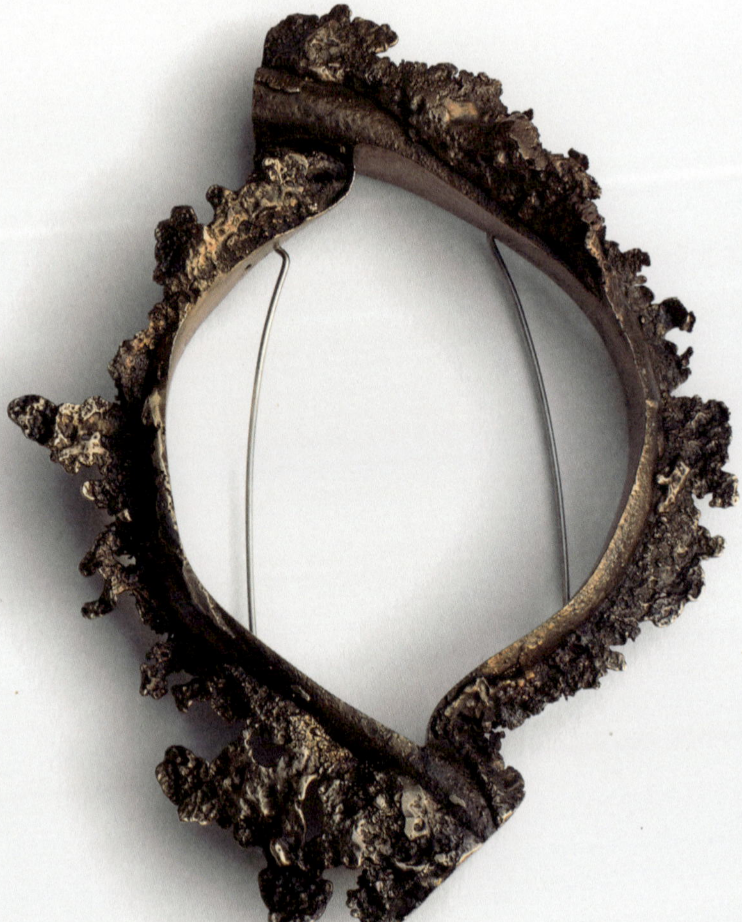

144
Brosche aus der Serie I brooch from the series
"Parerga", 2018
Bronze (Gußkanal einer Skulptur), Silber, Stahl
bronce (casting sprues of a sculpture), silver, steel
11 × 8,5 × 1,5 cm

146
Brosche aus der Serie I brooch from the series
"What will Kosmos say", 2013–2015
Bimsstein (Insel Yali, Griechenland), Edelstahl
pumice stone (Yali island, Greece), stainless steel
5 × 7 × 8 cm

147
Brosche aus der Serie I brooch from the series
"What will Kosmos say", 2013–2015
Bimsstein (Insel Yali, Griechenland), Edelstahl
pumice stone (Yali island, Greece), stainless steel
6 × 6 × 10 cm

Brosche aus der Serie I brooch from the series
"What will Kosmos say", 2013–2015
Bimsstein (Insel Yali, Griechenland), Edelstahl
pumice stone (Yali island, Greece), stainless steel
6,5 × 8 × 9 cm

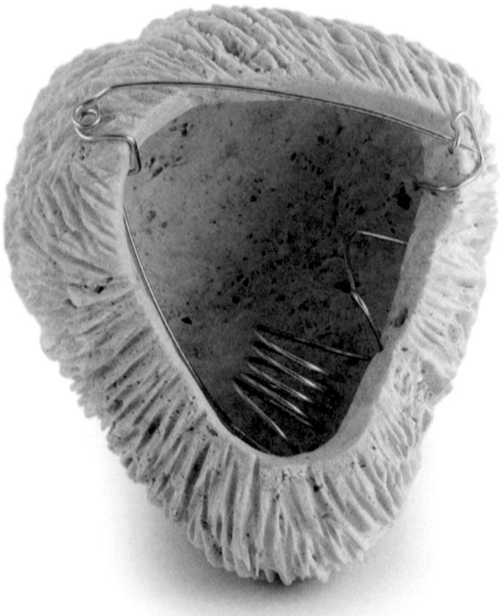

Das im Titel erwähnte Wort Kosmos (κόσμος) bezieht sich gleichzeitig auf das altgriechische Wort für Schmuck wie auch auf die neugriechische Bedeutung: Kosmos = das Volk. Ermöglicht durch eine Sondergenehmigung wurde das verwendete Bimsgestein auf der Insel Yali in Griechenland von Vivi Touloumidi gesammelt. Dies fand im Jahr 2012 statt, während die Ausmaße der griechischen Wirtschaftskrise die Europäische Gemeinschaft erschütterten. Die Schmuckstücke von Vivi Touloumidi verweisen auf das Potential des Schmucktragens als ein Medium des kollektiven Protests. KP

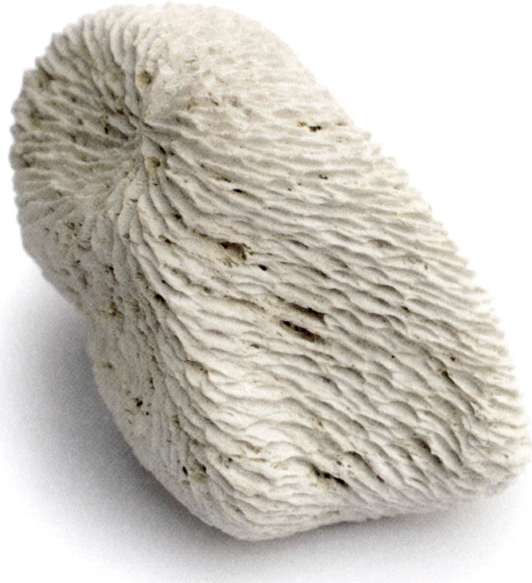

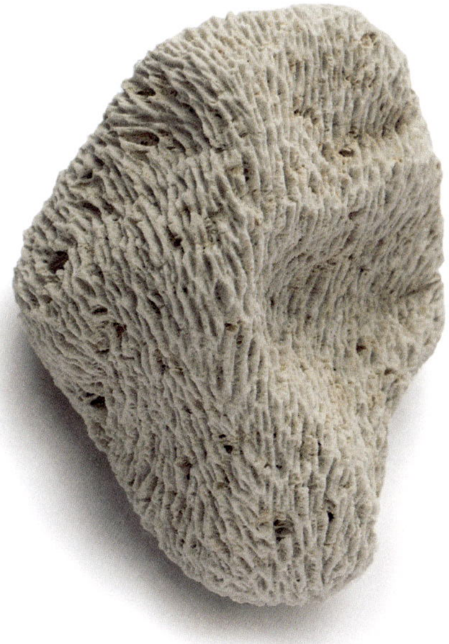

The word kosmos (κόσμος), used in the title, refers simultaneously to the ancient Greek word for jewelry and to the contemporary meaning in Greek language; cosmos = the people. With a special permit, Vivi Touloumidi was able to collect the pumice stone she used herself on the island of Yali in Greece. This took place in 2012, the year in which the extent of Greece's economic crisis shook the European Union. Vivi Touloumidi's works point to the potential of wearing jewelry as a means of collective protest. KP

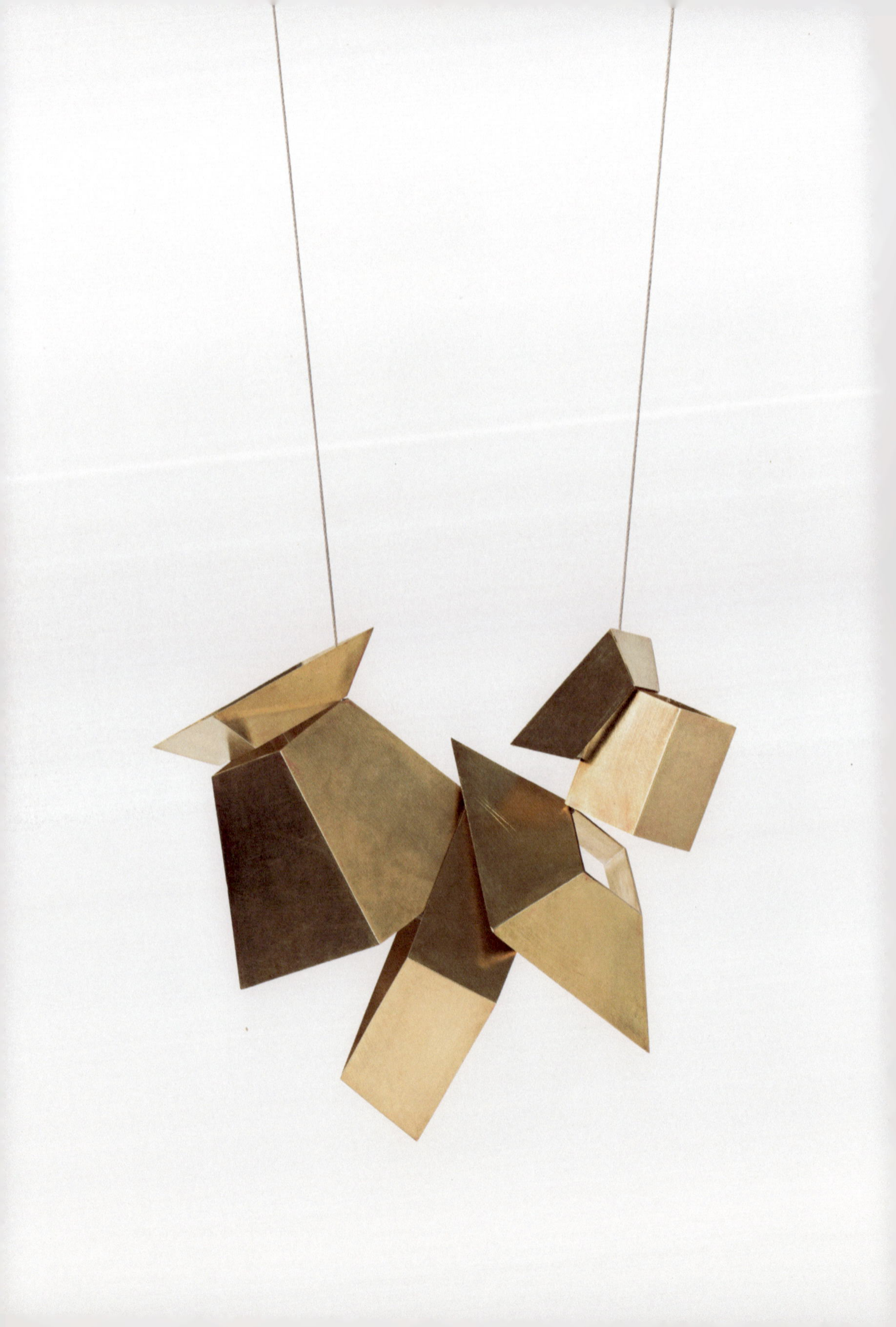

148
Halsschmuck I necklace "Ich bin keine Vase", 2018
Messing, Baumwolle I brass, cotton
Ø 7 cm (max.), H. I h. 17 cm

150
Halsschmuck I necklace "Ich bin keine Vase", 2017
Messing, Baumwolle I brass, cotton
9 × 18 × 7,6 cm

151
Halsschmuck I necklace "Ich bin keine Vase", 2017
Messing, Baumwolle I brass, cotton
10 × 16 × 7,6 cm

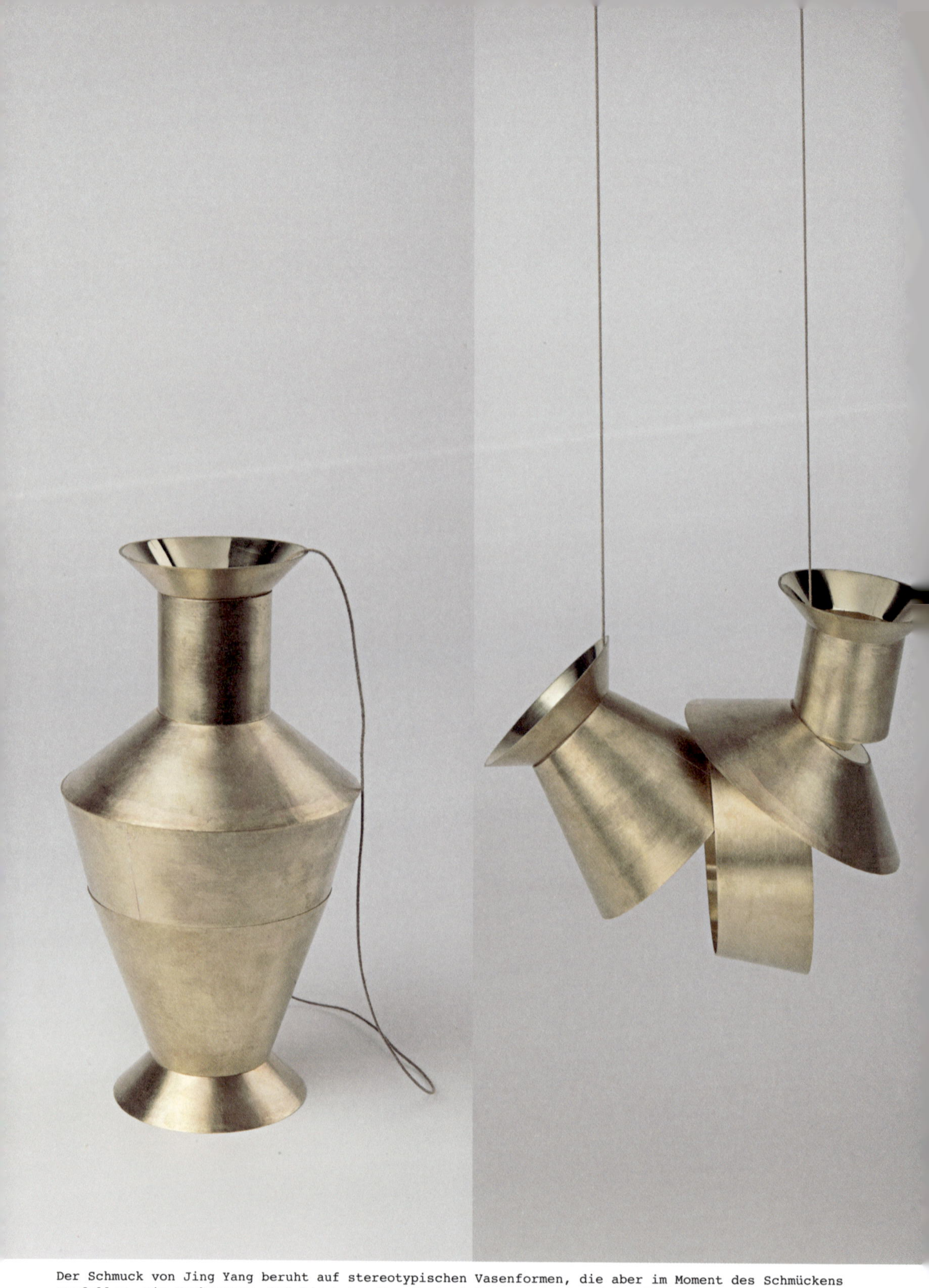

Der Schmuck von Jing Yang beruht auf stereotypischen Vasenformen, die aber im Moment des Schmückens zerfallen. Die Werkgruppe „Ich bin keine Vase“ nimmt Bezug auf eine chinesische Redensart. Als eine „Vase“ bezeichnet man Frauen, die zwar als optisch schön, aber gleichzeitig als intellektuell „hohl“ eingeschätzt werden. Die Arbeiten weisen darauf hin, dass Geschlechterrollen genauso wie Schönheitsbegriffe auf Normen beruhen, die innerhalb einer Gesellschaft immer wieder neu ausgehandelt werden müssen. KP

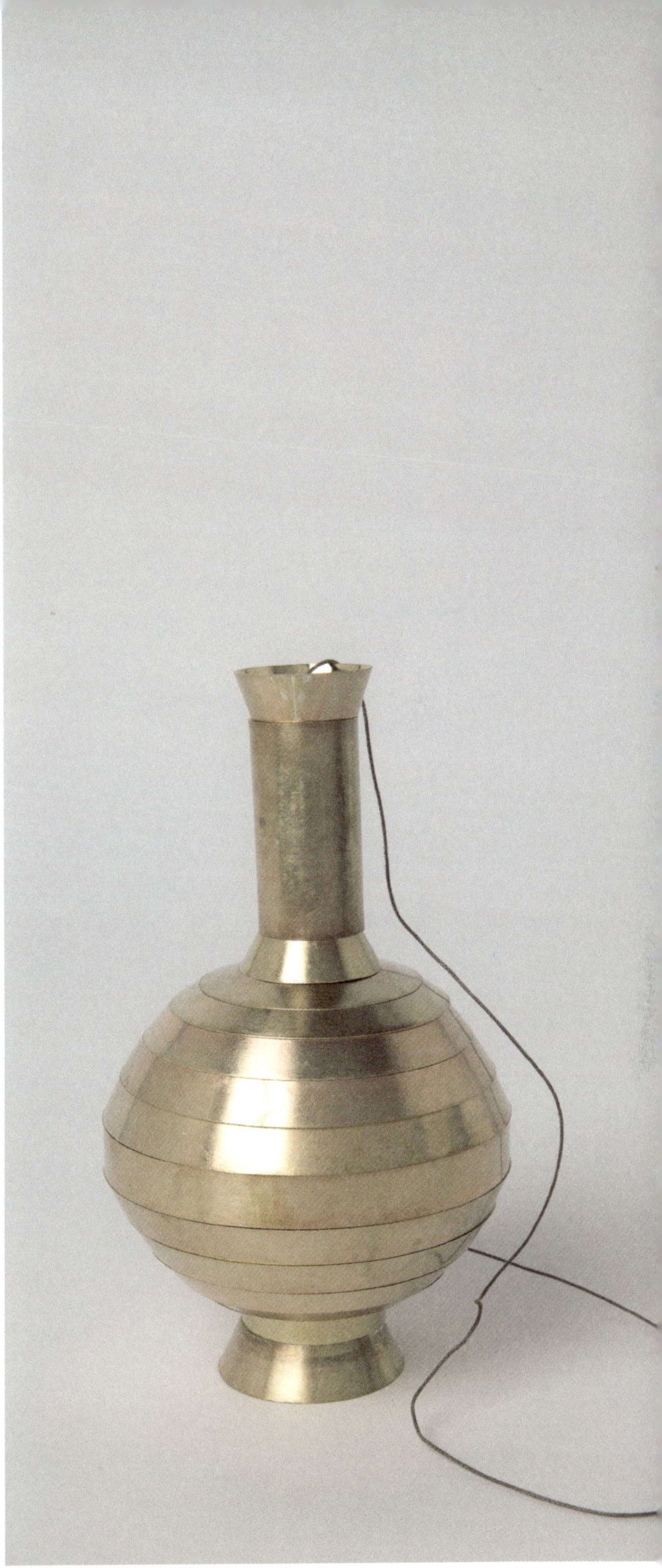

Jing Yang's jewelry is based on stereotypical vase shapes, which however will fall apart at the moment of adorning. The work group "I am not a vase" refers to a Chinese saying: Women who are considered visually beautiful while also intellectually "hollow" are referred to as a "vase." The work points out that gender roles as well as notions of beauty within a society are based on norms that have to be renegotiated time and again. KP

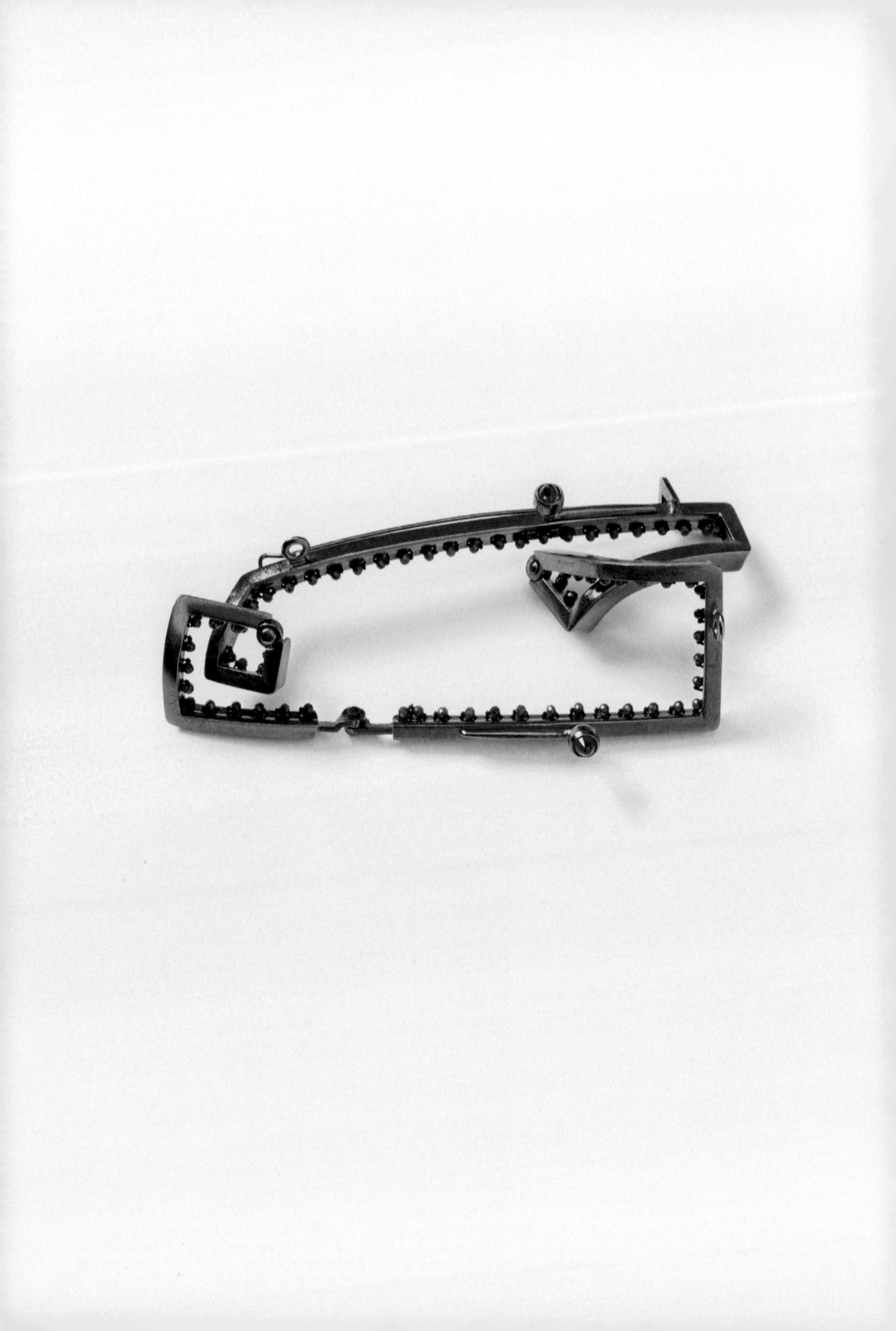

PETRA ZIMMERMANN

152
Brosche o.T. | brooch untitled, 2018
Alpacca, Glassteine, Saphire, Metallperlen, Seide
alpaca, glass stones, sapphires, metal beads, silk
12 × 5,5 × 4 cm

154
Brosche | brooch "Important Meeting", 2003
Polymethylmethacrylat; Strasssteine; Blattgold; Silber, geschwärzt | polymethylmethacrylate; rhinestones; gold leaf; silver, blackened
10 × 11 × 1,8 cm

Brosche | brooch "Happy Heidi", 2003
Polymethylmethacrylat; Strasssteine; Pyrit; Blattgold; Silber, geschwärzt | polymethylmethacrylate; rhinestones; pyrite; gold leaf; silver, blackened
11,4 × 6,4 × 1,8 cm
Privatbesitz

155
Brosche | brooch "Pin-Up I", 2003
Polymethylmethacrylat; Strasssteine; Pyrit; Blattgold; Silber, geschwärzt | polymethylmethacrylate; rhinestones; pyrite; gold leaf; silver, blackened
11,1 × 8 × 1,7 cm

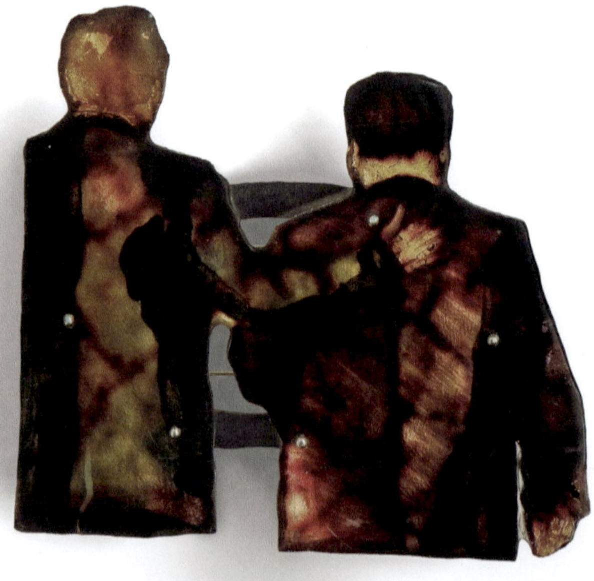

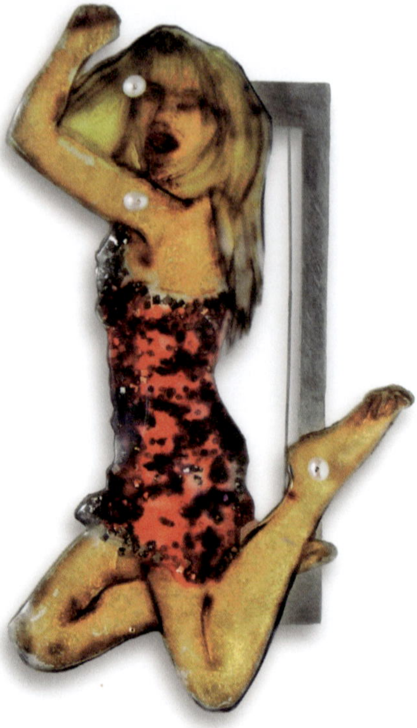

Pin-Ups and Cut-Outs ist der Überbegriff für Petra Zimmermanns Werkgruppe. Fotos aus Zeitungen werden zwar verfremdet, aber nur insofern, als dass das stereotypische Bild erkennbar bleibt; durch die Bearbeitung werden Politiker und Models auf ähnliche Weise als kulturelle Oberfläche dargestellt. Durch den ästhetischen Ausdruck der Broschen wird jeglicher Sentimentalität oder Romantisierung der Motive widersprochen und die postmodernen Plattitüden offengelegt. KP

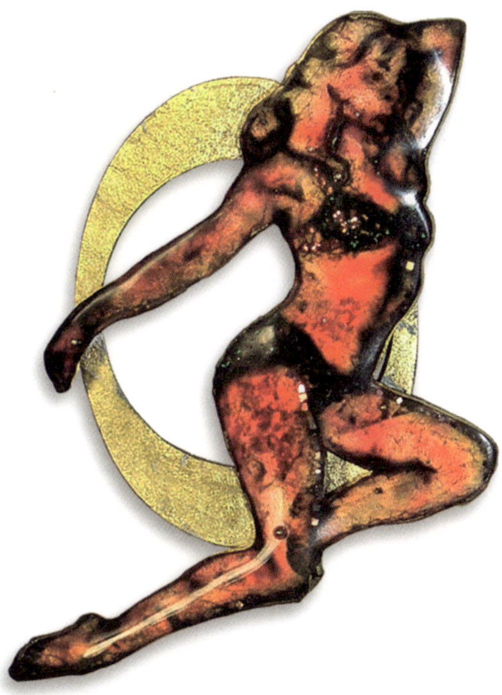

Pin-Ups and Cut-outs is the overarching term for Petra Zimmermann's group of works. The artist manipulates photos from newspapers, but only to the extent that the stereotypical image remains recognizable. Through this manipulation politicians and models are presented to be cultural surfaces in a similar way. The aesthetic expression of the brooches contradicts any sentimentality or romanticizing of the motifs, thus exposing postmodern platitudes. KP

"The moment jewellery finds its place
in the contemporary world as an act of resistance
and as an expression of autonomy
with respect to a norm, it triggers off
the ancient project of self-enhancement."
Pravu Mazumdar

"Through the visual clues of adornment humans
are able to convey subtle messages
about their social and cultural identity.
This information may be of a particularly personal nature,
decipherable only by members of a closed group,
or it may operate a cultural level conveying information
about group identity to other groups at large."
Michèle Hayeur-Smith

Pravu Mazumdar, *Jewellery And Hybridity1: On Human Nature And The Future Of Jewellery*, http://www.junctures.org/index.php/junctures/article/view/251/474 (25.01.2019).
Michèle Hayeur-Smith, *Dressing the Dead: Gender, Identity, and Adornment in Viking-Age Iceland*, Historic Sites Association of Newfoundland and Labrador, Inc., St. John's, Canada, 2000, S. | p. 228.

„Clothes and other bodily adornments are part of the vocabulary with which humans invent themselves, come to understand others and enter into meaningful relationships with them."
Joanne Entwistle

"Dress and body adornments may also be seen as symbolic and rhetorical devices, having the ability to move people to act in culturally prescribed ways."
Michelle I. Marcus

"The decoration of the body, far from being a frivolous and insignificant expenditure of time and resources, can be a highly practical, efficacious and necessary activity. Without it we would have great, perhaps insuperable, problems creating and maintaining those networks of social and cultural relationships, which have always been and will always be the foundation of human accomplishment."
Ted Polhemus

Joanne Entwistle, *The Fashioned Body*, Polity Press, Cambridge, 2000, p. 182.
Michelle I. Marcus, *Dressed to Kill: Women and Pins in Early Iran*, Oxford Art Journal, vol.17, nr. 2, Oxford, 1994, S. I p. 3.
Ted Polhemus, *BODYSTYLES*, TBS The Book Service Ltd., Colchester, 2018, p. 110 (first edition: Lennard Publishing, London, 1988).

Impressum
Imprint

Die vorliegende Publikation erscheint anlässlich der Ausstellung „SCHMUCKISMUS“, Die Neue Sammlung – The Design Museum, Pinakothek der Moderne, München 16.03.2019–16.06.2019

This book is published on the occasion of the exhibition “SCHMUCKISMUS“, Die Neue Sammlung – The Design Museum, Pinakothek der Moderne, Munich 16.03.2019–16.06.2019

Herausgeberin
Editor
Angelika Nollert

Katalogkonzept
Catalog concept
Angelika Nollert, Karen Pontoppidan

Autor*innen
Authors
Paul Derrez, Hanne Loreck, Angelika Nollert, Karen Pontoppidan

Mitarbeit
Assistance
Nelly Stein

Fotonachweis
Photo credits
Alexander Laurenzo (Die Neue Sammlung) 20, 22, 23, 25, 40, 44, 48, 52, 56, 60, 64, 68, 72, 76, 80, 84, 88, 96, 100, 104, 108, 112, 116, 124, 128, 132, 136, 140, 148, 152
Tobias Alm 54, 55, 102, 103
Enrico Bartolucci 86, 87
Yosef Bercovich 98, 99
Beatrice Brovia / Nicolas Cheng 90, 91
Federico Cavicchioli 126, 127
Carolina Gimeno 119
Christine Graf 50, 51
Karina Hagemann 130, 131
Sophie Hanagarth 78, 79
Silke Helmerdig 31
Jon Hertov 110, 111
David Huycke 123
Hannah Joris 120, 122
Eva Jünger (für Danner-Stiftung) 142
Göran Kling 134, 135
Sanna Lindberg 74, 75
Jana Matzakow 42, 43
Karin Olanders 106, 107
Lassi Rinno 82, 83
Travis Rozee 115
Henning Spranger 138, 139
Gisbert Stach 143
Mirei Takeuchi 47, 58, 59, 63 (oben | above), 66, 70, 71, 92, 94, 95
Vivi Touloumidi 144, 146, 147
Justine Wagner 62, 63 (unten | below)
Jing Yang 150, 151
Robert Zahornicky 7
Petra Zimmermann 154, 155

Übersetzung
Translation
Jeremy Gaines

Lektorat
Copy editing
Sabine Klinkert (dt.), Jeremy Gaines (engl.)

Grafische Gestaltung
Layout
Yvonne Quirmbach, Berlin

Arnoldsche Projektmanager
Arnoldsche Project Manager
Matthias Becher

Offset Reproduktion
Offset reproductions
Repromayer, Reutlingen

Druck
Printed by
GTS, Kranj

Papier
Paper
150 gsm Tauro Offset

Bibliografische Information der Deutschen Nationalbibliothek
Die Deutsche Nationalbibliothek verzeichnet diese Publikation in der Deutschen Nationalbibliografie; detaillierte bibliografische Daten sind im Internet über www.dnb.de abrufbar.

Bibliographic information published by the Deutsche Nationalbibliothek
The Deutsche Nationalbibliothek lists this publication in the Deutsche Nationalbibliografie; detailed bibliographic data are available on the Internet at www.dnb.de.

ISBN 978-3-89790-551-1

Wenn nicht anders bezeichnet, befinden sich die Schmuckobjekte im Besitz der Künstler*innen.
If not otherwise stated, the jewelry objects are in the property of the artists.

Eine Ausstellung der Neuen Sammlung – The Design Museum
An exhibition of Die Neue Sammlung – The Design Museum

Kuratorin
Curator
Karen Pontoppidan

Ausstellungskonzeption
Exhibition concept
Angelika Nollert, Karen Pontoppidan

Ausstellungsgrafik
Exhibition grafics
Yvonne Quirmbach
Rainer Schmitzberger

Restauratorische Betreuung
Conservation department
Tim Bechthold, Julia Demeter, Helena Ernst, Christian Huber, Franziska Schittler

Museumstechnik
Technical department
Michael Daume, Cornelius von Heyking, Florian Westphal

Registrar
Waltraud Wiedenbauer

Mitarbeit
Assistance
Nelly Stein

Presse- und Öffentlichkeitsarbeit
Press and public relations
Tine Nehler, Jette Elixmann, Pressestelle der Pinakotheken
Jana Walter, Digital Manager, Pinakothek der Moderne

Unser Dank gebührt den beteiligten Schmuckkünstler*innen
Thanks to the cooperating jewelry artists

sowie allen Leihgebern
as well as all lenders

THE DESIGN MUSEUM DIE NEUE SAMMLUNG

PINAKOTHEK DER MODERNE